S0-AIQ-873

HIGH
AND
INSIDE

AN A-TO-Z GUIDE TO THE LANGUAGE OF BASEBALL

Joseph McBride

CB
CONTEMPORARY BOOKS

Library of Congress Cataloging-in-Publication Data

McBride, Joseph.
High and inside : an A to Z guide to the language of baseball /
Joseph McBride.
p.   cm.
Includes bibliographical references (p.   ) and index.
ISBN 0-8092-3023-2
1. Baseball—United States—Terminology.   2. Baseball—
United States—Slang.   3. Baseball—United States—History.
I. Title.
GV862.3.M33   1997
796.351'014—dc21   97-25318
                                                CIP

Cover design by Todd Petersen
Cover background image copyright ©1997 PhotoDisc, Inc.
Interior design by Paula Weber
Interior illustrations by Dan Krovatin
Back-cover photo by Kendall Hailey
An earlier version of this book was published by Warner Books in 1980 as
High and Inside: The Complete Guide to Baseball Slang

Copyright © 1980, 1997 by Joseph McBride
Published by Contemporary Books
An imprint of NTC/Contemporary Publishing Company
4255 West Touhy Avenue, Lincolnwood (Chicago), Illinois 60646-1975 U.S.A.
All rights reserved. No part of this book may be reproduced, stored in a
retrieval system, or transmitted in any form or by any means, electronic,
mechanical, photocopying, recording, or otherwise, without the prior
permission of NTC/Contemporary Publishing Company.
Manufactured in the United States of America
International Standard Book Number: 0-8092-3023-2
17   16   15   14   13   12   11   10   9   8   7   6   5   4   3   2   1

In memory of my parents,
Marian Dunne McBride and Raymond E. McBride,
and my grandfathers,
John G. McBride and Pierce Joseph Dunne;
and for my children,
Jessica and John

CONTENTS

Contents

PREFACE

Casey Stengel inspired this book. One Saturday morning in the spring of 1962, when I was a fourteen-year-old baseball fan and the "Old Perfesser" was a seventy-one-year-old legend marking his fiftieth anniversary in the major leagues, I spent an unforgettable hour standing next to the New York Mets' dugout at Milwaukee County Stadium, eavesdropping on a Stengel monologue. Casey gave no sign of being aware of my presence as he rattled on and on to a baffled-looking fellow who occasionally chimed in with a few words of broken English. It was a wonderful monologue, one that would have brought a grin to the saturnine face of Ring Lardner, and I couldn't understand a word of it. Casey Stengel ostensibly spoke the English language, but sportswriters always referred to his rambling, whimsical, sagacious, and thoroughly colorful lingo as "Stengelese." Whatever it was, it fascinated me, and not long thereafter I began jotting down the notes on baseball slang that eventually came together to make up this book. When I had finished, as Casey used to say, "You could look it up."

The lengthy evolution of *High and Inside* parallels my own maturation process as a writer. My parents, Raymond and Marian McBride, were newspaper reporters in Milwaukee, and under their influence I gravitated toward the writing profession. At the time I began my research for this book in May 1963, as a sophomore in high school, I already considered myself a professional writer, because I had received money for my writing on baseball. My first published article, "The *Lightfeet* Top 'Em All!," which earned me $40, was written in 1960 for the *Young Catholic Messenger* about Greg Spahn, the son of Milwaukee Braves pitching ace Warren Spahn. Greg was one of my Little League teammates on the Wauwatosa Lightfeet, and one night while Greg was pitching, his father, my hero of heroes, served as our third-base coach. With that article under my belt (thanks greatly to my mother's help as my editor and unofficial agent), I had no doubt that I could pursue a writing career, and it seemed natural that the next step would be a book about baseball.

When I started collecting information for what originally was titled *Baseballese*, I was putting myself through Marquette University High School by working as a vendor at Braves games, shouting my changing voice raw while peddling all the junk that baseball fans consume so voraciously. I could almost shout it in my sleep even today: "Hey, hot dogs! Hey, get your red hots here!" Or, the longest litany: "Peanuts, popcorn, pennants, scorecards, yearbooks!" The money I made from the job was important to me, but more crucial was that the job allowed me free access to the ballpark. Some games were so thrilling that I spent most of my time watch-

ing the field and neglected to peddle my wares. From the day
my father took me to see Lew Burdette shut out the Yankees,
1–0, in the fifth game of the 1957 World Series, I had been
thinking of little else but baseball.

Day in and day out, I was either watching baseball, playing baseball (very badly), listening to baseball on the radio,
getting baseball players' autographs, talking about baseball,
reading about baseball, or trying to write about baseball. As
if that degree of monomania wasn't enough (a misspent
youth? I don't think so), my friend Bobby Kidera and I spent
literally thousands of our adolescent hours together playing
a complex and surprisingly accurate baseball table-game called
APBA, which gave us the heady pleasure of "managing" every
recent major-league team, as well as such fabled teams of the
past as the 1914 Athletics, the 1927 Yankees, and the 1934 Cardinals. We were experiencing the vividness of baseball's history, which, as Roger Angell observes in his eloquent book
The Summer Game, is what distinguishes it from all other
American sports. Baseball, he writes, is "a game of recollec-
tions, recapturings, and visions. This inner game—baseball
in the mind—has no season."

Baseball's past and present were equally important to
me, and I was lucky to have fleeting personal contact with
such legendary figures as Stengel, George Sisler, Satchel Paige,
Carl Hubbell, and Lefty Gomez. I wrote a letter to Ty Cobb
shortly before his death in 1961 and received an autograph
from him in reply (Bobby Kidera, who wrote Cobb a few

days before I did, received a priceless handwritten letter giving him tips on how to hit). It became a living thing to me, the history of this sport. The old-time players I read about and heard about became almost as real, in my imagination, as Warren Spahn, Henry Aaron, and the other future Hall of Famers I watched on the field in my youth—Luis Aparicio, Ernie Banks, Yogi Berra, Lou Brock, Roberto Clemente, Don Drysdale, Whitey Ford, Bob Gibson, Al Kaline, Sandy Koufax, Mickey Mantle, Juan Marichal, Eddie Mathews, Willie Mays, Willie McCovey, Stan Musial, Phil Niekro, Satchel Paige, Robin Roberts, Brooks Robinson, Frank Robinson, Red Schoendienst, Enos Slaughter, Duke Snider, and Billy Williams. I remember that in the waning shadows of one late afternoon at County Stadium in 1963, I mentally pinched myself to imprint on my memory before leaving the park the image of Stan Musial's batting crouch, because I knew that in the future I would value that image as much as I did the imagined memory of Babe Ruth, Ty Cobb, Lou Gehrig, and Christy Mathewson.

After Casey Stengel gave me the clue (Understand what the hell they're talking about!), I began to realize that it was in the language of baseball, its oral tradition, that I would find the familiarity I desired with the total experience of baseball history. Understanding would bring the past alive and make the present and future more comprehensible; since one of the functions of slang is to separate the insider from the outsider, I had to learn it to become an insider. When I started my research, many of the slang expressions and nicknames that interested me were mysterious: people had been using them for years without knowing why, and I felt it was necessary to penetrate these mysteries to participate in the inner meaning of baseball, just as I found it necessary to know as much as possible about each player's personality and career to get the maximum enjoyment from watching a game.

Surprising as it seemed, I found that there had been no comprehensive attempt to catalog and explain the derivations of baseball slang. Dictionaries of baseball had been published—and others would appear while I was continuing my research in the 1960s and 1970s—but all were limited to definitions, none delving into the *origins* of the slang. At the time *High and Inside* was first published in 1980, Dizzy Dean's observation about baseball slang was still true: in a whimsical booklet published in 1943 under the title *The Dizzy Dean Dictionary and What's What in Baseball*, the celebrated screwball complained, "The trouble is, I figgered, that there ain't no good expert source where you kin look up some of them words. I mean the real tecknicle words that's used by the players and has growed right out of baseball."

I had to perform my own laborious detective work to discover the derivations of such commonly used but linguistically obscure baseball expressions as "charley horse," "fungo," and "rhubarb," as well as such famous nicknames as "Cy" Young, "Pie" Traynor, and "Satchel" Paige. It took years of sifting slowly through hundreds of scattered printed sources and through the memories of many past and present players, sportswriters, team executives, and other experts in baseball lore before the job could be completed. Memory is often fallible, of course, and baseball since its inception has been a playground for prankish leg-pulling by players and writers alike. Varying versions of word and nickname origins from different sources had to be traced, compared, and evaluated, for frequently the commonly accepted version of how a word or nickname originated was mistaken. For example, the two-page article on nicknames in *The Official Encyclopedia of Baseball* erred on the derivation of seven nicknames—Charles (Gabby) Hartnett, John (Muggsy) McGraw, John (Grandma) Murphy, Harold (Tookie) Gilbert, William (Jap) Barbeau, John (Pretzels) Pezzullo, and Leroy (Satchel) Paige—all of whom are represented here, along with 892 other players, managers, and teams whose nicknames bear explaining.

My preliminary research was completed by 1966, with the unwitting help of my father, who patiently answered my questions about baseball slang without knowing I was writing a book on the subject (I didn't want to tell my parents what I was doing behind my closed bedroom door, because I was afraid they would call a halt to the project). Once the first version was completed, I didn't know how to go about selling it. The manuscript sat in a drawer for years while I moved on to other writing projects, but my father kept nagging me to do something with it. I revised and updated the manuscript substantially before its first publication by Warner

Books. I have updated the book again for this second edition, taking into account the nicknames of players who have entered the game since then, as well as other recent additions to baseball slang and fresh research by other historians and scholars. It was not until Paul Dickson published his *Dickson Baseball Dictionary* in 1989 that there existed a fully comprehensive reference work on the language of baseball, giving not only definitions but also etymologies for some 5,000 baseball terms; I have drawn upon Dickson's scholarship in revising and updating this more anecdotal volume (which, in deference to Dickson and other scholars who have come after me, no longer bears the subtitle attached to the original edition of *High and Inside: The Complete Guide to Baseball Slang*).

In cases where a derivation remains obscure or more than one explanation is plausible, I have so noted. In addition to the nicknames, I have given detailed explanations of how 416 of the most interesting and unusual baseball terms came to be coined (leaving aside the obvious and self-explanatory terms). I've also included, in boxes scattered throughout the text, several dozen of the most memorable quotations from the history of baseball, because lines like "Say it ain't so, Joe," "Nice guys finish last," and "If you build it, he will come" are also integral parts of the game's language.

The section on baseball terminology is alphabetized, but some related or synonymous expressions are included under the principal headings. Although the section on baseball nicknames is alphabetized by the last names of the players, in many cases additional players with the same or similar nicknames are grouped under one heading to avoid repetition; usually, the heading is that of the most famous or the first player to receive the nickname. All slang expressions and players mentioned in the book are listed in the index. Also included are the nicknames of every current major-league ballclub and the two 1998 expansion teams (alphabetized by the name of the city or state where the team is located), and important predecessor clubs are grouped under those headings. There are also a few odd nicknames referring to groups of players or specific teams, such as "Murderers' Row" and "The Gas House Gang." With the exception of players from the old Negro Leagues, the individual nicknames in the book are limited to those of major-league players, managers, umpires, and team executives. Thanks to the greatly increased attention paid to the Negro Leagues by baseball scholars in recent years, I have been able to expand my coverage of those players to acknowledge the full extent of their role in the creation of the language of baseball.

PART 1

BASEBALL
TERMINOLOGY

INTRODUCTION TO
BASEBALL TERMINOLOGY

"The history of baseball terms deserves to be investigated, for many of them have entered the common speech of the country." So wrote H. L. Mencken in the 1936 edition of his monumental work *The American Language*. The list of slang expressions stemming from baseball is a long one—*home run, foul ball, strike out, assist, hit, screwball, curveball, fastball, spitball, batting average, bench warmer, on base, off base, hit-and-run, box score, shutout, major leagues,* and *minor leagues* are only a few of the words so familiar that they serve a multitude of descriptive and metaphorical purposes in everyday American speech. And these are only the simplest of baseball expressions. Words with more esoteric origins—such as *bonehead, bullpen, bush leaguer, charley horse, fan, hot dog,* and *rhubarb*—have found equal acceptance in dictionaries of the American language, to the extent that many people probably don't even realize that they were created or popularized by baseball.

The rules and the essential terminology of baseball were borrowed from the English game of rounders. They were codified for American use in 1845 by Alexander J. Cartwright and, aside from a few modifications (such as the designated hitter rule), have remained remarkably consistent since the 1870s, when professional baseball took hold in the United States. Most of the essential words of the game—*bat, hit, play, strike, run, foul, field, team, mound,* and so forth—were words long in use in Great Britain, with roots in Old English. (The word *baseball* itself stems from Middle English root words— *base* plus *bal*—that in turn can be traced back to the Latin *basis* and the French *balle*.) Cartwright saw no need to meddle with the simple and direct Anglo-Saxon vocabulary of rounders in transplanting the game to America, but baseball imbued those words with a new freshness, color, and emotional impact.

The more peculiarly American baseball slang expressions—the ones that, as Dizzy Dean put it, "has growed right out of baseball"—first flowered in the mid-1880s, when newspaper coverage of baseball took an imaginative leap beyond simple descriptions and boldly regarded itself as an art form. Such pioneer sportswriters of the period as Charlie Seymour of the *Chicago Inter-Ocean* and Lennie Washburn of the *Chicago Herald* were credited by another early baseball writer, Hugh S. Fullerton, with inventing or popularizing such baseball slang as *circus play, shutout,* and *southpaw.* Within the next few years, the trend toward colorful baseball writing was epidemic.

"Baseball writing really began to develop, as a science, and also as an entertaining feature, about 1890," sports reporter William A. Phelan wrote in a 1908 issue of *Baseball Magazine.* "Washburn brought the comedy portions of baseball writing to its pinnacles, and today every press stand is full of keen-witted, clever boys who make their stuff entertaining, but the grade of their copy has not advanced since 1892, while it is ten times better reading than the dull descriptions that were published in 1885."

From the glory days of the 1880s and 1890s we derive such indelible expressions as *Annie Oakley, barnstorming, bleachers, bonehead, charley horse, fan, hot corner, ladies' day, pinch hitter, rain check, rooter,* and *Texas Leaguer.* Most of those terms were created by sportswriters such as Charley Dryden and Ren Mulford, or popularized by them after being bandied about on the playing field. They quickly entered the lingo of baseball fans, and from there, as baseball grew in popularity during the early 1900s, it was only a short step to entering the everyday language of the average American. Recognizing the impact the game's slang was having, *The American Magazine* in 1912 published an early lexicon of baseball terminology, written by Hugh S. Fullerton.

The trend, however, alarmed many grammarians and other literary oracles of the time. Though the vitality of the American language has always stemmed from its receptivity to a wide range of influences, from foreign languages to regionalisms to specialized vocabularies, the guardians of "proper" speech failed to recognize the lasting impact baseball slang would have on the language. They saw it as a fad, and they deplored it. A major debate erupted in 1912 and 1913 over the advisability of using baseball slang terms in newspaper reports. Most sportswriters, it should be admitted, were trying so hard to load their stories with neologisms and fancy lingo that, when read today, they are all but unintelligible. Here is one brief sample from a *Washington Post* story by Joe Campbell: "And Amie Rusie made a Svengali pass in front of Charlie Reilly's lamps and he carved three nicks in the weather." More simply stated, this meant that pitcher Amos Rusie had mesmerized batter Charlie Reilly into striking out.

Editorial writers in newspapers and magazines split sharply on the issue. Those against the use of baseball slang were in the unhappy position of trying to lock the barn doors after the cows had escaped. As *The Nation* huffily protested in 1913:

> One of the most puzzling problems of this puzzling era is the effect wrought upon our native speech by contact with the national game. Why is it that when it essays to tell what happened at the Polo Grounds or Ebbets Field between the hours of 3:20 and 6:00 P.M., the English language stands on its head and tries to convey its meaning by waving its hands and feet, instead of speaking like one sane man to another? Surely, here is material worthy the attention of the philologist, not to say the psychopath; and yet up to the present moment no one has undertaken a scientific investigation of the case. Its difficulties, indeed, are enough to daunt the boldest.

In a more enlightened vein, the *Charleston News and Courier* took the side of modernism:

The injury which is now proposed is the abolition of the language of baseball. This, as all the world knows, is a distinctive and peculiar tongue. It is not English. It is not precisely slang. It is a strange patois, full of idiomatic eccentricities, rich in catchphrases and technical terms, wonderfully expressive and in the highest degree flexible. Against this patois the voice of the purist has been raised. He would have us give up this "lingo" in which for years events in the baseball world have been chronicled by the press. He would have the editor of every dignified sheet order his baseball reporters to use nothing but conventional English in the sporting columns. . . . It is to be hoped, and it may reasonably be expected, that the movement will not accomplish the results which its more radical advocates desire.

The grammatical purists won the battle, for newspapers began to discourage the more extravagant whimsies of baseball reporters. But the purists lost the war, because many of the words considered "peculiar" and "vulgar" by grammarians in 1913 were deemed acceptable English within just a few years. That process was accelerated by the increasing literacy and sophistication in the press box. Ring Lardner, with his "busher" stories for the *Saturday Evening Post* in the mid-1910s, became the first writer to turn baseball language into enduring literature. Lardner's satiric, yet affectionate and deeply knowledgeable, employment of the illiterate language of the ordinary ballplayer recognized the vitality of baseball slang and helped validate it for educated readers. This gave a new self-consciousness to baseball slang and eased the path toward its acceptance into everyday American speech.

Before long, grammarians had done an about-face and were rushing to study "Baseball-American," as Lardner termed it in a brief section he contributed to the 1921 second edition of Mencken's *American Language*. The slang that educated people had despised so recently was now seen as a boon to the nation's vocabulary. Lexicographer Edward J. Nichols, in his 1939 Pennsylvania State College doctoral thesis "An Historical Dictionary of Baseball Terminology," cataloged more than 2,500 baseball slang expressions (including no fewer than 100 synonyms for the verb "to hit"), and expressed surprise that so few of the words had fallen into disuse. By the time Paul Dickson published his *Dickson Baseball Dictionary* in 1989, the number of baseball terms had doubled, and even so not many of them had become archaic.

Baseball slang today can be said to have transcended, in large part, the definition of slang as "words not acceptable in formal, standard usage but often used in colloquial speech; the transitory bywords of a language." It could be argued that one of the reasons baseball slang has had such a remarkable impact on American speech is that it has remained so consistent over the years. The vocabularies of most other games and professions are updated constantly to reflect innovations, but the terms used in baseball today, by and large, are the same ones used at the turn of the century. That has always been a key to baseball's appeal—baseball is one of the last remaining strongholds of tradition in American life, a living link to our imagined Garden of Eden, our pioneering, pre-industrial past. In the first (1980) edition of this book, I wrote that "the danger in tradition is stagnation. It cannot be denied that as baseball and its language have become more respectable, they have lost much of their early vitality." Russell Baker similarly complained in a 1979 *New York Times* column:

> Until quite recently the language spoken by baseball's practitioners and hangers-on crackled with terseness, vibrancy and metaphor. Now it is becoming as arid as the tongue of the Federal bureaucrat and shows alarming signs of drift toward the mumbo-jumbo jabber of sociology. . . . Why baseball American should be so impoverished at a moment when the sport is flourishing as never before is anyone's guess. Mine is that it is going through a period of highbrow pretension, brought on perhaps by the hordes of college men cluttering up the locker rooms and the advent of high-falutin' sportswriters too self-conscious about their master's degree in creative writing to risk playing a kid's game at the typewriter. . . . It is enough to make a man pine for Dizzy Dean, who, having been struck in the foot by a batted ball, waited on the mound while a doctor examined him. "This toe is fractured," the doctor said.

To which Dean replied, "Fractured, hell! The damn thing's broken." In those days nobody could have said anything else.

Baker's point is still well taken: Too much about modern American life, baseball included, has had the living color bleached out of it. Baseball could use a strong reinfusion of the linguistic exuberance of Dizzy and his semiliterate confreres. But it now seems that the threat to the language of baseball, and to the game itself, comes not from stagnation but from the wanton disregard of tradition. As the players become ever wealthier, more self-important, and more distant from the concerns of the fans who pay their salaries, and as the owners become ever more conglomerated and greedy, what is in danger of being lost is a sense of the continuity of baseball's past and present. While most fans still cherish the glorious memory of baseball's distant immortals, many of the players know or care less about their bygone predecessors and the words they lived by. All too often, the bottom line seems the major motivating factor for both owners and players, as was demonstrated so disillusioningly by the disruptive baseball strike of 1994. In committing the previously unthinkable cultural crime of canceling the World Series, baseball symbolically severed its most precious link with tradition. Whether that link can ever be fully repaired remains to be seen. A major part of what is at stake is the continued vitality of the language of baseball, the surest barometer of the average fan's immersion in the game's living tradition.

Ace

Most of baseball's early terminology came from the British game of rounders, one of its predecessors. In the first baseball rule book, approved on September 23, 1845, by a committee headed by New York amateur ballplayer Alexander Cartwright, the rounders terms "ace" and "count" were used interchangeably to indicate what today is called a run; a "hand" meant an out. As the game evolved, and the old rounders terms were generally discarded, "ace" took on another meaning. Asa Brainard pitched every game for the 1869 Cincinnati Red Stockings, baseball's first professional team, and compiled a 65–0–1 record that season. The next year, in his honor, a pitcher hurling an especially good game was called an "Asa," a term later condensed into "ace." It was one of the first baseball expressions to find its way into more general American usage, as both a noun and an adjective connoting skillful performance.

Alibi Ike

One of Ring Lardner's unforgettable baseball characters lent his nickname to everyday speech. Frank X. Farrell ("I guess the X stood for 'excuse me'") was the constantly apologetic title character in Lardner's 1914 short story "Alibi Ike," a phrase that came to be applied to anyone who avoids taking responsibility. The expression was further popularized by the 1935 movie *Alibi Ike*, starring comedian Joe E. Brown. Perhaps the classic "Alibi Ike" remark in baseball history was Dodgers pitcher Billy Loes's explanation of why he misplayed a ground ball in the 1953 World Series: "I lost it in the sun."

All-Star Game

The All-Star Game, the popular midsummer contest between the best players of the American and National Leagues, was the brainchild of *Chicago Tribune* sports editor Arch Ward. He suggested a "Dream Game" as part of the ballyhoo surrounding the 1933 Chicago Century of Progress Exposition. The concept was so popular that the All-Star Game became an annual event. The first All-Star Game, played at Chicago's Comiskey Park on July 6, 1933, featured a home run by Babe Ruth and resulted in a 4–2 AL victory. Fans choose the players through ballots, though many in baseball find that this practice leads to undue local favoritism. After a 1957 scandal involving ballot stuffing by Cincinnati fans, the squads were chosen by the rival All-Star team managers until the old practice was resumed in 1970. Between 1959 and 1962, there were two All-Star Games each year, but that backfired by diluting the impact of the event.

American League

After the National League was founded in 1876, several rival major leagues came and went, including the American Association, the Union Association, and the Players' League. The one competitor that lasted was the American League, an outgrowth of the Western Association and its successor, the Western League. Under the presidency of Byron (Ban) Johnson, the Western League built up its forces throughout the 1890s until it was ready to mount an all-out challenge to the NL following the 1899 season. There was talk at that time of reviving the American Association, but Johnson cleverly checkmated that move by renaming his circuit the "American League." This new, nonsectional title coincided with his expansion into eastern cities, and the strategy was successful. The AL played its first game on April 24, 1901. The cities represented that year were Chicago, Boston, Detroit, Philadelphia, Baltimore, Washington, Cleveland, and Milwaukee. Feuding with the NL continued until 1903, when the AL was recognized as an equal competitor.

Angel

Outfielders often complain that high fly balls are hard to judge because the sun plays havoc with their eyes. They welcome clouds, because as Rollin Lynde Hartt explained in a 1908 *Atlantic Monthly* article, "Pitilessly the sun beats down from a sky, broken only by the fleecy-white clouds that the players call 'angels,' because they afford so benevolent a background for the batted ball." Such clouds are also known as "guardian angels."

Annie Oakley

At Buffalo Bill's Wild West shows in the late nineteenth century, one of sharpshooter Annie Oakley's favorite stunts was to shoot holes in playing cards as they were tossed into the air. Since free passes to the show had holes punched in them, as do complimentary tickets to baseball games, some press agents remarked that Annie must have shot holes in them. Ban Johnson, founder of the American League, was the first to call a free ticket an "Annie Oakley," and the term was later used to refer to bases on balls, or "free passes." During the John Dillinger era, a synonym for "Annie Oakley" was "machine-gun ticket."

Apple

Players and writers weary of repeating the word "baseball" began to compare it to other round objects, coming up with such names as "pellet," "pill," and "sphere." By the 1920s they had even begun to use "apple," "cantaloupe," "onion," "orange," "potato," "tater," and "tomato," of which "apple" is most commonly used today. "Tater" in contemporary players' usage has become a slang expression for a home-run ball, formerly called a "long tater." Baseball lexicographer Paul Dickson believes the expression may have originated in the old Negro Leagues as "long potato"; it entered the majors when George Scott came to the Red Sox in 1966 and referred to his homers as "taters."

Around the Horn

The infield ball-tossing ritual and the 5–4–3 double play are both referred to as "around the horn." The phrase was old nautical lingo for the long voyage between the Atlantic and Pacific oceans, with its center point at South America's Cape Horn.

Ash

A bat is called a "bludgeon," "cudgel," "hickory," "lightning," "lumber," "mace," "oak," "pine," "shillelagh," "stick," "thunder," "wagon tongue," "wand," "weap," and "willow"—but not often an "ash," of which it usually is made today. In the early days of the game, all combinations of wood were used for bats, but an 1893 rule stipulated that bats must be entirely composed of hardwood. White ash is preferred for the manufacture of modern bats, although hackberry and hickory also are used.

At Bat, on Deck, in the Hole

On August 6, 1872, the Boston Red Stockings visited the seafaring town of Belfast, Maine, to play the Belfast Pastimes. The scorers for both teams took turns announcing the batters. When Boston was up, the team scorer would yell, "George Wright at bat, Leonard and Barnes next." But in Belfast's half of the inning, the local scorer would announce, "Moody at bat, Boardman on deck, Dinsmore in the hold." The scorer from Boston liked the nautical terms and brought them to his city. Eventually the third phrase was corrupted in baseball usage to "in the hole." Belfast, by the way, lost the historic game by a score of 35–1 but left an enduring legacy in the sport's lexicon.

Bad Head

The phrase "bad head" has nothing to do with brains; bench jockeys use it in reference to an ugly player. Yogi Berra, often the target of such insults, found the perfect riposte when Mike Ryba called him the ugliest man in baseball. Berra merely shrugged and said, "So what? Ya don't hit the ball with your face." Clubhouse comedians today are fond of selecting "all-ugly" teams from among the ranks of "bad heads."

Baltimore Chop

The guileful, cunning Baltimore Orioles of the 1890s delighted in thinking up trick plays. One of their favorites, used most expertly by place-hitter Wee Willie Keeler, became known as the "Baltimore chop." As the *Baltimore News* explained in 1896, "The Baltimore Club has already originated several distinctive plays which have made it famous and which had been copied with more or less success by others. Foremost among these are the 'hit and run' tactics. Now a new style of hitting will be recorded in the baseball history of '96 and credited to the Orioles. It is 'chopping' the ball, and a chopped ball generally goes for a hit. It requires great skill in placing to work this trick successfully, and it is done in this fashion: A middle-height ball is picked out and is attacked with a terrific swing on the upper side. The ball is made to strike the ground from five to ten feet away from the batsman, and, striking the ground with force bounds high over the head of the third or first baseman. In nearly every game lately has this little teaser been successfully employed, and yesterday two such hits were made." Today the play is seldom used intentionally, but when it occurs it is still called a "Baltimore chop." Casey Stengel, who encour-

aged his players to use it, called it the "butcher boy," because
of the batter's downward, chopping motion.

Bandbox

A bandshell, or bandbox, was a familiar sight in the town
squares of America in the early 1900s. Its compact size suggested a comparison to unusually small ballparks, such as
Baker Bowl, the old tin-walled Philadelphia stadium that was
a dream for batters and a nightmare for pitchers. Ebbets
Field, the home of the old Brooklyn Dodgers, was often
called a bandbox. The term is seldom used today, at least in
the major leagues, because the modern stadiums are more
spacious and symmetrical than those in the early days of the
game. Synonyms for "bandbox" are "cigar box" and "flea
box."

Banjo Hit

A pop fly that falls safely has long been called a "Texas
Leaguer," but it remained for Ray (Snooks) Dowd, playing
for Jersey City in 1924, to christen a fluke-hit grounder. Since
the ball "plunks" off the bat, he called it a "banjo hit." Other
names for it include "bleeder," "blooper," "drooper," "humpback," "humpie," "nubber," "plunker," "pooper," "Punch-and-
Judy hit," "punker," "sinker," "squib," and "stinker." A ball
hit directly to a fielder, on the other hand, is called an "atom
ball"—because it's "right at 'im."

Barber

Bench jockeys, like barbers, are notorious for their steady stream of banter, and the use of "barber" to connote a loquacious player entered baseball slang via chatterbox pitcher Waite Hoyt. The word became more popular when voluble Red Barber began broadcasting Brooklyn Dodgers games. A variant meaning for "barber" is a pitcher who, like Sal (The Barber) Maglie, specializes in "close shaves," or pitches close to the batter's whiskers. Such pitches are also called "gillettes," derived from the razor-blade brand name, and "dusters," because they have a tendency to dump a batter into the dust. "Barbers" are sometimes known as "headhunters."

Barnstorming

Itinerant actors who usually performed on farms (the "silo circuit") were first called "barnstormers" around 1884. Eventually the term was used to describe any kind of traveling showmen, and was applied to ballplayers on one-night stands with major-league teams during spring training or with traveling teams such as the bearded House of David or the black Indianapolis Clowns.

Baseball

The legend that Abner Doubleday invented baseball in 1839 endures today, even though historians have found that games using balls and bats date back to ancient times and stem from primitive religious rituals. The medieval French game of *la soule* was a close forerunner of baseball, and the English developed it further into "stoolball" and rounders. An American derivation of rounders in the early 1800s was called the "Massachusetts game." Robert William Henderson's definitive study *Ball, Bat and Bishop* concludes that baseball stemmed chiefly from rounders, which used wooden posts for "goals" or "bases." The first known printed reference to baseball was in *A Little Pretty Pocket Book*, published in 1744 by Londoner John Newberry. It carried a woodcut of a children's baseball game, showing a pitcher, a catcher, a batter, and a runner at first. First, second, and third bases were marked with posts. Accompanying the illustrations was a snatch of doggerel under the heading "Base Ball": "The ball once struck off / Away flies the boy / To the next destined post / And then home with joy." The first American book mentioning baseball was Robin Carver's *Book of Sports*, published in 1834, which describes the rules for a game closely resembling rounders but called "base, or goal ball." The rules of baseball as we know it today were codified by Alexander J. Cartwright in 1845.

Bat Day

Special "days" and "nights" honoring popular players have long been a part of baseball tradition, but the first "bat day" wasn't held until 1952. It was a brainstorm of Rudie Schaffer, Bill Veeck's top assistant when Veeck owned the St. Louis Browns. After obtaining about 12,000 bats at bulk rate from a supplier who was closing out his stock, Schaffer arranged for their distribution to fathers and sons at a June doubleheader, which drew a large (for the Browns) crowd of 15,600. The promotional gimmick spread through the majors and has spawned such variants as "photo days," "ball days," "autograph days," and even a "mustache day," held by Charles O. Finley in 1972 to reward his A's for sprouting facial whiskers. An equally unusual occasion, antedating Schaffer's invention of bat day, was held by Veeck and his Cleveland Indians in 1948. A fan had written a letter to the *Cleveland Press* complaining that players were given "days" and "nights," while fans, who gilded the players' pockets, were ignored. He signed the letter "Good Old Joe Early." So Veeck announced a "Good Old Joe Early Night," presenting Early with an outhouse, a trick Model-T, a swaybacked horse, a new convertible, and a truckload of gifts donated by local merchants, while female fans were presented with a total of 20,000 Princess Aloha orchids.

Veteran minor-league manager Spencer Abbott lost three different starting second basemen to the Army in 1942. "They must be going to fight this darned war around second base," he moaned.

Battery

In military parlance, a battery consists of two pieces of artillery acting as a unit. In baseball usage, it means the pitcher and the catcher. The term, originally applied to the pitcher (considered the key weapon in the team's arsenal), had evolved to its present use by 1868.

Beanball

The use of "bean" as slang for the head is not original to baseball, but "beanball" is an offspring of the sport. It was used to mean a pitch aimed at the batter's head as long ago as 1906, when sportswriter Charley Dryden observed of the great Chief Bender, "While pitching Mr. Bender places too much reliance on the bean ball." The pitch is also called a "beaner," the verbal form is "to bean," and in the early days, a batter dazed from being hit in the head by a pitch was described as "beany." The one major leaguer who died as a result of a beaning was Cleveland shortstop Ray Chapman, who died on August 17, 1920, after being struck by an underhand pitch thrown by the Yankees' Carl Mays. As sportswriter Fred Lieb, an eyewitness, described the incident, "There was a sickening thud as the ball hit the left side of Chapman's head at the temple. He got up after a few seconds, and I could see the left eye hanging from its socket. With a ball player's instinct, he took two steps toward first, then fell in a heap."

Berraism

The argot of Yogi Berra is so unusual that a word had to be coined to identify it. Not long after Berra joined the Yankees, sportswriters began saying, "Have you heard the latest Berraism?" Yogi's utterances have even been collected into a book, *The Wit and Wisdom of Yogi Berra*, by Phil Pepe. Perhaps the classic Berraism came when St. Louis, Yogi's hometown, threw a night for him while he was visiting with the Yanks in 1947. After being avalanched with gifts, Berra lumbered to the microphone and said, "I want to thank all you fans for making this night necessary." And Joe Garagiola still tells about the occasion when Yogi, never punctual, arrived ten minutes late for an appointment. When Garagiola chastised him, Berra replied, "But this is the earliest I've ever been late!" Another time, Berra was interviewed on TV and was given a $100 check made out "Pay to Bearer." He objected, "This ain't the way to spell my name." And when Yogi was named manager of the Yankees in 1964, he was asked what qualified him for the job. "You observe a lot watching," he replied. Among Berra's other oft-quoted words of wisdom are: "Baseball is ninety percent mental. The other half is physical." . . . "In baseball you don't know nothing." . . . "It's déjà vu all over again." . . . and "It ain't over till it's over."

Biff

William T. Hall, a Chicago sportswriter, coined "biff" in the October 4, 1902, issue of *Sporting Life*. His reason for picking the word is obscure, but it may be that the onomatopoeic "biff," meaning to hit a ball hard, is the opposite of "whiff," to strike out.

The Big Bang Theory

Staking his entire offensive strategy on the likelihood of his batters' blowing a game wide open with a big inning, feisty Orioles manager Earl Weaver came up with what he called "The Big Bang Theory." Rather than trying to nibble away at the opposition with bunts and hit-and-run plays, Weaver encouraged his hitters to swing away and maximize the chances of a bases-clearing homer. Puckishly christened after the cosmological theory that the universe was created in a single explosion, Weaver's "Big Bang Theory" may have seemed an inelegant form of strategy, but, coupled with superior pitching, it helped the Orioles win four pennants and one World Series under his tutelage.

Bill Klem

The famous statement attributed to umpire Bill Klem, "I never missed one in my life," made "a Bill Klem" synonymous with an umpire or player who considers himself infallible.

After Klem retired, he said he had been misquoted, and that what he actually had said was "I never missed one—in my heart." He never corrected the mistake during his thirty-five-year National League umpiring career because, as he later explained, "What a happy day it was for me when the baseball world tied that egomaniacal sentence to my coattails and never let me forget it. It was worth a million dollars in publicity for me because for all time it singled me out from the other umpires." The umpire who *did* claim he never missed one was the ebullient Silk O'Loughlin. After an argument, he would often tell a player, "Get out of here. I never missed one in my life. Too late to start now. The Pope for religion, O'Loughlin for baseball; both infallible."

The most famous double-play combination in baseball history—though, in point of fact, far from the best—was Tinker to Evers to Chance. Chicago Cubs shortstop Joe Tinker, second baseman Johnny Evers, and first baseman Frank Chance enjoy their legendary reputation because of some doggerel written in 1908 by Franklin P. Adams of the *New York Globe*. FPA's often-quoted lines:

These are the saddest of possible words:
　　"Tinker to Evers to Chance."
Trio of bear cubs and fleeter than birds,
　　"Tinker to Evers to Chance."
Ruthlessly pricking our gonfalon bubble,
Making a Giant hit into a double—
Words that are heavy with nothing but
　　　　trouble:
　　"Tinker to Evers to Chance."

How many double plays did the famous trio execute that year? Only eight. And if "Evers to Tinker to Chance" twin killings are added, the total still is only sixteen. Over the four seasons between 1906 and 1909, the trio executed a grand total of fifty-four double plays. The holders of the record for most double plays in a single season are the infielders of the 1949 Philadelphia Athletics, who made 217 DPs. Eddie Joost was the shortstop, Pete Suder and Nellie Fox divided second-base duties, and Ferris Fain was the first baseman. But the 1949 A's finished in fifth place, whereas the 1908 Cubs won the pennant (or "gonfalon," in FPA's quaint usage)—and of such stuff legends are made.

Bingle

Neither of the two theories for the origin of "bingle"—meaning any kind of hit, but most often a single—can be conclusively proved or disproved, and it is likely that both contributed to the word's derivation. The first theory calls "bingle" a combination of the onomatopoeic "bang" or "bing" with "single," the basic type of hit. The other theory refers to the old joyful exclamation of "bingo!" which, conceivably, could have been combined with "single" to make "bingle." This theory is supported by the early use of "bingo" to mean a hit, as in a 1902 *Sporting News* article that noted that " 'Truck' Egan is showing his form of other seasons, playing a swell short and getting his timely bingoes as of yore." The first recorded use of "bingle" occurred in the same year.

Bird Dog

Scouts are sometimes called "bird dogs" because they are adept at tracking down good prospects. More precisely, the term describes men on commission who merely inform regular scouts about amateur talent, letting the pros evaluate and sign the players. Scouts are also called "ivory hunters," because they track down the baseball equivalent of "big game."

Black Betsy

Athletes often have pet names—usually female—for their equipment, such as golfer Bobby Jones's "Calamity Jane" putter. The favorite weapon of Shoeless Joe Jackson, who terrorized American League pitchers from 1910 to 1920, was his big, dark bat, nicknamed "The Black Betsy" by its manufacturers, A. G. Spalding and Company. Today the term is applied to any strong bat. Another feminine term that entered baseball lingo was "Old Sal" (short for "Old Sally"), the swiftly hopping "jump ball" thrown by the Giants' Joe McGinnity. The pitch was also known as the "Sal-raise."

Bleachers

Baseball's cheapest seats were once called "rocks" because of their hardness. Later they became known as "bleaching boards" because of their exposure to the sun. "Bleachers" has been traced as far back as 1888. Since the late 1960s, the raucous fans in the bleachers of Chicago's Wrigley Field have been called "bleacher bums." *Bleacher Bums* is the title of a long-running play conceived by Joe Mantegna and written by the members of the Organic Theater Company of Chicago, who first performed it in 1977.

Blind Tom

An unwritten law in baseball forbids ballpark organists to play "Three Blind Mice" in the presence of umpires. But players still taunt them about their eyesight ("Blind Tom," "Mr. Guess," "guesser"), their integrity ("robber," "dog robber," "Jesse James"), their outfits ("boy blue"), and their haughty position ("empire," "Hizzoner," "Hizzumps"). An umpire who seems to be unjustly favoring the home team is scorned as a "homer."

Blue Darter

A sharp, low hit is called a "clothesliner," a "frozen rope," or a "darter." Researcher Edward J. Nichols has traced the expression "blue darter," presumably a metaphor for speed, back to the Baltimore Orioles of 1891.

Bonehead

This derisive expression for someone who makes mistakes, or "boners," was coined by cartoonist "Tad" (T. A. Dorgan) and first used in baseball to refer to Philadelphia Phillies owner Colonel John I. Rogers. George Stallings applied it to Rogers after being released as manager of the Phillies in 1898. Today the names of Fred Merkle, whose baserunning blunder cost the Giants the 1908 pennant, and Babe Herman, the daffiest Dodger, are synonymous with "bonehead." Committing a boner on the field is sometimes called "pulling a Merkle."

> After Ping Bodie was thrown out by several yards at second base in a 1917 game, reporter Arthur (Bugs) Baer wrote, "His heart was full of larceny, but his feet were honest."

The Book

Baseball's most valuable book is the unpublished one that exists in the heads of managers. "The Book," for example, decrees that left-handed batters face right-handed pitchers, and vice versa. An informal codification of baseball experience and tradition, The Book tells managers which move, in a given situation, will more often be correct. Manager Grady Hatton of the Houston Astros once made an attempt to summarize such dicta in an instructional handbook for his players called *Organizational Policy*. Another meaning for "The Book" is the list of official baseball records.

The Boudreau Shift

Cleveland Indians manager Lou Boudreau gave long thought to finding a way of stopping slugger Ted Williams in the

1940s. Finally, knowing that Williams always pulled the ball to right and refused to place-hit to left, Boudreau shifted all of his fielders except the left fielder to the right of second. Other teams began to copy the shift, but Cleveland's remained the most exaggerated.

Bullpen

When the National League started in 1876, the grandstand price was fifty cents. Some teams, however, had roped-in areas adjoining the outfield with an admission price of ten cents. Because the fans (and later the relief pitchers) were herded into it like animals, writers called the outfield practice area the "bullpen," the "pen," or the "corral." The later practice of painting large "Bull Durham" tobacco advertisements on outfield walls encouraged use of the term but did not, as many believe, originate it. An antiquated term for bullpen was "ice box"—the place where fresh pitchers were "kept on ice."

Bunt

Early-baseball authority Hugh S. Fullerton traced the origin of the bunt to shortstop Richard (Dickey) Pearce, who began using it in 1866. As Fullerton wrote in his 1912 article on baseball slang for *The American Magazine*, "Batters formerly turned their bats quickly and struck the ball with the small end, dropping it to the ground. Later many held their bats loosely in the hands, and merely let the ball hit it and fall. The faster ball now in use compelled a change and now most of them push or hook the ball with their bats, striving to control its direction and to roll it at medium speed past the pitcher, yet so slowly the infielders have difficulty in reaching and handling the ball." Other sources credit weak-hitting Boston infielder Tim Murnane with helping popularize the bunt in 1876; Murnane whittled one side of his bat flat and practiced "butting" the ball, an expression eventually corrupted into "bunting." Casey Stengel had a word of his own, "buntation," which he defined while managing the Mets: "Buntation is anything so they don't strike out. Bunt, hit and run, slap the ball, because nothing is more disgraceful than for a major league hitter to strike out."

Bush Leagues

In baseball's early days, small-town fields were not kept in very good condition. This, coupled with the rustic nature of most minor-league towns, led to a number of derogatory terms for the minors: "alfalfa leagues," "the sticks," "the woods," "the tall timbers," "the cob-fence route," "the high-grass leagues," "the rhubarbs," "the deep bushes," and "the bushes." Eventually, "bush leagues" became the generally used insult for the lower minors, and players on such teams were called "bushers." Any form of crude, amateurish play or behavior in baseball is still described by the adjective "bush." Another old expression for the minor leagues was "trolley leagues," because the teams in the league were "only a trolley ride apart."

Can of Corn

Since at least the 1920s, a high, lazy fly ball has been called a "can of corn." According to baseball lexicographer Paul Dickson, "The phrase has long been assumed to have come from the old-time grocery store where the grocer used a pole or a mechanical grabber to tip an item, such as a can of corn, off a high shelf and let it tumble into his hands or his apron, which was held out in front like a fire net." Dickson also cites alternate theories, including announcer Bob Prince's explanation that catching such a fly ball is "as easy as taking corn out of a can."

Charley Horse

The origin of "charley horse," meaning a stiffness of the leg muscles, has puzzled etymologists for years, and many different theories have been advanced. The most plausible theory is also a complicated one: King Charles I of England used to palm off his aging guards, or "Charleys," onto the London police force; broken-down horses, like broken-down cops, came to be known as "old Charleys"; baseball parks used to keep old workhorses on the premises, usually referring to them as "Charley"; and a hobbling ballplayer was said to walk like the team's horse, or to have a "charley horse."

An anecdote that supports this theory appeared in a *Cincinnati Enquirer* item of June 30, 1889, concerning a player named Joe Quest, who had left the majors three years earlier: "When Joe Quest was employed as an apprentice in the machine shop of Quest & Shaw at New Castle, Pennsylvania, his father, one of the proprietors of the firm, had an old white horse named Charley. Doing usage in pulling heavy loads had stiffened the animal's legs so that he walked as if troubled with strained tendons. Afterward, when Quest became a member of Chicago, he was troubled, along with other players, with a peculiar stiffness of the legs, which brought to his mind the ailment of the old white horse, Charley. All players hobbled like the old horse, and since no one knew what the trouble was, Quest dubbed it 'charley horse.'" So although Quest may not have been the first ballplayer to use the expression, there is evidence that he at least played a major role in popularizing it.

Chicago Slide

The early version of the hook slide was invented by Mike (King) Kelly (of "Slide, Kelly, Slide" fame), who, instead of dropping feet-first into a base, would fall away from the baseman and hook the corner with his toe. Since Kelly was a star on the Chicago Nationals, it became known as the "Chicago Slide."

> Pet phrases dot the speech of most base-
> ball announcers, and often they become
> widely used among fans and the general
> public alike. The most famous exclamation by
> an announcer was Dodgers radio broadcaster
> Walter (Red) Barber's "He's sittin' on the cat-
> bird seat!" That meant a player was in a good
> position, usually on the base paths. James
> Thurber used the expression for the title of
> one of his short stories, ensuring Barber's
> immortality in the literary world. Another of
> Barber's trademarks was, "They're tearin' up
> the pea patch!," which he'd say when the
> Dodgers were staging a rally.

Chinese Homer

The Sporting News has claimed that New York cartoonist
Thomas A. (Tad) Dorgan originated the term "Chinese
homer" or "Chinese fly," meaning a cheap home run, in reference to homers hit down the short foul-lines of the old Polo
Grounds. Many a pitcher was defeated by the bloopers that
traveled the necessary 280 feet (to left) or 258 feet (to right).
San Francisco sportswriters, however, have insisted that the
term "Chinese homer" was coined in their city prior to World

War 1. California, which has always had a large Asian popu-
lation, paid notoriously low wages in the nineteenth century
to Chinese coolie laborers, and as a result, whites insultingly
used the word "Chinese" to refer to anything cheap. Similarly, a cheap hit in the old days of the Pacific Coast League
was known as a "Chinese liner" or a "Japanese liner."

Choke-Up

Baseball's most despised player is one whose "Adam's apple
comes up," or who "chokes up," becoming nervous in a tight
situation. The derisive "choke" sign, directed at someone who
feels the pressure "choking" his throat, is made by clutching
the neck or, in some cases, by wrapping a towel around the
throat. There are few quicker ways to get in trouble or start
a fight in baseball than to give the choke sign. During the
1958 World Series, Yankees pitcher Ryne Duren, incensed at
an umpire's call, grabbed at his throat. Commissioner Ford
Frick, watching the game on a hospital television set, saw the
gesture and slapped Duren with a long-distance fine.

Circus Play

Baseball players who make easy plays seem difficult in order
to milk applause are said to "showboat," or to make a "circus play" or "circus catch," since their behavior smacks of
corny show-biz antics. *Chicago Inter-Ocean* sportswriter Charlie Seymour is believed to have coined the phrase "circus

play"; its earliest known appearance in print was in one of his articles, on July 15, 1885. Three years later, in a book called *The Krank: His Language and What It Means* ("krank" was an early term for sports enthusiast, antedating "fan"), Thomas W. Lawson defined "circus catch" facetiously as "catching the ball between the upper and under eyelid." Players who make such catches, usually outfielders, are also called "grand-standers," because they are "playing to the grandstands." Sometimes, however, "circus catch" is used in praise of a gen-uinely spectacular play, such as Willie Mays's famous over-the-shoulder catch of a long Vic Wertz drive to deep center in the Polo Grounds during the 1954 World Series. Another phrase for "circus catch" is "Jawn Titus," believed to have been derived from the name of John Titus, a 1903–13 National League outfielder renowned for his sensational fielding.

Clubhouse Lawyer

In military usage, a "guardhouse lawyer" is a pop-off who usually winds up confined to the guardhouse, where he con-tinues to agitate against his superiors. Baseball's equivalent is the "clubhouse lawyer," which refers both to rebellious mal-contents and to players prone to making long disquisitions on how "we was robbed." With the increasingly independent attitude of ballplayers in recent years, clubhouse lawyers have become more commonplace and more vocal, often airing their complaints in the press. The Yankees of the late 1970s under volatile manager Billy Martin were notorious clubhouse lawyers, particularly slugger Reggie Jackson. But the classic clubhouse lawyers in baseball history were the 1940 "Crybaby Indians," who lost both manager and pennant because of intramural dissension.

Cockeye

Left-handed people have been targets of irrational abuse and suspicion for ages (the word "sinister" derives from *sinistra*, the Latin word for "left"), and baseball is no exception to this prejudice. In the early days of the game, southpaw gloves were rare, and as a result, lefties were strange sights on the diamond. Although a recent survey showed that about 20 percent of all major leaguers now throw left-handed, they are still taunted with such terms as "cockeye," "crooked arm," "corkscrew arm," and "twirly-thumb."

Country-Fair Hitter

In the old days of the game, most players punched, chopped, and pushed the ball. Free-swingers were rare and usually found among the strong country boys. Since the plow jockeys played ball at country fairs, a swing-from-the-heels batter became known as a "country-fair hitter," or, in a later corruption, a "pretty fair country hitter," meaning any kind of adept batter. Sometimes "country-fair player" is used derisively, like "grandstander," in reference to a show-off.

Cousin

Some batters, claimed Waite Hoyt, helped his career so much they could have been his cousins. The Yankees pitcher was the first to use the term for pushover hitters, and it was applied later to a pitcher easy to hit.

Cripple

With a count of 3–0 or 3–1 on the batter, a pitcher must put the ball over the plate to avoid a walk, so the situation "cripples" his effectiveness in shaving the corners and using tricky deliveries. Such a pitch thus is called a "cripple."

Cup of Coffee

In September, major-league rosters are expanded to carry extra players, since the minors close their season early to give the parent clubs a chance to test rookies under big-time conditions (and so the minors won't play to empty seats during the end of pennant races and the start of the football season). For many players, the September whirl is their only major-league experience—barely long enough to "drink a cup of coffee" with the team.

Whenever baseball is used as a metaphor for the meaning of life—a play that American intellectuals, with ample reason, find hard to resist—one is sure to find some words written in 1954 by the philosopher Jacques Barzun: "Whoever wants to know the heart and mind of America had better learn baseball . . ." (Less often cited is the sentence's concluding clause: "the rules and realities of the game.")

Curveball

William A. (Candy) Cummings is acknowledged to be the inventor of the curveball. Although some pitchers previously had used curves without understanding why they were breaking, Cummings was the first to learn the technique of intentionally curving pitches. His claim was verified by Henry (Father) Chadwick, the first recognized baseball authority. As a youngster of fourteen in 1862, Cummings practiced curving clamshells across his Brooklyn backyard until he perfected the trick of gripping the ball firmly with the middle finger and snapping the wrist to make it break down and away from the direction it is thrown. The pitch, originally called the "out-curve," acquired prominence after Cummings used it in 1866 for the Excelsior Juniors of Brooklyn against the Harvard varsity team in Cambridge, Massachusetts, according to

Tim Murnane in an 1896 copy of the *Boston Globe*. Cummings entered the major leagues in 1872, but no one else knew how to throw the pitch until 1874. As Cummings explained in an 1898 letter to *Sporting Life*, "I taught Ham Avery how to curve the ball and explained the theory to the entire satisfaction of Professor Eaton, of Yale." Strange as it now seems, it took a while for people to believe that such a pitch could be thrown. As an unidentified sportswriter observed around the turn of the century, "For years the scientific men laughed at the idea of a man making a ball curve in the air; but the prejudice has passed away, as many of the learned men of the day can go out on a field and fully illustrate the science of curve pitching themselves." Today the curve is alternately called a "breaking ball." Other names for a curveball include "fish," "hook" or "fish hook," "jughandle," "pretzel," "dipsy-do," "roundhouse," and "snake." A curve is also called a "mackerel," because after watching fastballs zing past their ears, batters think a curve looks "dead as a mackerel." "Number two," another synonym, arises from the common use of two fingers by a catcher when signaling for a curve. A pitcher who has lost his speed and must rely on his mackerel is said to have "two fingers only."

Daniel Webster

A player adept at riding umpires is respected for his forensic ability, which may be compared to that of the Massachusetts orator Daniel Webster. A less imposing name is given to another type of player—the loner, the guy who becomes unpopular because he won't horse around or pick up the check. Since such a player never makes his presence known, he is given the anonymous name of "a Dick Smith."

Designated Hitter

The designated hitter rule, adopted by the American League in 1973 as a means of beefing up the teams' hitting potential, was first proposed, ironically enough, by a president of the National League. John Heydler suggested in 1928 that the majors adopt what he called a "ten-man team," with a batter designated to hit in place of the pitcher, thus eliminating the weak spot at the bottom of the batting lineup. The American League laughed down the proposal at the annual baseball meeting in 1928, but Ed Hughes of the *Brooklyn Eagle* presciently observed that "Heydler's idea of an official pinch hitter operating throughout a game for the pitcher has many advocates as well as scoffers. A good many baseball players seem to think well of the proposed innovation, too. At any rate it wasn't considered ridiculous all around, which means the thing may some day come to pass." Irrepressible Oakland A's owner Charles O. Finley, the man who brought facial hair back to baseball and unsuccessfully tried to have the ball tinted orange, revived the DH idea in the early 1970s and managed to win approval by his league. It was first tested in the minors in 1972 and was introduced in the AL the following year. Many baseball traditionalists deplored the new rule, and the National League has stubbornly refused to adopt it, although it is used in the All-Star Game and the World Series every other year. Finley even went so far as to hire a player unofficially known as his "designated runner"— sprinter Herb Washington, who was used by the A's in 1974 and 1975 purely as a pinch runner. Washington had never played a single game in organized baseball before Finley hired him, and during most of his time with the A's he did not even own a glove.

Ducks on the Pond

One of baseball's more whimsical expressions compares runners on base—usually with the bases loaded—to ducks on the "pond" (i.e., the diamond). Cornball radio announcers love to exclaim, "Ducks on the pond, folks, ducks on the pond!"

Duffy's Cliff

When Boston's Fenway Park was constructed, the outfield surface was about four feet lower than the surface of the street bordering the fence. For reasons of haste or economy, the builders accommodated the existing conditions by leaving a portion of the higher ground in the left-field playing area, which was about three feet higher than the main surface of the field and had a slight incline. The team's left fielder when the park was opened in 1912, George (Duffy) Lewis, played

the hill so well that it became known as "Duffy's Cliff."
When the park was rebuilt in 1933–34, the hill was made less
precipitous, but Fenway Park still has an elevation in left field
to warn outfielders that they are approaching the "Green
Monster," the players' name for the park's imposing thirty-
seven-foot-high left-field wall. Red Sox star outfielder Carl
Yastrzemski became as expert at playing the incline as Duffy
Lewis was long before him.

Eephus Ball

After the big toe on his right foot was damaged in a hunt-
ing accident on December 7, 1941, Pittsburgh pitcher
Truett (Rip) Sewell had to find a new pitching motion. He
developed a unique pitch that ballooned high into the air,
falling just in time to nick the strike zone. The first time he
used it was against Dick Wakefield of the Tigers in a 1942
exhibition game at Muncie, Indiana. Sewell later explained the
origin of its name: "After I threw my new pitch all the newspapermen wanted to know what its name was. I said, 'I don't
name them—I just throw them.' One of the outfielders,
Maurice Van Robays, told the sportswriters that the pitch was
an 'eephus ball.' They wanted to know what 'eephus' meant,
and he told them that 'it don't mean nothing, and that's what
that pitch is—nothing.'" Baseball lexicographer Paul Dickson points out that prior to 1942, "ephus, e-phus, or ephus
ophus was used as slang for dependable information; the low-
down or the right 'dope.'" Umpires initially looked askance

at the eephus ball, but they eventually accepted its use by Sewell, who turned it into a potent weapon in back-to-back 21-victory seasons in 1943 and 1944. The only batter who ever homered off Sewell's eephus ball was Ted Williams, in the 1946 All-Star Game. Other names given to the pitch by sportswriters were the "balloon ball," the "blooper ball," and the "rainbow pitch."

> After diminutive Dodger outfielder Al Gionfriddo made his fabled catch of a Joe DiMaggio long ball in the sixth game of the 1947 World Series, the writers clustered around the previously unknown player. Teammate Hank Behrman, listening in, cracked, "What are you all excited about? He makes catches like that every day during batting practice."

Fadeaway

In modern baseball usage, "fadeaway" refers to a slide developed by Ty Cobb in which the runner falls (or "fades") away from the base and hooks a corner of it with his toe or trailing foot, thus eluding the tag. For a long time, though, "fadeaway" was the name of Christy Mathewson's most potent weapon, a slow curveball that took a sharp break away from the plate just as it reached the batter. According to Fred Lieb, sportswriter Bozeman (Boze) Bulger of the *New York Evening World* probably was responsible for giving the pitch its name. Today the closest approximation of the fadeaway is the screwball, a pitch thrown with the rotation opposite to that of the curveball, making it twist in and out like a corkscrew. Giants lefty Carl Hubbell, one of the great pitchers of the 1930s, is generally credited with its invention, although the phrase "corkscrew twist" was used in a baseball context in the May 8, 1891, *Chicago Herald*. Hubbell certainly was the man who made the screwball popular. Players also call it the "scroogie."

Fan

More controversy has raged around the origin of "fan" than of any other baseball term, with the possible exception of "charley horse." Before "fan" came into general use in the 1890s, the common term for a baseball enthusiast was "crank" or "krank." Many claim that "fan" is a shortened version of "fanatic." This theory often traces it back to Chris von der Ahe, an eccentric German who owned the St. Louis Browns in the nineteenth century and was known for his mispronunciations of the English language. Connie Mack's theory was that spectators were called "fans" because they usually fanned themselves in hot baseball weather (he was famous for using one himself). Most modern etymologists, however, trace the word from "the fancy," a British term in use since about 1810 to designate patrons of boxing events. The expression was successively corrupted to "fance," "fans," and "fan."

The first recorded use of "fan" to mean a baseball enthusiast was by Cincinnati writer Ren Mulford in an 1888 copy of *The Sporting News.* A secondary meaning of "fan" is as a verb meaning "to strike out"—to "fan" the air with the bat. In the early 1900s, "fanning" also meant gabbing about baseball, and players were fond of postgame "fanning fests."

Fantasy Baseball

For many years, baseball fans have been able to "manage" their favorite teams vicariously by playing games based on actual ballplayers' statistics. The granddaddy of sophisticated tabletop games, APBA, was created by Richard Seitz in 1932 (the initials refer to the original American Professional Baseball Association). APBA fanatics (including, in his boyhood, the author of this book) have spent long, dreamy hours lost in such fantasies. Robert Coover's highly acclaimed 1968 novel *The Universal Baseball Association, Inc., J. Henry Waugh, Prop.* satirized that kind of obsession with an imaginary game played on a diamond conjured up out of dice and cards. What Coover's protagonist loved was "not the actual game so much—to tell the truth, real baseball bored him—but rather the records, the statistics, the peculiar balances between individual and team, offense and defense, strategy and luck, accident and pattern, power and intelligence. And no other activity in the world had so precise and comprehensive a history, so specific an ethic, and at the same time, strange as it seemed, so much ultimate mystery." Since the 1970s, the fantasist J. Henry Waugh has been cloned many times over through the proliferation of what has come to be called "fantasy baseball," "virtual baseball," or "Rotisserie League Baseball." Fantasy players organize their own leagues to compete in what is now a major American leisure-time activity, abetted by the proliferation of personal computers (even APBA has been computerized). "Rotisserie League Baseball," the seminal modern fantasy-league game, was created in 1979 over dinner at New York's La Rotisserie Française by a group of fanatics headed by baseball historian Dan Okrent. Another recent phenomenon (dating from 1983) is the "fantasy baseball camp," in which fans pay for the privilege of actually playing ball with their favorite big-league players from the past.

Farm System

Branch Rickey of the St. Louis Cardinals originated the farm system of minor-league clubs in order to "grow our own talent," as he told owner Sam Breadon. "We can round up promising young prospects and develop them on our own minor-league clubs," Rickey explained. After constructing a framework of teams for his system, Rickey instructed his scouts to round up young players, telling them to ask themselves simply, "Can he run? Can he throw? Can he hit?" The farm club, rather than the elaborate farm system familiar today, antedated Rickey, however. And although "farming" players to the minors was a term used even in the nineteenth century, deriving partly from the rustic nature of most towns in the minors, or "bushes," it confused major leaguers as late as 1915. When Rogers Hornsby joined the Cardinals that year, manager Miller Huggins told him he should be sent to a farm to develop. Hornsby, taking the advice literally, worked as a farmer during the winter, developing strong muscles for baseball.

Fireman

The primary baseball meaning of "fireman" is a relief pitcher who "puts out the fire" late in a game by squelching an enemy rally. The term was first applied to the Yankees' Johnny (Grandma) Murphy, who pitched from 1932 to 1947. Another Yankee, reliever Joe Page, was nicknamed "The Fireman." Hoyt Wilhelm and Elroy Face were two of the greatest firemen. Mike Marshall, while with the Dodgers in 1974, became the first fireman to win the Cy Young Award. Among the most prominent in recent years have been Jeff (The Terminator) Reardon, Lee Smith, Dennis Eckersley, Rollie Fingers, Sparky Lyle, Kent Tekulve, and Bruce Sutter. The secondary meaning of "fireman" is a fast dresser. Some ballplayers linger in the clubhouse for hours after a game, but others leave as quickly as possible. Don McMahon, when he was a relief pitcher for the Milwaukee Braves, set a pace a real fireman would admire: he once took off his uniform, showered, and dressed in 4½ minutes—undoubtedly an all-time record.

Flake

Eccentric players in the early days of baseball were often called "Dizzy," "Bugs," "Goofy," or other nicknames connoting craziness. The nicknames of John (Cuckoo) Glaiser, Clyde (Mad) Hatter, and Ray (Filbert) Pierce are typical of that era. In the 1950s, because of the beatnik subculture, the word "kook" came into wide use for oddball characters, but by the late 1950s "flaky" had entered the slang lexicon. Outfielder Jackie Brandt probably was the first ballplayer to be called "Flaky," a nickname given to him in 1957 by a Giants teammate who said that "things seem to flake off his mind and disappear." The adjective became a noun ("flake") by the early 1960s. "Baseball gave the word its current meaning," William Safire acknowledged in 1979 in his *New York Times* column "On Language." Today every player exhibiting the slightest variation from establishment habits is called a "flake." Among the more famous baseball flakes of recent years have been Bill (The Spaceman) Lee, Mark (The Bird) Fidrych, Doug (The Red Rooster) Rader, Al (The Mad Hungarian) Hrabosky, Ross (Crazy Eyes) Grimsley, and Bill (Looney Tunes) Faul.

Fly

If a ballplayer uses the word "fly" with a disparaging tone of voice, he's not referring to a fly ball but rather to a fan who pesters him like a persistent insect. Female groupies who hang around ballplayers are called "green flies" (supposedly an even less discriminating breed than the common fly), or, less insultingly, "baseball Annies."

Foggin' It Through

Dizzy Dean showed up in spring training as a Cardinals rookie and wowed everyone by "foggin' through" his fastball. It was so hard to see his pitches when he reached back for "sumthin' extra" that they seemed to be coming out of a fog. Whether or not Dean was the first to use "foggin' it through" in that sense is not certain, but he made the expression popular. Another version is "radio ball": you can hear it but you can't see it. Batters who faced Walter Johnson often went back to the bench muttering the famous phrase of Senators catcher Cliff Blankenship, "You can't hit what you can't see," and the batters even claimed they caught colds from the breezes stirred by Johnson's pitches, which they called "pneumonia balls." In one celebrated incident, the Indians' Ray Chapman (later to die after being beaned by Yankees pitcher Carl Mays in 1920) took two called strikes from Johnson and headed for the dugout. "Wait a minute," the umpire said, "you've got another strike coming." Chapman replied, "Never mind. I don't want it." Besides "fog," "pneumonia ball," and "radio ball," other synonyms for fastball include "smoke," "smoker," "heat," "BB," "pea," and "aspirin," the latter three because the ball appears so small when it crosses the plate. Throwing a fast pitch is called "putting the mustard on it," because it "stings."

Foot in the Bucket

A batter who moves his forward foot away from the plate as he swings is said to have his "foot in the bucket"—usually considered a bad batting habit—an exaggeration meaning that such a hitter would put his foot in the water bucket near the team bench. The term is still used today even though water coolers have replaced water buckets in dugouts. One batter not hurt by the habit was Al (Bucketfoot) Simmons, who wound up in the Hall of Fame with a .334 lifetime batting average after twenty seasons of "spiking the water bucket," as players used to say.

Forkball

Invention of the tricky forkball pitch has usually been attributed to Red Sox right-hander Bullet Joe Bush. While practicing in 1920 with catcher Al Walters, Bush happened to grip the ball between his index and middle fingers. He later recalled that the ball "did things"; after throwing it a few more times he knew he "had something." While Bush certainly deserves credit for popularizing the pitch, evidence brought forth by readers of *The Sporting News* has indicated that he did not invent it. A pitcher named Bob Troy, who appeared in only one major-league game (for Detroit in 1912) and was killed in action during World War I, threw a pitch in which the ball was held between the index and middle fingers. And one reader of the paper claimed that sandlotters threw a similar pitch called a "V-ball" in Buffalo as early as 1905. The most famous forkballer in baseball history was Pittsburgh reliever Elroy Face, who learned it from Joe Page of the Yankees. Asked how he knew which way the pitch would break, Face replied, "I don't, but neither does the batter."

Fungo

Fungo is the name of a practice game in which a batter hits flies to outfielders or (sometimes) infielders. The type of wood used in the fungo bat accounts for one theory of the word's origin: the bats, with very narrow handles and extra-thick heads, were so soft that they seemed to be made of fungus. Another theory is that the batter in the old version of the practice game would yell, "One go, two goes, fun goes," before hitting the ball; the expression "fun goes" may have been derived from cricket, in which it referred to practice strokes. "Fungo" has been traced as far back as 1867. Though a fungo bat is hardly an imposing weapon, Henry Miller of the Northern League used one in 1916 to wallop a ball 438 feet, 2 inches. Later, California Angels coach Jimmy Reese became known as the "King of the Fungoes" because of his uncanny ability with that type of bat. He often gave exhibitions of his specialty before Angels games.

Washington manager Joe Cantillon had been hearing wild tales in 1908 about a young hayseed from Weiser, Idaho, who was touted as "the greatest pitcher in baseball." He tried to ignore them, but after several months he became fed up and sent Cliff Blankenship, a catcher on the injured list, to scout the youngster. "And bring your bat with you," instructed Cantillon. "If you can get even a loud foul off him, leave him there." After a few days a telegram arrived in Washington beginning with words often heard in later years: "YOU CAN'T HIT WHAT YOU CAN'T SEE. I'VE SIGNED HIM AND HE'S LEAVING TODAY." "He" was Walter Johnson.

Gateway

Not content with the ordinary name of first base, writers began calling it the "gateway," since it is the first destination of a runner on his trip home, hence the "gateway" to a score. Similarly, second base is known as the "keystone," since as the middle of the road to the plate, it is the key base to reach if one is to be in scoring position.

Giving It the Arlie Latham

Walter Arlington (Arlie) Latham was a scrappy infielder who played regularly from 1880 to 1895, with brief appearances stretching his career to 1901. One day he and a St. Louis Browns teammate, Doc Bushong, argued over who could throw a ball farther. Club manager Charles Comiskey foolishly offered $100 to the winner of the contest. Although Latham won the prize, he pulled a muscle because he had failed to warm up sufficiently, and his arm was permanently injured. Near the end of his career, it was so weak that "'giving it the Arlie Latham" meant making a halfhearted attempt at fielding a grounder. The hit that resulted was known as an "Arlie Latham hit." After his playing career ended, Latham became notorious for his yelling and his wild gesticulations in the coaching box, and that kind of behavior, a common tactic to distract pitchers in the early days of the game, became known as "doing an Arlie Latham."

Glass Arm

A player with a history of arm trouble is said to have a "glass arm," because it is so fragile. This nineteenth-century term is still used today, despite a premature declaration in the *New York Sporting Times* of June 20, 1891: "The term 'glass arm' is becoming obsolete. 'Crockery limbs' is the proper caper now."

Glove Man

Although it is sometimes used as a compliment, the phrase "glove man" is just as often a backhanded insult, because it can be a form of damning with faint praise: a glove man in that sense is a weak hitter who survives on the strength of his fielding ability. Synonymous is "leather man," while a good-hit-no-field player is called a "wood man."

Gopher

Vernon (Goofy) Gomez first called home-run pitches "gophers" because they "go fer" homers. The term "gopher" previously had been coined to refer to a flunkie, an underling who is told to "go fer" something. In baseball, common practical jokes include telling a gullible rookie or young clubhouse attendant to go for a "bucket of steam," find "the key to the mound," or "get the bull out of the pen."

Grapefruit League

The first spring-training trip by a pro baseball team was a journey to New Orleans in February 1870 by the Chicago White Stockings. Other teams began to move south in the late-winter months, and the first team to visit Florida, according to Lee Allen, was the Washington National League club in 1888, which made Jacksonville its training base. Florida became the most popular state for preseason workouts, and the jocular term

"Grapefruit League" gradually came into use to designate the spring-training exhibition circuit. The teams that play in the Southwest are said to make up the "Cactus League."

Greenberg Gardens

When Hammerin' Hank Greenberg joined the Pirates in 1947 after a long American League career, the club erected a shorter fence in left field as a target, and the area became known as "Greenberg Gardens." Later when Ralph Kiner was the resident slugger, it was called "Kiner's Korner." The irrepressible Bill Veeck practiced the ultimate in fence manipulation while running the minor-league Milwaukee Brewers. He devised a fence that could be moved forward or backward depending on the batting power of the visiting club. Umpires and league officials disapproved. Veeck said in his own defense, "I try not to break the rules but merely to test their elasticity." Just before the 1964 season opened, Athletics owner Charles Finley put up in Kansas City's Municipal Stadium a wooden fence shaped like a V. The point of the V was exactly 296 feet from home, the same distance as Yankee Stadium's right-field foul pole was at that time. Since Finley claimed that the New York wall unfairly boosted the Yanks into championships, he called his apparatus a "Pennant Porch." Forced to remove it, he modified it to a "One-Half Pennant Porch," covered by a roof made of burlap and wood that extended twenty-seven feet into the field. But the umpires made him dismantle that one, too.

Hogan's Brickyard

Just as "Murphy" was once synonymous with cop, another Irish surname, "Hogan," was a widely used slang expression for building contractor. "Hogans" kept their bricks and other supplies in rough, bumpy yards, which ballplayers compared to unkempt minor-league parks. "Hogan's Brickyard," or "Hogan's Back Yard," went into baseball usage to describe a lumpy diamond. Similar in meaning is a "home-brew field"— one that has plenty of "hops."

Horse-and-Buggy League

Jet travel has its drawbacks for modern players, who often feel the effects the next day, but it's heaven in comparison with team transportation in "the sticks," where often a bus is used. Minor leaguers still say they are playing in a "horse-and-buggy league," even if this once-accurate expression is no longer literally true.

Horsecollar

Draft horses used to wear big, bulky stuffed collars over the backs of their necks. When a player goes hitless in a game, he figuratively carries a similar burden, or a "horsecollar," on his shoulders.

Officially, Ping Bodie's 1920 Yankee roommate was Babe Ruth. However, noting Ruth's constant curfew violations, Bodie shrugged and said, "I'm rooming with a suitcase."

Hot Corner

This colorful expression, usually meaning "third base," dates back to 1889, when Cincinnati sportswriter Ren Mulford covered a game in which Reds third baseman Hick Carpenter had an amazingly tough time. Carpenter was almost ripped apart by seven line drives, each waist-high and each the third out of the inning. Mulford wrote, "The Brooklyns had Old Hick on the hot corner all afternoon and it's a miracle he wasn't murdered."

Hot Dog

Concessions man Harry M. Stevens originated the "hot dog," a frankfurter on a bun, around 1900 at the Polo Grounds. The day was cold and windy and soft drinks were selling badly, so Stevens bought up all the franks and rolls in the ballpark area. After boiling the wieners and splitting the buns, he started yelling the soon-to-be-famous line, "Get 'em while they're hot!" Later, sports cartoonist "Tad" (T. A. Dorgan) drew humorous pictures of the franks, poking fun at their supposed contents by drawing them as dachshunds. Tad's gibe was suggested by a then-popular nickname for a sausage, "barker," from a popular song about a Dutchman's dog. The "hot dog" industry profited from the catchy phrase. (Among other slang expressions coined or popularized by Dorgan were "bonehead," "23 skidoo," "the cat's pajamas," and "yes, we have no bananas.") "Hot dog," like "hot shot," is also used to describe a player who shows off and tries to dominate the fans' attention. The Yankees' Reggie Jackson was the epitome of a "hot dog." A former teammate, Darold Knowles, once said of him, "There isn't enough mustard in the world to cover Reggie Jackson."

Hot Stove League

The "Hot Stove League," also called the "Winter League," refers to the cold period between baseball seasons in which fans figuratively sit around the fire and replay the games of the past. Baseball historian Ernest J. Lanigan said that "Hot Stove League" was coined around 1900. The phrase may have originated with Ren Mulford, who wrote winter baseball columns in Cincinnati. Some claim the term originated with devotees of horse racing.

Iron Man

Many baseball aficionados think of Lou (The Iron Man) Gehrig or marathon pitcher Joe (Iron Man) McGinnity when the term "iron man" is mentioned. Besides connoting a durable player, most often a pitcher, the term is also used to mean the price of admission to a ball game. Silver dollars were once called "iron men," and $1 was formerly a common price for a general-admission ticket. "Iron Mike" is the name of the mechanized pitching machine used in spring training and other periods of batting practice.

Jaker

According to nickname researcher Thomas P. Shea, "jaker" (or "jake") dates back to Garland (Jake) Stahl, a famous player-manager of the early 1900s. Stahl, unwilling to play first base for the 1913 Red Sox because of a bad foot, was chastised by his teammates as a loafer, and "jaker" went into slang usage as a result. Another version, favored by *The Sporting News*, holds that Stahl was so famous that "Jake" became synonymous with the word "stall," even though he usually was a hustler. Shea defines "jaker" as a "ballplayer who stalls, or fakes sickness to keep from playing." A player who doesn't let injuries keep him from playing is known admiringly as a "gamer," because he is "game."

John Anderson

"Honest" John Anderson was an average first baseman and outfielder for the old New York Highlanders, the predecessors of the Yankees. In 1904, however, he immortalized himself by stealing second with the bases loaded. Since then runners pulling the same boner are said to have done "a John Anderson."

Junk Man

The same pitchers whom fastballers scorn for their fancy deliveries are often those who achieve the greatest success. "Junk pitches" include the knuckler and all other varieties of the slowball. The deliveries look easy to hit from the stands, but they often tie the big sluggers into knots. Ed Lopat of the Yankees was the first such pitcher to be labeled a junk man, in the 1940s, but Dizzy Dean earlier threw what he called his "nuthin' ball," a junk pitch, after his fastball motion was ruined when a line drive broke his toe in the 1937 All-Star Game. Perhaps the most renowned junk man was diminutive Stu Miller, who relied so much more on junk than on strength that he was blown off the mound by a stiff wind during the 1961 All-Star Game at San Francisco's Candlestick Park (Miller wound up as the game's winning pitcher). Giants publicity director Garry Schumacher called Miller's version of the fastball a "Wells Fargo pitch," explaining, "It comes to you in easy stages." Super-slow Hoyt Wilhelm, a wizard with the knuckler, was another famous junk man.

K

The scorer's symbol for a strikeout, "K," was first used by *New York Herald* baseball writer M. J. Kelly, who was also the editor of the 1868 *DeWitt Baseball Guide*. Kelly assigned "K," the last letter in "struck," to strikeout in order to avoid confusion with "S," the symbol for sacrifice and, formerly, for shortstop.

> The great Brooklyn Dodgers catcher Roy Campanella, before his playing career was ended in a 1958 automobile accident, told a gathering of the nation's businessmen, "You have to be a man to be a big leaguer, but you have to have a lot of little boy in you, too."

Knothole Club

Every respectable ballpark used to have several knotholes in its wooden fence, privileged vantage points for the kids of the neighborhood. In the 1920s, progressive Cardinals executive Branch Rickey started a St. Louis "Knothole Club," in which youngsters were admitted for nothing. The practice, with some modifications, including nominal admission charges, is now common throughout baseball as a means of nurturing the interest of budding fans who someday will have the privilege of paying full ticket prices.

Ladies' Day

Handsome Irishman Tony (Count) Mullane was a star Cincinnati pitcher in the late nineteenth century. The team's owner, Aaron Stern, noticed that swarms of women attended every game Mullane was scheduled to pitch. So, early in the summer of 1889, Stern ran an advertisement stating that Mullane would pitch every Monday, when all ladies accompanied by male escorts would be admitted free of charge. Unlike ladies' day promotions tried briefly by various teams in 1883, the Reds' event became a regular attraction. The practice spread quickly after owners realized it was good business to expand the ranks of potential fans in what was originally considered a sport for male spectators only.

Lowdermilk

Grover Cleveland Lowdermilk was a below-average pitcher for six teams from 1909 to 1920, with a 21–39 lifetime record. But his wildness became almost legendary, and as a result wild young pitchers are sometimes called "Lowdermilks," whereas the names of better pitchers of the 1910s are forgotten.

Magic Number

A small box that appears in daily sports sections toward the end of the season features the "magic number," which isn't really magical, just sound mathematics. So called because it seems the magic formula to unlock the door to a championship, the magic number is the total number of games the leading team must win and/or the second-place club must lose in order for the leader to clinch the division title. For example, if the Dodgers' magic number is eight, four Dodgers wins plus four Reds losses equals Dodgers divisional title. George Phair, writing in the old *New York American*, composed a memorable ditty making fun of the magic number: "If the Giants win but two of four / And the Dodgers six of ten / The Phillies, as in days of yore, / Will finish last again."

Manicurist

A good groundskeeper is so important to a team's success that he is often considered its most valuable nonplayer, next to the manager. The veterans have dozens of ways to "manicure" the playing field to suit their teams' strengths and weaknesses. Pitching mounds are often tampered with to suit the styles of local hurlers. For example, the Indians' Bob Feller liked a heightened mound because it gave him more leverage for his fastball. Ed Lopat, however, while pitching for the White Sox and the Yankees, wanted a flattened mound for his slow "junk" pitches. Base paths can also be conveniently altered:

When the Sox' Luis Aparicio was having a base-stealing spree in 1959, the team's manicurist made the baselines about two feet shorter. When a slow-running team plays host to fast-running opponents, the base paths are often watered down so the visitors will drag their heels. And in ballparks that still use real grass instead of artificial turf, the manicurist will sometimes let the grass grow longer to slow down the grounders of stronger-hitting visiting teams.

McGrawism

Rowdy baseball is sometimes known as "McGrawism." The term was more common in the early days of the sport, when John McGraw was a slashing, bruising third baseman on the tough Baltimore Orioles. Using his spikes, his tongue, and any other available weapon, "Muggsy" set the pace for the era's do-or-die battles. Later, as player-manager of the Orioles and the New York Giants, "Little Napoleon" encouraged his men to use the same hard-hitting tactics.

Meal Ticket

Synonymous with "meal ticket" is the name of Carl (Old Meal Ticket) Hubbell, the Giants' great lefty of the 1930s, who was known as the man who "kept the groceries on his manager's table." Another term for pitchers of Hubbell's stature is "stopper," a pitcher who can always be counted on to stop losing streaks. Warren Spahn was a famous stopper for the Milwaukee Braves in the 1950s and 1960s.

Money Player

The traditional meaning of "money player" in baseball is a player who performs best when the chips are down. A classic example was Athletics pitcher Chief Bender, of whom manager Connie Mack once said, "If I had one game to play and one pitcher to pick, I would choose Bender to hurl that game." Today, however, the astronomical salaries paid to top players, and the fact that they often seem to care more about their contracts than about team loyalty, have given a less complimentary meaning to "money player." The term was frequently used in the 1970s to refer to Reggie Jackson and his fellow Yankees, a collection of expensive prima donnas known as "The Best Team Money Could Buy."

Morning Glory

Every spring-training camp has "another Babe Ruth" and "another Sandy Koufax." But by opening day the young "phenom" (short for phenomenon, and coined by Garry Schumacher in 1947 to describe the Giants' Clint Hartung) is just another busher. These rookies, who are impressive in spring training but fizzle later, are called "morning glories," or "early bloomers," by the players. The classic morning glory was the mythical rookie who wrote his mother from Florida, "I'll be home soon, Ma. They've started throwing curves."

Morning Journal

Baseball players are notorious hotel lobby-sitters, and one of the few things to do in a hotel lobby is to read the morning newspaper. Since newspapers are printed on a cheap kind of wood pulp, "morning journal" became baseball slang for a bat with poor wood. Such a bat is also called a "banana stick."

Moxie

"Moxie," meaning courage, nerve, or skill, derives from the name of a soft drink first sold in the East in 1884. Ballpark vendors would cry out, "Ice-cold Moxie!" and the connection was soon drawn with "ice-cold nerves." A similar case of a commercial expression entering sports lingo was the cereal slogan, "He's had his Wheaties today," which came to describe physical strength.

Muff

"Muff," meaning to fumble the ball or to mess up a play, has been traced back to 1869 and stems from "muffin," a name earlier given to someone who played the game poorly and

One of baseball's most infamous quotations was uttered in April 1987 by Los Angeles Dodgers general manager Al Campanis. Appearing on ABC-TV's *Nightline* program to commemorate the fortieth anniversary of Jackie Robinson's breaking the major-league color bar with the Brooklyn Dodgers, Campanis revealed an attitude that was still all too prevalent in baseball's hierarchy. He told interviewer Ted Koppel, "The reason baseball has no black managers or general managers is that I truly believe that they may not have some of the necessities to be, let's say, a field manager. Why are black men, or black people, not good swimmers? Because they don't have the buoyancy." Those remarks caused an uproar, cost Campanis his job, and started a long-overdue reexamination of modern baseball's conscience about progress toward equal opportunity. Although African Americans are still underrepresented in baseball's executive suites and managerial posts, some progress has been made in those areas, ironically spurred along by the embarrassment caused by Campanis.

entirely for fun. "Muffin" was to baseball what "duffer" is to golf.

National League

Capitalizing on the popular appeal of professional baseball as demonstrated by the first pro team, the Cincinnati Red Stockings, a group of ten club representatives formed the first major league in 1871, calling it the National Association of Professional Base Ball Players. The league soon ran into trouble with contract disputes and gambling. When Chicago businessman William A. Hulbert took over the presidency of the NA's White Stockings team in 1875, he challenged the circuit's Eastern domination by raiding player-manager A. G. Spalding and other big names from rival clubs. The situation became bitter, but Hulbert countered it by proposing the formation of a new, more tightly controlled league. While plotting his coup with Spalding, Hulbert said, "Let us get away from the old, worn-out title 'National Association of Base Ball Players,' and call it 'The National League of Professional Base Ball Clubs.'" His strategy succeeded, and the National League was organized in New York City on February 2, 1876. The eight charter members were Boston, Chicago, Cincinnati, Hartford, Louisville, New York, Philadelphia, and St. Louis. Because it predated the American League (the "Junior Circuit"), the National League is referred to as the "Senior Circuit." That term is not to be confused with the Senior League, an organization of superannuated pros founded in 1989 by Colorado real estate developer Jim Morley.

Cleveland shortstop Ray Chapman, hit on the head by a pitch thrown by the Yankees' submarine-ball pitcher Carl Mays on August 16, 1920, died the next morning. Regaining consciousness in the clubhouse before going to the hospital, he murmured to a friend, "I'm all right. Tell Mays not to worry."

Negro Leagues

Baseball's great disgrace is the fact that African American players were barred from the major leagues for sixty years by a "gentleman's agreement." The color bar lasted from 1887 until 1947, when Branch Rickey brought Jackie Robinson to the Brooklyn Dodgers. Racial segregation forced black and Latino players to form their own teams, both for barnstorming games and, eventually, for organized leagues. Some of the finest players of that era—such as Satchel Paige, Josh Gibson, Pop Lloyd, Martin Dihigo, Oscar Charleston, and Cool Papa Bell—starred in what became known as the Negro Leagues. Playing to loyal, largely black audiences in cities throughout the Midwest, Northeast, and South, the "blackball" players also faced major leaguers in exhibition games and often had the satisfaction of beating the best players white baseball had to offer (Negro Leaguers won 268 of 436 such games). Although the first black professional team, the touring Cuban Giants, was formed in 1885, it was not until 1920 that the first Negro National League was organized by Andrew (Rube) Foster, who is considered the father of Negro Leagues baseball. Other Negro leagues included the Eastern Colored League, the American Negro League, the East-West League, the Negro Southern League, the Negro American League, and a second Negro National League (after the first one collapsed). Although the Negro Leagues were rendered obsolescent by Robinson's entry into major-league ball, the Negro American League continued playing until 1960, the year after the last major-league team (the Boston Red Sox) finally fielded a black player. The National Baseball Hall of Fame belatedly began admitting players from the Negro Leagues in 1971, when it elected the legendary Satchel Paige (who had come to the majors in 1948 at age forty-two). With an unfortunate choice of symbolism, the Hall of Fame initially had announced a separate "display" for the Negro Leagues players, prompting Paige to observe, "The only change is that baseball has turned Paige from a second-class citizen to a second-class immortal." The ensuing controversy finally brought Paige and his fellow Negro Leagues players into the same hall with the other immortals.

Nile Valley League

Although obsolete now, the term "Nile Valley League" was frequently used by players in the early 1900s. As defined by sportswriter Hugh S. Fullerton, it was "a mythical league in which all the wonderful plays ever heard of took place. Whenever a player tells some extraordinary yarn concerning a play, the other players instantly inquire if it happened in the Nile Valley League."

One-Cushion Shot

Just as pool sharks must practice endlessly the proper way to play shots off the cushions, outfielders soon learn that it isn't easy to play "caroms" off the walls, also known as "one-cushion shots." Hack Wilson was one who learned the hard way. One day as his Dodgers played the Phillies in the old Baker Bowl, the Tin Lizzie of ballparks, Wilson chased liner after liner, which wasn't easy for him on a good day, let alone a day when he was hung over and Walter (Boom-Boom) Beck was pitching. Finally, as manager Casey Stengel plodded out to the mound to hoist Beck, Wilson rested and started to enjoy the scenery. The angry Boom-Boom, refusing to leave, fired the ball with all his might at the right-field wall. Wilson, stunned out of his lethargy by the reverberations from the tin wall, jumped up, chased down the ball, and made a perfect throw to second. They still talk about it in Philadelphia.

Orchard

Another baseballese name for a ballpark is "orchard," a term more commonly applied to the outfield. Synonymous with the latter meaning are "garden" and "pasture." Outfielders are called "orchardmen," "gardeners," or "pastureworkers." Sharp ground balls hit safely to the outfield are known by such pastoral expressions as "daisy clipper," "daisy cutter," "grass clipper," "grass cutter," and "lawn mower."

Pancake

Frank (Home Run) Baker and Joe DiMaggio were discussing fielding on the day in 1955 when both were inducted into the Baseball Hall of Fame. Baker, one of the slickest fielders of all time, a member of the A's "$100,000 Infield," pulled out a shriveled scrap of leather that, he told DiMaggio, was his glove. DiMaggio was incredulous. "Nobody today," he said, "could catch a ball with that thing." Today many players have trouble digging the ball out of their gloves, which are often huge, shiny leather scoops called "bushel baskets." Oldtimers, on the other hand, used to have trouble digging their gloves out of their pockets. Any thin, flat, undersized glove was mockingly called a "pancake."

Pebble Picker

Whenever an infielder lets a grounder go past him, he gropes for an excuse. Some even pick imaginary pebbles off the ground around them, claiming the ball took a bad hop. The outfield counterpart to the infield "pebble picker" is the fellow who claims that the ball "hit an air pocket."

The Peggy Lee Fastball

Singer Peggy Lee's bluesy lamentation "Is That All There Is?" inspired underhand relief ace Dan Quisenberry to give her name to a fastball that is fast in name only. In the early 1900s, another pitcher, Eddie Siever, called his languid delivery "The Lady Godiva pitch," because it "had nothing on it." A 1970s variant was Phil Hennigan's "nudist ball."

Pepper Game

Before each game there are bound to be several groups of men playing "pepper," a series of short, brisk throws and bunts in rapid succession, designed to limber up the muscles and tune up the reflexes. The name originated because the game is "peppy" or "peppery."

Pickle

One of baseball's most exciting plays is the rundown, in which a runner is trapped between two fielders who toss the ball back and forth until one makes the tag. This is also called a "pickle," from the expression "in a pickle," meaning to be in a tight situation.

Piece of Iron

Although the rules of baseball state that no foreign substance may be embedded in a bat, ballplayers used to rig their bats with pieces of iron, nails, and anything else they could get away with. Today, "piece of iron" has come to have a figurative rather than a literal meaning, denoting any bat with exceptionally good wood.

> Explaining why he went along with gamblers who persuaded him and seven other members of the Chicago "Black Sox" to throw the 1919 World Series, pitcher Eddie Cicotte said, "I done it for the wife and kiddies."

Pinch Hitter

Shortly after the rule permitting substitutions was passed in 1892, sportswriter Charley Dryden coined the term "pinch hitter," because the hitter in that situation is in a tight spot, or "in a pinch." Johnny Doyle of the Cleveland Spiders was the first pinch hitter.

The Pine Tar Incident

One of baseball's most telegenic controversies erupted in Yankee Stadium on July 24, 1983, after the Kansas City Royals' George Brett hit a two-run homer against New York pitcher Goose Gossage. The homer put the Royals ahead 5–4 in the top of the ninth inning. But wily Yankees manager Billy Martin, who had been patiently waiting for just such an opportunity, claimed that Brett was using an illegal amount of pine tar on his bat. An examination of the bat by umpire Tim McClelland showed that Brett, indeed, had more than the allotted eighteen inches of the black goo on the lower part of his bat. The umpire invalidated the homer, and in a memorable display of outrage broadcast on nationwide television, Brett charged the umpires, waving his arms hysterically, and had to be restrained by his teammates. The controversy only deepened after the Royals appealed and American League president Lee MacPhail overruled his umpire's decision. The game eventually was completed, the Royals' margin of victory stood, and "The Pine Tar Incident" (or "The Pine Tar Game") won an immortal place in baseball lore, abetted by Brett's spectacular, often-replayed outburst.

Pittsburgh Chopper

The world-champion Pittsburgh Pirates of 1960 were a team with little batting power, specializing instead in choppy hits. One key to their success was the rock-hard Forbes Field infield, which made chopped balls bounce over the heads of infielders. Pitchers were the usual victims of "Pittsburgh choppers," as such hits came to be called, but during the World Series that year, Yankees shortstop Tony Kubek was taken to a hospital after a chopper hit him in the windpipe. After the season, a Philadelphia sportswriter gave waggish recognition to the "Pittsburgh chopper" by casting his Most Valuable Player vote for the Bucs' groundskeeper.

Prayer Ball

Like a football player who has only "a punt and a prayer," all a pitcher has near the end of his career is "a glove and a prayer." A "prayer ball" is equivalent to Dizzy Dean's feeble but valiant "nuthin' ball."

Rabbit Ball

Following Babe Ruth's emergence as a phenomenal home-run hitter in 1919, major-league baseball introduced what was widely considered a hopped-up new ball in order to stimulate public interest in the game. The American League first used the "lively ball" in 1920, and the National League the following year; the resulting excitement helped counteract fan disenchantment following the 1919 Black Sox Scandal. Replacing what in retrospect was called the "dead ball," the new lively ball appeared to have such a tendency to jump off bats that there was said to be a "rabbit in the ball"—hence the term "rabbit ball." Whenever home-run hitting dramatically increases in baseball, speculation becomes rife that something has been added to the official major-league baseball to turn it into a "rabbit ball."

Rain Check

The "rain check," a ticket stub saved for future admission if a game is canceled because of rain, has been used in baseball since the 1880s. Abner Powell, owner of a New Orleans ball club, was one of the earliest to employ the device. In those days, most clubs used hard cardboard tickets that were turned in at the games and resold for the next game. If rain halted a game before the fifth inning, the spectators lined up to receive tickets for the next day. But freeloaders and fence-climbers joined the line as well. "Usually," Powell said, "there were more fans in line than there were tickets in the box. The situation became so acute that, despite weekday crowds of 5,000 and Sunday throngs of 10,000, we were losing money." He adopted the practice of ripping off part of the ticket when a fan entered the park, and it soon spread throughout baseball. In today's domed stadiums, only power failure or a similar emergency can postpone a game. Customers thus retain their "cancellation checks."

Razzberry

The term signifying an expression of contempt blown through the lips was originally "raspberry," a play on the word "rasp," meaning to make a harsh, unpleasant sound. Popular usage later modified it to "razzberry" or just "razz." In New York, where it enjoyed the most popularity, a razz is known as a "Bronx cheer." Not to be confused with the razz is "strawberry," a large, livid bruise, also called a "slider," usually acquired on the base paths.

Rhubarb

New York newspaperman Garry Schumacher may have been the first to use "rhubarb," in its present meaning, in print, though the word was not original with him. In his definition, a rhubarb is "a hurly-burly ruckus that later is the occasion for laughter." During a 1939 Dodgers-Reds game at Cincinnati, Schumacher witnessed an altercation involving the umpires, several players, and (of course) Leo Durocher. He laughed, and said, "What a rhubarb!"—and Dodgers broadcaster Red Barber used it on the radio, giving credit to Schumacher. "That the word was a common memory with many people of my age in Brooklyn is indicated by its prompt acceptance when Red Barber used it on the air," Schumacher later explained. With interest aroused in the derivation of the word—which had been out of use for decades but was now acquiring a fresh currency—Schumacher began checking with old boyhood friends, coming up with the following explanation: "Our mothers regarded rhubarb as a springtime tonic for youngsters, something that was good for them. Naturally, we kids didn't like it, but unfailingly we got it every day in the spring, spread upon bread, upon our return from school. Most of the time we'd hurry out onto the street with it, to get our games organized. It followed that now and again a ruckus would develop and the handiest weapon was a rhubarb-smeared bread. It added to the hilarity and fun, something to laugh about—but afterward it wasn't quite so funny to the lad who had to get the rhubarb out of his hair. . . . When the incident occurred on the field at Cincinnati, somehow the word popped out of one of the hidden recesses of my memory."

Rooter

The first recorded use of "rooter," according to researcher Edward J. Nichols, was in the July 8, 1890, issue of the *New York Press*. It was used, apparently, because a true fan sometimes is so close to his team that he seems "rooted" to it.

Roundhouse Curve

Often the curves that are the bane of rookies are the delight of veterans. Such a pitch is the "roundhouse curve," the widest of them all. Named after a railroad roundhouse, which has a revolving floor to turn train cars in opposite directions, the pitch looks confusing as it sweeps a wide arc, but it is easy to hit if the batter times his swing properly. It is also known as a "jughandled" or "rainbow" curve.

Sabermetrics

Baseball has always appealed to people with a fondness for statistical record keeping. But until Bill James came along in the 1970s, the art of baseball stats was still in its infancy. Introducing modern statistical methodology to the field of baseball history, James combined numerical analysis with a true obsessive's passion for the arcane. His books, including his 1986 magnum opus, *The Bill James Historical Baseball Abstract*, and his 1994 critique of the Hall of Fame, *The Politics of Glory*, bristle with iconoclastic analyses of frequently mind-boggling complexity. But James helped elevate the study of baseball history to a popular science, and he has attracted a host of followers. Many also are members of the Society for American Baseball Research—SABR, pronounced "saber"—a broadly based organization of scholars founded in 1971 by L. Robert (Bob) Davids. SABR publishes journals and holds gatherings that tend to focus on neglected or esoteric aspects of the game, only some of which, however, have to do with statistics. After popularizing the terms "sabermetrics" and "sabermetrician" in reference to his own pioneering work, Bill James wrote somewhat apologetically in his 1984 *Baseball Abstract*, "The Society for American Baseball Research has very little to do with sabermetrics. . . . The misidentification of SABR and sabermetrics has been an unfortunate side effect of using the word to describe what I do for a living. . . . I think that some people in SABR think that I have given the public a mistaken idea of who they are and what they are doing, and that's probably true, and [they] resent it. I have no defense, but you must understand that at the time I began using the term, I had no idea that this whole thing would get as large as it has. I thought I was writing to a few hundred people who were interested in the subject, most of them already SABR members; it turned out that the audience was much larger than I thought."

Ty Cobb struck fear into the hearts of infielders with his spikes-high slides and with his bold declaration, "The baseline belongs to me."

Seeing the Barrels

Many baseball superstitions begin when an unusual event coincides with a hot day at the plate. "Turkey Mike" Donlin of the New York Giants, arriving at the Polo Grounds for a game in the early 1900s, noticed a horse-drawn wagon of empty barrels going past. He then went out and made three hits. The next day he was horsecollared, and he moaned that the reason was that he hadn't seen any barrels before the game. His wily manager, John McGraw, hired a truck of empty barrels to circle the park before every game. Donlin, overjoyed at his "good fortune," went on a batting rampage to lead the Giants to the pennant, and the superstition of "seeing the barrels" was born.

Seventh-Inning Stretch

Some sources place the origin of the "seventh-inning stretch" as late as 1910, but the practice actually has been traced back to 1869, the first year of professional baseball. Harry Wright, captain and center fielder of that year's unbeaten Cincinnati Red Stockings, wrote a letter to his friend Howard Ferris stating that "the spectators all arise between halves of the seventh, extend their legs and arms, and sometimes walk about. In so doing they enjoy the relief afforded by relaxation from a long posture upon the hard benches." The practice was started, apparently, by superstitious fans who felt the seventh inning to be lucky (seven has been considered a lucky number since ancient times), as well as an opportune time for a stretch.

Shagging Flies

Chasing down outfield fly balls is often called "shagging," and the verb form is "to shag." Originally, around 1890, the slang expression used by ballplayers was "shack," a variant of "shake" (as in the more modern expression for hustling behavior, "shake it"). By 1914, popular usage had modified "shack" to "shag."

Shine Ball

Among the countless ways pitchers in the early days doctored the ball was to throw a "shine" ball. This was done by sprinkling the ball with resin, spitting on it, and spreading the wet powder over part of the ball, making a shiny spot about the size of a half-dollar. The spot distracted the batter by reflecting the sun into his eyes. The pitch, also called the "emery" ball and the "talcum" ball because of other ways of making the ball shine, was outlawed in 1920 along with the spitball and other so-called freak deliveries. As precisely defined in the official rules, this means the pitcher shall not: "apply a foreign surface of any kind to the ball; (2) expectorate either on the ball or his glove; (3) rub the ball on his glove, person, or clothing; (4) deface the ball in any manner; (5) deliver what is called the 'shine' ball, 'spit' ball, 'mud' ball, or 'emery' ball." Of course, pitchers today continue to find ways of sneaking "freak deliveries" past the umpires by spitting on the ball surreptitiously or making a "greaseball" by rubbing the ball with pine tar, pitch, Vaseline, and other substances secreted in the hair, glove, or uniform. A pitcher applying a foreign substance to the ball is said to be "loading it up," and he is often called a "doctor" because he "doctors the ball." Catchers also collaborate in the trickery by scraping the ball on their sharpened uniform clasps or shin guards. Such tactics produce the "scuffed ball" or "cut ball." Gaylord Perry had a pitch he called the "powder puff ball"; he filled his hand with resin by juggling the bag up and down, with the result that the pitch came at the batter "out of a powder puff."

The Shot Heard 'Round the World

"The Giants win the pennant! The Giants win the pennant! The Giants win the pennant!" Russ Hodges, the radio announcer for the New York Giants, shouted incredulously. On October 3, 1951, Bobby Thomson's 280-foot home run in the bottom of the ninth inning off Dodgers pitcher Ralph Branca climaxed baseball's most celebrated comeback. The Giants had rallied from 13½ games behind the Dodgers in August to beat Brooklyn in the final game of a three-game playoff. Thomson's homer was so dramatic that it became known as "The Shot Heard 'Round the World," a phrase borrowed from Ralph Waldo Emerson's poem about the American Revolution, "Concord Hymn" ("By the rude bridge that arched the flood, / Their flag to April's breeze unfurled, / Here once the embattled farmers stood / And fired the shot heard 'round the world").

Slider

The pitch that Ted Williams called "the hardest to hit" is also one of the hardest to define. The closest description of a slider is "a fastball that breaks just as it crosses the plate." Waite Hoyt claimed that "George Uhle taught it to me when we were together at Detroit in 1930." Some historians, however, say that the pitch was first named by batters who faced George Blaeholder of the St. Louis Browns, one of the first to use it, in 1936. Hitters remarked that it "slid" across the plate. Before it became respectable, the slider used to be called the "nickel curve," since it was considered a bit of a cheap trick. The other meaning for "slider" is a bruise acquired in sliding, also called a "strawberry."

The Snodgrass Muff

Like Fred (Bonehead) Merkle, another unfortunate Giant of the same era, center fielder Fred Snodgrass committed a blunder that forever clouded his name. It happened to Snodgrass on October 16, 1912, at Boston's Fenway Park, in the tenth inning of the last game of the World Series between the Giants and the Red Sox. The Giants went into the bottom of the inning with a 2–1 lead (ironically, it was Merkle who drove in the lead run), and the first batter up for Boston was Clyde Engle, pinch-hitting for pitcher Smokey Joe Wood. As Snodgrass recalled in Lawrence S. Ritter's book *The Glory of Their Times*: "He hit a great big, lazy, high fly ball halfway between Red Murray in left field and me. Murray called for it first, but as center fielder I had preference over left and right, so there'd never be a collision. I yelled that I'd take it and waved Murray off, and—well—I dropped the darn thing." Engle wound up on second, eventually scoring the tying run, and the Sox went on to win, 3–2. The fielding lapse immediately became known as "The Snodgrass Muff" or "The $30,000 Muff," in terms of what losing the Series cost the Giants, but Snodgrass always resented taking sole blame for the loss, and he was backed up by manager John McGraw. In his book *My Thirty Years in Baseball*, McGraw commented, "Often I have been asked to tell what I did to Fred Snodgrass after he dropped that fly ball in the World Series of 1912, eleven years ago. Well, I will tell you exactly what I did: I raised his salary one thousand dollars."

Soup Bone

A pitcher's arm is the most valuable limb on a team, so it has been likened to a soup bone, which is used as the basis of the soup and is indispensable to it. The term was in baseball usage as early as 1910. Pitching is sometimes called "soup-boning," and synonyms for soup bone include "old souper," "wing," "whip," and "salary wing" or "salary whip."

Southpaw

Just who invented the term "southpaw," meaning a left-handed pitcher, has never been firmly established. It is generally agreed that, as Hugh S. Fullerton wrote in 1912, "the term is derived from the fact that most baseball grounds are laid out so the pitcher faces west, and a left-handed pitcher's arm is to the south." That alignment (not always used in modern parks) was designed to maximize the amount of afternoon shade for patrons in the more expensive grandstand seats. H. L. Mencken in *The American Language* cited the account of *Chicago Times* publisher Richard J. Finnegan, who wrote that "southpaw" was coined in the 1880s by *Chicago Inter-Ocean* sportswriter Charlie Seymour. Devotees of humorist Finley Peter Dunne, on the other hand, claim that he coined "southpaw" while covering baseball in 1887. However, the word was used in the January 14, 1885, issue of *Sporting Life,* which referred to a pitcher named Morris and his "quick throw over to first with that south-paw of his." Regardless of who actually originated the term, Dunne and Seymour were among those who helped to popularize the expression. Earlier terms for a lefty, in the days when the game enjoyed most of its popularity in New England, stemmed from nautical lingo. They included "portsider," "port flinger," "port paw," and "sidewheeler." The port side of a boat is the left side, and because the right side is the "starboard" side, a right-handed pitcher was called a "starboard slinger."

Spitball

The invention of the now-illegal spitball, or spitter, is still a matter of dispute, although its reintroduction in the twentieth century is generally attributed to Brooklyn pitcher Elmer

Stricklett. Hugh S. Fullerton wrote in 1912 that "Smiling Al" Orth, a pitcher who won 205 games between 1895 and 1909, may have originated the spitter while doing underhand pitching in 1892. Before him, Tom Bond, another early star, was said to have been the first to grease the ball, using glycerin during an 1876 game in New Bedford. In any case, it is well established that George Hildebrand, later an umpire, experimented with spitball pitching in 1902, while he was an outfielder with Providence of the Eastern League. He called it a "wet ball." Hildebrand joined Sacramento later in 1902 and became a teammate of Stricklett, who was about to be released from the club because of a sore arm. Stricklett learned the pitch from Hildebrand, prolonging Stricklett's career, and he in turn passed it on to the Yankees' Jack Chesbro and the White Sox' Big Ed Walsh, who was probably the greatest spitballer of all time. The term "spitball" has been traced to 1905, and "spitter" to 1908. More fanciful terms for the pitch included "aqueous toss," "damp sling," "expectoration pellet," "humidity dispenser," "pump pellet," and "soggy delivery." Though the erratically breaking pitch was banned in 1920—except for seventeen pitchers who were allowed to continue using it until they retired, the last one being Burleigh Grimes in 1934—that hasn't stopped crafty pitchers from using it since, much to the distress of opposition batters and managers. Hall of Famer Whitey Ford admitted throwing spitballs regularly during his illustrious career with the Yankees. Preacher Roe, Lew Burdette, and Don Drysdale were widely suspected of it (when Drysdale became a TV broadcaster, manager Gene Mauch commented, "He talks very well for a guy who's had two fingers in his mouth all his life"). The spitter enjoyed a kind of surreptitious renaissance in the 1960s, leading to clamor either for its legalization or for a tougher crackdown. In 1968 it became illegal for a pitcher even to touch his mouth with his pitching hand while on the mound. Pitchers found that the reputation of throwing spitters is often enough to intimidate batters into thinking they're seeing one. Gaylord Perry, Don Sutton, and Tommy John were among the prime targets of umpire vigilance, and Perry even capitalized on his reputation by writing a book called *Me and the Spitter.*

American League president Ban Johnson suspended a White Sox outfielder for three days and then took a fishing trip. He sent Chicago president Charles Comiskey his best catch, but Comiskey was still angry about the suspension. He wired Johnson, "Do you think I can play that fish in left field?"

Stanza

Not content with "inning," baseball buffs have stolen "stanza" and "canto" from music, "round" from boxing, and "chukker" from polo as substitutes. Another name for inning is "frame," which dates from the time when scoreboards were set by hand, with a number on a piece of wood fitting into a frame for each inning.

Statue of Liberty

The name of a tricky running play in football, "Statue of Liberty" in baseball refers to a batter who stands immobile, like a statue, while taking a called third strike with his bat on his shoulder. The term was derived from an earlier baseball-slang expression for such a lapse, "statue stunt." Another expression for a batter who doesn't swing is "wooden Indian," after the cigar-store Indians that were familiar sights in the early 1900s.

Stengelese

Casey Stengel uttered many memorable one-liners, such as "I couldna done it without my players" and "Most people my age are dead," but the full glory of his unique language, "Stengelese," can be savored only by quoting a Stengel monologue. Fortunately, Clay Felker has preserved many choice examples of Stengelese in his book *Casey Stengel's Secret*. For example, when asked in the Yankees' spring-training camp one year who his regular third baseman would be, Stengel replied: "Well, the feller I got on there is hitting pretty good and I know he can make that throw, and if he don't make it that other feller I got coming up has shown me a lot, and if he can't, I have my guy and I know what he can do. On the other hand the guy's not around now. And, well, this guy may be able to do it against left-handers if my guy ain't strong enough. But I know one of my guys is going to do it." In case that wasn't clear: "the feller" of the first sentence was Gil McDougald; "that other feller" was Andy Carey, then a rookie; and "my guy" referred to Bobby Brown, who wasn't around at the time because of his medical studies. Some who studied Stengelese viewed it as a form of deliberate obfuscation: Gayle Talbot of the Associated Press wrote in 1954, "By talking in the purest jabberwocky he has learned that he can avoid answering questions and at the same time leave his audience struggling against a mild form of mental paralysis." But some discerned a higher purpose. In his book *Five Seasons,* Roger Angell made an eloquent defense of the method behind Casey's apparent madness: "I think that a demurrer should be entered on the subject of Stengelese, which too many of his biographers seemed to consider as nothing but a comical difficulty with the English language. It always seemed to me that Casey's nonstop disquisition—stuffed with subclauses, interruptions, rhetorical questions, addenda, historic examples, shifted tenses, and free-floating whiches—constituted a perfect representation of the mind of a first-class manager. Almost every managerial decision during a ball game—the lineup, who is to pitch, when to pinch-hit and with whom, when to yank a pitcher, who should pitch to the new pinch hitter—is, or should be, the result of a dozen or two dozen pressing and often conflicting reflections, considerations, and ancient prior lessons." That would have sounded good to the "Old Perfesser."

Subway Series

When the Dodgers were in Brooklyn, a city World Series with the Yankees was almost standard October entertainment. Traveling from one park to another was easily done by riding the subways. A "subway series" was also called a "nickel series," because of that era's subway fare, and a "trolley series." The term "subway series" was revived in New York with the onset of interleague play in 1997.

Sweetheart

While some players try to monopolize the headlines, the most popular with their teammates are those who do their job oblivious to glory. A typical "sweetheart," as such players are called, was Charlie Gehringer, who played second base for Detroit from 1924 to 1942. The "Mechanical Man" was so consistently great that he often escaped notice; in fact, when Gehringer was elected to the Hall of Fame in 1949, some fans expressed surprise that he had retired. The modest and affable Lou Gehrig was another "sweetheart," playing in the shadow of Babe Ruth, and both Henry Aaron and the late Roberto Clemente also were taken for granted by the fans throughout too much of their careers. Clemente, who died in a 1972 plane crash, was not fully appreciated until his batting and fielding heroics paced the Pirates to a world championship in 1971. Aaron's relaxed, consistent hitting style seemed so easy that fans didn't sit up and take notice until they realized he was getting close to breaking Babe Ruth's career home-run record, which he topped on April 8, 1974.

Tape-Measure Shot

In 1953 Mickey Mantle hit one of the most prodigious home runs in the history of baseball. His shot, off Chuck Stobbs of the Senators, was hit so hard that Yankees public relations director Arthur (Red) Patterson hurried from the park and, after locating a boy who saw the ball hit the ground, measured the distance of the drive at 565 feet. Although a few other players, including Babe Ruth, have hit longer homers, Mantle's feat made the press and public more curious about

Rex Barney, a hard-throwing but wild Dodgers pitcher of the 1940s, never lived up to the brilliance predicted for him. Sportswriter Bob Cooke perfectly summarized his problem: "Rex Barney would be the league's best pitcher if the plate were high and outside."

what came to be called "tape-measure shots," a phrase now solidly embedded in baseball tradition.

Tenney

Fred Tenney, a National Leaguer from 1894 to 1911, mostly with the Boston Nationals, was one of the game's greatest fielders. The glove he used was small, fat, and almost circular, a sharp contrast to the "pancakes" most players used. When others began to imitate Tenney by using similar gloves, the gloves were called "tenneys" in his honor.

Texas Leaguer

Art Sunday, a onetime star with Houston of the Texas League, played for Toledo of the International League after his old league folded. In 1890 he hit .398 for Toledo, but many of his hits were short flies that dropped between the infielders and outfielders, a favorite trick play in Texas, where it was called a "plunker." Describing Sunday's performance, a Toledo sportswriter noted that he had delivered "another one of those Texas League hits." The phrase soon went into widespread baseball usage as "Texas Leaguer." Franklin P. Huddle, in a 1943 *American Speech* article, noted that the term had regional variants, usually with derogatory connotations, in different minor leagues: "Sheeny Mike" and "banjo" (International League), "humpback liner" (Southern Association), "Japanese liner" (Pacific Coast League), "drooper" (Western

League), "looper" (American Association), and "special" (Eastern League). Some of these terms were used interchangeably for "banjo hit," a fluke-hit grounder. Also synonymous with "Texas Leaguer" are "leaping Lena" and "percentage hit." A hit that lands safely after caroming off a rock or a pebble is called a "base on stones."

Tools of Ignorance

It used to be that catchers were big, strong brutes with muscles everywhere—especially in the head. The catcher's mask, chest protector, shin guards, and glove were dubbed the "tools of ignorance" by well-educated catcher Herold (Muddy) Ruel, who was a lawyer in the off-season. Today the demand is for backstops (another "brutish" phrase for catchers) with good baseball heads—one of the reasons they often become managers.

Two O'Clock Hitter

The anachronism "two o'clock hitter" is still used to describe a player who hits well in batting practice but fizzles in the game itself. The term dates from the days when games began at 3:00 P.M. and batting practice at 2:00 P.M.

Wally Pipp

Because he had a headache on June 1, 1925 (he was beaned during batting practice), Yankees first baseman Wally Pipp found himself unexpectedly out of a job. For that was the day a youngster named Lou Gehrig filled in for Pipp at first. Gehrig didn't leave the Yankees' lineup until amyotrophic lateral sclerosis felled him on May 1, 1939, ending his record consecutive-game playing streak at 2,130 games (later broken by Cal Ripken, Jr.). "I took the two most expensive aspirins in history," Pipp said in looking back on the day Gehrig filled in for him. Ever since then, a regular who takes a day off is said to be running a similar risk, or doing "a Wally Pipp."

Whitewash

To "whitewash" a team, a term that can be traced back as far as 1851, is to obliterate it, just as whitewash does to the previous coloring of a fence. The word used today is "shutout." Synonyms for "whitewash" were "kalsomine" and "calcimine," both obsolete now. Another antiquated slang expression for a shutout was "Chicago," probably because of the ability of an early Chicago club to keep opponents from scoring. "Shutout" came from racing lingo. In the July 3, 1879, issue of the *Troy (New York) Times,* a baseball reporter wrote, "The Troys have at last been whitewashed—'shut out,' as the horsemen say."

No more colorful personality than Dizzy Dean has ever played major-league baseball. His improbable manipulations of the English language have delighted fans and outraged grammarians for decades. After his playing career ended, Dizzy continued to malaprop madly as a radio and television announcer. Some of his favorite expressions were "The pitcher is presspiring freely," "The empire is dusting off home plate," and "The players are headed for their respectable positions." Hard-to-pronounce names, such as that of George Metkovich, also passed through the Dean meatgrinder: "That Moklovich singles to right and how wouldja like to have nine guys named Moklovich on your ball club?" Dean was somewhat perturbed by English teachers' complaints over his choice of words: "What if I did say 'he slud into third' or 'he was throwed out at second'? Besides, where do folks get off criticizing my grammar? Shucks, I only went up to the second grade, and if I'da gone up to the third, I'da passed my old man!"

Wolves

A term first used by the players themselves, "wolves" means fans who direct unmerciful heckling at individual players. For some peculiar psychological reason, wolves are prone to vent their worst abuse on members of the home team. Among the most notorious baseball wolves are those at Boston's Fenway Park. They gave the treatment to outfielder Carl Yastrzemski in his early years with the Red Sox, forcing Yaz to put cotton in his ears. And before that, they loved to hate the man Yaz replaced, Ted Williams. Williams, despite his brilliance at the plate, was disliked by many locals because of his haughty attitude, and they let him have it with a vengeance. Legend has it that Williams once took his revenge by fouling seventeen consecutive pitches at an especially obnoxious wolf in Fenway Park. And after closing his great career with a home run on September 28, 1960, Williams circled the bases with his typically impassive expression, refusing to tip his hat or otherwise acknowledge the fans' wild but belated cheers. As John Updike commented, "Gods don't answer letters."

World Series

Championship series of various kinds have been played in major-league baseball since 1882. From 1894 through 1897, the contest was between the National League pennant winner and the runner-up; it was called the "Temple Cup Series," after Pittsburgh sportsman William C. Temple, who donated a cup given to the winning club. There was a break in postseason competition from 1898 to 1903, when the National League made its peace with the fledgling American League, founded in 1901 amid bitter wrangling over "raiding" of players and teams' territorial rights. The first modern World Series was called the "World's Championship Games" or "World's Championship Series" when it was played that fall between Boston of the AL and Pittsburgh of the NL. In the first game, Pittsburgh's Deacon Phillippe beat Boston's Cy Young, 7–3, and Boston went on to win the best-of-nine series, five games to three. Popular usage gradually shortened the name of the championship series to "World Series." In recent years, some have argued that the name or the nature of the Series should be changed to acknowledge the importance of Japan on the world baseball scene. A common synonym for World Series is "fall classic," and players sometimes jocularly refer to it as the "World Serious," a phrase popularized in 1914 by Ring Lardner's short story "Alibi Ike," where it appears as "world's serious."

PART 2

BASEBALL
NICKNAMES

INTRODUCTION TO
BASEBALL NICKNAMES

Nicknames are as much a part of baseball as hot dogs and salted-in-the-shell peanuts. As the veteran sportswriter Fred Lieb put it, "Babe went as naturally with Ruth as ham goes with eggs." When a nickname captures the fancy of players, fans, sportswriters, and broadcasters, it becomes an indelible part of a player's personality—so much so that his first name is often forgotten. Dizzy Dean, Yogi Berra, Satchel Paige, Tug McGraw, Three-Finger Brown, Home Run Baker, Chili Davis, Bonehead Merkle, Cool Papa Bell, Pee Wee Reese, Oil Can Boyd, Ducky Medwick, Pie Traynor, and Duke Snider are seldom referred to by their real names, and the colorful nicknames helped promote their popularity.

It isn't only the great players who have memorable nicknames. Some of the best ones have been given to players who hardly made a name for themselves in any other way, such as Bow-Wow Arft, Pea Ridge Day, Boom-Boom Beck, Suitcase Seeds, Creepy Crespi, Arbie Dam, and Never Sweatt. A nickname stimulates the public's imagination and piques its interest in a player. As Elijah (Pumpsie) Green once boasted, "Someday I'll write a book and call it *How I Got the Nickname Pumpsie* and sell it for a dollar, and if everybody who ever asked me that question buys the book, I'll be a millionaire." (To save everybody the dollar, his nickname is explained within these pages.)

Probably the most common incentive for a nickname is the spirit of camaraderie among the players themselves. Calling a teammate by a nickname, even a derisive one, helps break down the barriers of formality and fosters a sense of belonging. Often a player is nicknamed because his real first name is disliked, dull, or inappropriate to his image. And many players bring with them nicknames from childhood, which is fitting, since, as Roy Campanella observed, "You have to have a lot of little boy in you" to play baseball for a living.

Baseball terminology tends to be coined more by writers than by players, but players have much more voice in the coining of nicknames, which are their richest contribution to the poetry of the game. Even so, to achieve lasting and widespread value, a nickname has to be put into circulation and kept there by writers and broadcasters. Many on-field and in-clubhouse nicknames never attain wide currency because they are clichéd or unimaginative. This book makes no attempt to catalog all the players with such common and easily understood nicknames as "Red," "Whitey," "Lefty," "Butch," "Buck," "Buddy," "Tex," "Scrappy," "Pep," "Rusty," "Spike," "Dutch," and the like. And neither is it necessary to discuss the many nicknames that are merely contractions of a player's first or last name.

The most enduring nicknames given by players (or by coaches, managers, team executives, and fans) usually are

short, punchy, and evocative, such as those of Casey Stengel,
Cy Young, Rabbit Maranville, Scooter Rizzuto, Cracker
Schalk, Junior Gilliam, Catfish Hunter, Mark (The Bird)
Fidrych, Pete (Charlie Hustle) Rose, and Mitch (Wild Thing)
Williams. Nicknames originated in the press box, on the
other hand, often are more fanciful and elaborately metaphor-
ical, such as those given to Frank (The Fordham Flash)
Frisch, Luke (Hot Potato) Hamlin, Christy (The Big Six)
Mathewson, Frank (The Big Hurt) Thomas, and John (The
Wild Horse of the Osage) Martin (Martin's more commonly
used nickname, "Pepper," naturally originated on the playing field). A sportswriter memorably dubbed the young strikeout artist Dwight Gooden "Doctor K," but the nickname was
shortened to the more casual "Doc" for everyday usage.

Sportswriters in the old days tried to outdo each other
in coming up with sobriquets for players, and though their
efforts sometimes got out of hand—such as calling Pepper
Martin's teammate Ed Heusser, a journeyman pitcher, "The
Wild Elk of the Wasatch"—surprisingly often the nicknames
they created caught the fancy of players and fans. Probably
the most prolific coiner of nicknames among all writers was
Charley Dryden, who was responsible for such memorable
nicknames as those of Fred (Bonehead) Merkle, Frank (Wildfire) Schulte, Joe (Pongo Joe) Cantillon, Charles (The Old
Roman) Comiskey, Eppa (Jephtha) Rixey, John (The Crab)
Evers, and Frank (The Peerless Leader) Chance.

There is no denying that nicknames today aren't as colorful as they were in Dryden's day, when ornate, hyperbolic

prose was the rule rather than the exception among sports-writers. While today's sportswriters are, in general, far more erudite than their precursors, they also tend to have a more prosaic bent. Unlike the old exponents of the "gee-whiz" school of baseball reporting, the modern practitioners are rel-atively cool and detached, with an aversion to the more flam-boyant (and more amusing) forms of linguistic corn and hyperbole. As a result, they tend to shy away from whimsi-cal slang and innovative nicknames.

Some recent players have had colorful nicknames—among them Ozzie (The Wizard of Oz) Smith, Mike (The Human Rain Delay) Hargrove, Steve (Bye-Bye) Balboni, and Mark (Amazing) Grace—but they are unusual. It isn't only the writers' fault. Their attempts to popularize nicknames for big-name players—such as Fernando (El Toro) Valenzuela and Hideo (The Tornado) Nomo—usually meet with indif-ference from the fans.

The late Bill Veeck, the premier showman of post–World War II baseball, thought the problem wasn't just with base-ball but with modern life in general: there just aren't as many offbeat characters now as there once were. And *Sporting News* editor C. C. Johnson Spink, in a 1979 editorial decrying the decline of nicknames in baseball, pointed to the changing economics of the game in the era of free agency: "The higher a man goes up in the economic scale, the less likely he is to have a nickname. You might call a $10,000-a-year worker 'Rocky,' but the $250,000-a-year president of a corporation is 'Mister.' It's that way in baseball, too, now that the players have become big-money men. The colorful nicknames of the past are pretty much a thing of the past." Sadly, exponentially increasing player salaries have made that observation seem even truer today. The free-agent system, while showering the players with riches, diminishes their loyalty to individual teams, and, indeed, to the game itself. The bonds of mutual identification that once bound fans to their hometown players have weakened, taking away much of the affectionate impetus that inspired memorable nicknames.

What gave old-time baseball its color and vitality was an element that has been lost, no doubt irretrievably, from the game of today—innocence. There was a childlike enthusiasm in the personalities and playing habits of players in bygone days. Today few grown men would want to go through life being called "Pie" or "Gabby" or "Dizzy." The players today, and the fans, are more sophisticated and better educated than their counterparts of the past. Illiteracy and social backwardness—which helped give such flavor to the slang, lore, and literature of early baseball—is uncommon among players now. And since they take themselves so much more seriously, the sense of playfulness that inspires nicknaming is less prevalent.

You can see the changes in the game quite vividly just by looking at the kinds of nicknames players aren't given anymore. Rustic nicknames—such as "Cy," "Cactus," "Rube," "Shoeless Joe"—are virtually obsolete. Fewer players today are nicknamed after cartoon characters—as were Available Jones,

Bing Miller, Nemo Leibold, Boob McNair, and so forth—
or animals, two of the most common methods of nicknaming players in the past. Player nicknames with ethnic
connotations are rarely used (at least in public) today, unlike
in the past, when names such as "Nig" Clarke, "Dago" Griffith, and "Jap" Barbeau were used without a blush. Even so,
despite increasing social pressure to avoid offending ethnic
sensibilities, there still are major-league ballclubs called the
Indians and the Braves, and Atlanta fans refuse to surrender
their war chant and "Tomahawk Chop."

Much less common in baseball now are nicknames deriving from players' hometowns, home states, or other regional
idiosyncrasies. A player today wouldn't be called "Arky" simply because he came from Arkansas, like Joseph (Arky)
Vaughan in the 1930s, and being from the South isn't likely
to give a player the name of "Dixie" or "Reb." With the wide
availability of air travel and the coming of television, regional
differences have become increasingly difficult to detect.
When Ted Turner began beaming Atlanta games throughout
the country by satellite, he unabashedly billed his players as
"America's Team." As the nation has become increasingly
homogeneous, so have its slang and its nicknames.

That's why baseball today needs more characters like the
late Charles O. Finley of the Kansas City and Oakland A's,
who was one of the rare modern owners to recognize the
image-building value of nicknames. Baseball seemed in the
throes of a near-terminal dullness when Charlie Finley came
along in the mid-1960s, thumbing his nose at conventions

and helping bring the game, kicking and screaming, into the contemporary world. How he did that, ironically, was to encourage a return to the colorful trappings of old-time baseball: mustaches and beards on the players, gaudy uniforms, and flamboyant nicknames. His team became known as "The Mustache Gang." If his players didn't have nicknames, Finley would coin new ones himself, as he did for "Catfish" Hunter, "Blue Moon" Odom, and other players.

Just how much importance Finley placed on nicknames was illustrated by a story told by the longtime Los Angeles Dodgers pitching ace Don Sutton. In 1964, when he was a nineteen-year-old free agent fresh from his home in Alabama, Sutton almost signed with Finley's A's. But a snag occurred as the youngster talked by telephone with the owner.

"Tell me, son," asked Finley, "do you have a nickname?"

"No, sir, I don't," Sutton replied.

"What? No nickname? Why, we've just signed three kids called 'Catfish' and 'Blue Moon' and 'Jumbo Jim.'"

"I'm sorry, sir. They just call me Don."

"Well," said Finley, "if you don't have a nickname, we can't give you the money."

Henry (Hammerin' Hank) Aaron

"Trying to sneak a pitch past Hank Aaron," teammate Joe Adcock once said, "is like trying to sneak the sunrise past a rooster." The man who broke Babe Ruth's career home-run record, finishing with 755 homers to Ruth's 714, Aaron was called "Hammerin' Hank" as a tribute to his batting power. The nickname was given earlier to the Tigers' long-ball hitter Hank Greenberg, and John Milner was called "The Hammer" because Aaron was his boyhood idol. Aaron was also known to his teammates as "Mr. Chips" or "Money in the Bank" because of his reliability in tight situations, and he was called "Bad Henry" toward the end of his career, when "bad" in black usage came to signify someone to be reckoned with. After surpassing Ruth in 1974, Aaron became "The New Sultan of Swat." "I don't want them to forget Ruth," Aaron said during his run for the record. "I just want them to remember me."

Charles (Babe) Adams

Adams, who pitched in the majors from 1906 through 1926, was the first famous baseball player to be nicknamed "Babe." When the baby-faced young man pitched for Louisville in his minor-league days, female fans would shout "Oh, you Babe!" whenever he went to the mound, and the nickname stuck. Others who have been called "Babe," some for their boyish looks and others as would-be challengers of George Herman (Babe) Ruth, include Herb Barna, Bill Borton, Floyd Herman, Ed Linke, Phil Marchildon, Ernest Phelps, Jay Towne, and Norman Young. Ellsworth (Babe) Dahlgren, whose main significance in baseball history is that he replaced the ailing Lou Gehrig at first base for the Yankees on May 2, 1939, was a hefty man who reminded teammates more of Ruth, whose last year in baseball was 1935. But Dahlgren wound up his twelve-year career with only 82 homers, and few players have dared to usurp the nickname of "Babe" since then.

Earl (Sparky) Adams

When the 5'4" infielder joined the Cubs in 1923, he was known as "Rabbit" because of his smallness and his speed. In 1925, however, James (Rabbit) Maranville became the team's manager and said, "Look here! We can have only one Rabbit on this team, and it's going to be me. You're a sparkplug, so we'll call you Sparky." Paul Molitor became known as "The Ignitor" because he jump-started the offense for the Milwaukee Brewers.

On July 5, 1946, Dodgers announcer Red Barber tried to make manager Leo Durocher admit that some tawdry Giants homers of the previous day were legitimate. "Why don't you admit they were real home runs?" asked Barber. "Why don't you be a nice guy for a change?" "A nice guy!" Durocher snorted. "A nice guy! I been around baseball for a long time and I've known a lot of nice guys." Gesturing toward the Giants dugout, Lippy Leo continued, "Nice guys! Look over there. Do you know a nicer guy than Mel Ott? Or any of the other Giants? Why, they're the nicest guys in the world! And where are they? In last place! Nice guys! I'm not a nice guy—and I'm in first place. Take it from me, nice guys finish last."

Walter (Smokey) Alston

The longtime Dodgers manager began his baseball career as a grade-school pitcher, and he put so much speed behind his pitches that pals nicknamed him "Smokey." In later life, the mild-mannered Alston, who came from Darrtown, Ohio, was also called "The Squire of Darrtown."

Anaheim Angels

When the expansion team was formed in the "city of angels" in 1961, it was called the Los Angeles Angels, adopting the name previously used by the city's Pacific Coast League team. In 1965, however, the year before the club made its move to nearby Anaheim, its name became the California Angels, making it the second team (after the Minnesota Twins) to use a state instead of a city name. *The Sporting News* dubbed the Californians the "Halos" or "Seraphs" (from "Seraphim") and its manager "The Archangel." After the 1996 season, the team changed its name to the Anaheim Angels. The Walt Disney Co., the team's parent company, also owns the Mighty Ducks of Anaheim hockey team, and including the city in the name of the sports franchises was part of Disney's sweetheart deal with Anaheim.

George (Sparky, Captain Hook) Anderson

While playing in the Texas League in 1955, the future manager was called "Sparky" by his Fort Worth teammates because, like Sparky Adams and others with that nickname, he had an aggressive temperament. Umpire Al Clark stubbornly called Anderson "George," explaining in 1986, "I refuse to call a fifty-two-year-old man Sparky." Anderson became known as "Captain Hook" because of his tendency to "hook" members of the Cincinnati Reds' pitching staff from the box when they showed any signs of tiring. The original Captain Hook was the villainous pirate in J. M. Barrie's *Peter Pan*.

Adrian (Cap) Anson

The Chicago Nationals' manager was called "Cap" because managers in his day were referred to as "captains" and he was the most prominent. The first white child to be born in Marshalltown, Iowa, Anson early in life had been dubbed "Baby" Anson or "The Marshalltown Infant." Since he played to the age of forty-six, he also acquired the title of "Pop." Known for his contentious personality, Anson was called "Cry Baby" by sportswriters. A Chicago writer, noting Anson's middle name of Constantine, named him "Uncle Constantchin" because of his constant "chin music" (complaining) in his later baseball years. (Today, "chin music" more often is used to refer to a knockdown or brushback pitch.)

Lucius (Luke, Old Aches and Pains) Appling

Although the durable Lucius (Luke) Appling played twenty years for the White Sox, finishing with a career average of .310, he always seemed to have some minor ailment. So, teammates called him "The Groaner" and "Old Aches and Pains." Appreciative fans and writers sometimes called him "Luscious Luke."

Arizona Diamondbacks

When it was announced in 1994 that Arizona would be awarded its first major-league baseball franchise, the owners of the Phoenix-based expansion team sought a nickname that evoked its southwestern desert surroundings. A fan contest was held through the Phoenix newspapers, and the most popular suggestions were the "Scorpions," the "Coyotes," and the "Diamondbacks." Previously used by a team of major-league hopefuls in the Arizona Fall League, the "Diamondbacks" nickname—referring to a type of rattlesnake common in Arizona—was adopted by the new National League team, which is scheduled to begin playing in the spring of 1998.

Richie (Putt-Putt) Ashburn

"Whitey," as the blond outfielder was called, chugged around the bases so fast that Ted Williams remarked that "Putt-Putt" had twin motors in his pants. Another swift runner, Ed Charles, was called "The Glider" because he "glided" around the base paths.

Atlanta Braves

Early Boston National League clubs were called the "Red Caps" and the "Beaneaters" or "Beanies" (because of Boston's culinary reputation as "Beantown"). While owned by Wilburn Russell, the team was sometimes called the

"Rustlers" after him. For two seasons, 1907 and 1908, it was known as the "Doves," after new owners George and John Dovey, and "Pilgrims" was the team name from 1909 through 1911. The lasting nickname "Braves" was chosen in 1912 after James E. Gaffney and associates bought the club. Gaffney, a contractor, was involved in the Tammany Hall political machine; Tammany was named after Delaware Indian chief Tammanend, and members of the organization were known as "braves." So, a partner of Gaffney's, John M. Ward, selected the name "Braves" for the baseball team in the new owner's honor. In 1936 a fans' contest selected another name for the club, the alliterative "Bees," but it was discarded after five seasons. "Braves" remained the nickname after the team moved to Milwaukee in 1953 and then to Atlanta in 1966.

Jim (Ole Sarge) Bagby, Sr.

Bagby received his nickname of "Ole Sarge" after the Indians went to a Broadway play. Since one of the characters was Sgt. Jimmy Bagby, the Indians began calling their teammate "Sarge" or "Ole Sarge."

Frank (Home Run) Baker

Although it is generally assumed that Baker's nickname was a result of his heroics for the Philadelphia Athletics in the 1911 World Series—winning the second game with a homer off Rube Marquard, and tying the third game with another, off Christy Mathewson—he actually had acquired it in the minors. Baker's statistics don't sound impressive by today's standards, but in that era of the "dead ball" he was considered a phenomenal slugger. He hit 96 homers in his major-league career, including 11 in 1911, when the entire A's team hit only 35. Baker's performance in the majors, leading the league in homers four times in a row, reinforced the suitability of his nickname, and for a while homers were called "bakers." Willard Brown, the first African American to hit a homer in the American League, acquired the nickname "Home Run" while playing in the Negro Leagues, as had Home Run Baker's contemporary Grant Johnson.

Johnnie (Dusty) Baker

The stylish, hard-hitting outfielder, who later became the manager of the San Francisco Giants, was nicknamed "Dusty" in childhood after his pet dog and the way Baker looked when they straggled home together.

Steve (Bye-Bye) Balboni

The slugging first baseman won his nickname in the minor leagues because he kissed so many baseballs good-bye with his bat. But he came to regret the alliterative appellation. "Every time I strike out or fly out," he complained, "you can hear them yelling, 'Bye-bye.' I can't seem to stop it, so I'm going to quit trying."

Jimmy Dykes, peeved at being called out on strikes, once asked plate umpire George Moriarty, "I beg your pardon, Mr. Moriarty, but would you mind telling me how you spell your last name?" The umpire fulfilled the request. "Just as I thought," said Dykes impishly, "only one 'i'." History does not record whether he remained in the game.

Charles (Lady) Baldwin

This nineteenth-century pitcher didn't smoke, drink, or swear, so, like some other sedate players of his time, he was derisively called "Lady."

Baltimore Orioles

The old Orioles of the 1890s and early 1900s derived their name from Maryland's state bird, and the St. Louis Browns inherited the nickname when they moved to Baltimore in 1954. The Orioles are also called the "Birds," and in Baltimore they are often referred to as the "O's."

David (Beauty) Bancroft

This slick-fielding shortstop invariably yelled "Beauty!" when a teammate made a good play.

Ernie (Mr. Cub) Banks

Ernie Banks virtually was the Chicago Cubs' franchise during his first fourteen years on the club, when he performed his hitting and fielding heroics for a team foundering in the second division. "Without Ernie Banks," said Jimmy Dykes, "the Cubs would finish in Albuquerque." By the time the team's fortunes improved in the late 1960s, Banks was firmly established as "Mr. Cub." Even on the windiest of Windy City days, Banks would exclaim to his teammates, "It's a great day for a game! Let's play two!"

Eros (The Old Home Remedy) Barger

Brooklyn sportswriter Tommy Rice called Barger "The Old Home Remedy" because the Dodgers pitcher was strong medicine against opposing teams. He was most commonly known as "Cy," because of his rustic upbringing in Kentucky.

William (Whispering Bill) Barrett

Barrett's nickname was ironic, because he actually was a loudmouth. "Whispering Roy" Hughes, on the other hand, was softspoken.

Walter (Boom-Boom) Beck

In Brooklyn, the pitcher was known as "Elmer the Great," because he reminded people of Ring Lardner's egotistical baseball character of that name. After Beck joined the Phillies, he was sarcastically dubbed "Boom-Boom" by Brooklyn sportswriter Edward T. Murphy because of the sound echoing from the tin walls of the old Philadelphia Baker Bowl whenever Beck was pitching. "I don't mind being called Boom-Boom," Beck once said. "Why, even my wife calls me Boom!" Slugger Willie Kirkland received the "Boom-Boom" nickname from a fan for the opposite reason, after he hit four homers in four days for St. Cloud of the Northern League in 1954. Another long-ball hitter, Cliff Johnson, was nicknamed "Boomer" by John Hollis of the *Houston Chronicle,* and slugger George Scott also was known as "Boomer."

Robert (Bo) Belinsky

Tough, cocky Belinsky, his New York street friends claimed, could fight like Bobo Olson, the former middleweight boxing champion.

James (Cool Papa) Bell

The legendary black outfielder, who played in the Negro
Leagues until he was forty-one (retiring in 1946, the year
before Jackie Robinson broke the majors' color barrier),
received his nickname in his rookie year of 1922 with the
St. Louis Stars. Bell combined pitching chores with his outfield duties at the start of his career, and teammates marveled
at the nineteen-year-old youngster's sangfroid in facing—
and striking out—slugger Oscar Charleston. As Bell recalled
in Donald Honig's book *Baseball When the Grass Was Real,*
"Some of the fellows said, 'Hey, that kid's mighty cool. He
takes everything cool.' So they started calling me Cool. When
I'd go in, they'd yell, 'C'mon, Cool,' like that. But that didn't
sound right. That's not enough of a name, they said, got to
put something else on it." So manager Bill Gatewood ampli-
fied the nickname to "Cool Papa" in tribute to the youngster's precocious maturity. Bell was voted into baseball's Hall
of Fame in 1974. His baserunning ability prompted a memorable tribute from Satchel Paige: "That man was so fast he
could turn out the light and jump in bed before the room
got dark."

Ray (Cal) Benge

The taciturn pitcher made his debut with the Indians in 1925,
when Calvin Coolidge was president, and they both seemed
worthy of the title "Silent Cal."

Joe (Blitzen) Benz

The smoke-throwing White Sox pitcher was compared to the speediest car of his day, the Mercedes-Benz, which "blitzed" down the road.

During his amazing rookie year of 1976, Tigers pitcher Mark (The Bird) Fidrych often made sportswriters shake their heads over his flaky utterances. The postgame remark most often quoted came when a New York reporter asked Fidrych why he always threw the ball back to the plate umpire after surrendering a base hit. "Well," explained The Bird, "the ball had a hit in it, so I want it to get back in the ball bag and goof around with the other balls there. Maybe it'll learn some sense and come out as a pop-up next time." Dizzy Dean couldn't have said it better.

Lawrence (Yogi) Berra

During Berra's boyhood on The Hill, the Italian section of St. Louis, he and his pals loved to attend the movies. One day they saw an Indian travelogue with scenes of a Hindu fakir. Since Berra crossed his legs while watching the movies,

Jack Maguire, later a Giants infielder, said, "You know, you look just like that yogi. That's what I'm going to call you—Yogi." Because of his squat, hirsute appearance, Berra was often taunted in his early major-league years by players who thought he looked like an ape, and he was called "Little Kong" after his Yankee precursor Charlie (King Kong) Keller. Berra's tendency to make outrageous malaprops (called "Berraisms") inspired sportswriter Milton Gross to label him "The Kid Ring Lardner Missed"; Lardner's baseball writings dote on characters who, like Berra, speak fractured English. Berra was such a well-known figure of fun that a cartoon character was named after him—"Yogi Bear."

Christian (Bruno) Betzel

Betzel's inseparable boyhood companion was a dog named Bruno, and he adopted the nickname because of his dislike for his first name, Christian. Another player with a canine nickname was Henry (Bow-Wow) Arft, whose last name suggested it.

Kurt (Dirty) Bevacqua

This utility player was known for the messy appearance of his uniform, which somehow was always dirty at the end of a game, even if he didn't play. Pitcher Dick Tidrow was called "Dirt" or "Dirty Dick" because of his similarly sloppy habits. A poll of players once named him the worst-dressed man in baseball, and his former teammate Ken Holtzman said, "He deserves it. He once wore a napkin for a tie."

The Big Dodger in the Sky

The team boosterism of Tom Lasorda knew no bounds in his rookie managerial year of 1977, when he led the Dodgers to a pennant. Lasorda declared that the number-one Dodger rooter was none other than God himself, or as Lasorda nicknamed him, "The Big Dodger in the Sky." The Yankees were too busy tallying up their championship purses after the World Series to dispute him.

The Big Red Machine

The Cincinnati Reds, after slipping in the mid-1960s, began to revitalize themselves in 1968 as Lee May, Tony Perez, and Johnny Bench led a slugging attack that was to propel Cincinnati back into first place by 1970. Sportswriter Bob Hunter of the *Los Angeles Herald-Examiner* and Reds star Pete Rose both claimed to have nicknamed the team "The Big Red Machine" in 1969, according to Bob Hertzel's book of that title. Rose told Hertzel, "I originated the name. Hunter? No way. It was at Crosley Field and I started calling us the Big Red Machine. At the time I had this red '34 Ford. That, I said, was the Little Red Machine and the team was the Big Red Machine." Hunter's version: "I hear Rose is claiming it, but I gave them the name. The Reds had just

finished winning a game, 19–17, from the Philadelphia
Phillies. I thought about the color of the uniforms and the
power they had, they were like a machine, big and red, that's
how it came about." Hunter first used the name in print after
the Reds went to Los Angeles following the 19–17 victory.
Reds manager Dave Bristol told him, " 'Big Red Machine.'
I like that. I like that. Keep using it." Hunter said, "That
convinced me to keep on with it." The Reds' players and
fans happily adopted the phrase, which is still used to
describe the team. The Reds took out a copyright on
the name, and sports cartoonist Jerry Dowling of the
Cincinnati Enquirer did a widely used drawing of
Rose, Bench, and Bristol riding a vehicle spewing out
home-run balls.

Max (Camera Eye) Bishop

The Athletics outfielder, also called "Tilly" because of his
girlish voice, had remarkably accurate eyesight, resulting in
many walks and his nickname of "Camera Eye."

Russell (Lena) Blackburne

The skinny Blackburne, who stood 5′11″ and weighed 160
pounds, was first known as "Slats," "Slivers," and "Lean."
During his rookie season at Worcester, Massachusetts, in
1908, he acquired another nickname that he could never
shake. The rival Brockton team had a player named Cora

Donovan, and after Blackburne made a fine infield play, a heckler in the stands shouted, "Oh, you Lena! Are you any relation of Cora Donovan?"

Ewell (The Whip) Blackwell

This long, tall Cincinnati pitcher, called "Blackie" by his fellow players, had an unusual sidearm, or "whiplash," pitching motion. His nickname of "The Whip" was especially appropriate because of his great speed.

John (Sheriff) Blake

First called "Sheriff," because of his stern personality, by manager George Stallings at Rochester in 1921, Blake reacquired the nickname in 1924. While he and some friends were talking in a Chicago hotel about Prohibition-era gangsters, another player referred to Blake as "Sheriff," and the nickname again became popular.

Frank (Ping) Bodie

The real name of the American League outfielder was Franceto Sanguenitta Pezzola. The family adopted "Bodie" from the name of the California mining town where his father worked. A friend of the Bodies, who to his dismay was nicknamed "Ping," dumped the nickname on the two-year-old Franceto.

Lynton (Dusty) Boggess

As a boy, this future umpire had "dusty" red hair as well as a habit of scooping dirt on his hands while at bat.

Lyman (Abdul Jibber Jabber) Bostock

Teammates of the popular California Angels outfielder thought he had the same aggressive, loquacious qualities as boxer Muhammad Ali and basketball star Kareem Abdul-Jabbar. Not long before Bostock's murder in September 1978, they nicknamed him "Abdul Jibber Jabber" by combining part of Kareem's name with the slang expression "jibber-jabber," meaning "to chatter."

Judge Emil Fuchs, owner of the Boston Braves from 1925 through 1935, was adept in the business world but hopelessly innocent about the intricacies of baseball strategy. When he heard that the Braves had won a game on a ninth-inning squeeze play, he was incensed. "I won't hear of it," he stormed. "Tell the manager we'll win honorably or not at all."

Boston Red Sox

Harry Wright's Cincinnati Red Stockings, the first professional baseball team, caught the imagination of the public in
1869, but the club had trouble making money—its profit for
the 1870 season was only $1.39. So, Wright pulled up stakes
and joined the new National Association with several former
Cincinnati teammates. They relocated to Boston in 1871,
continuing to use the nickname "Red Stockings," but the NA
lasted only five years. When the American League was organized in 1901, the Boston franchise was known as the "Som-
ersets," in honor of owner Charles W. Somers, as well as the
"Puritans," "Plymouth Rocks," and "Speed Boys." The present nickname was chosen in 1904 by John Taylor, who was
named president of the team after it was purchased by his
father, General Charles H. Taylor. The way was cleared for
the club to become the "Red Sox" when the Boston Nationals (later known as the Braves) decided to abandon their red
stockings for white hose because manager Fred Tenney said
that the dye used in the colored cloth caused infections to
players suffering from spike wounds. *The Sporting News* refers
to the Red Sox as the "Hub Hose," and they are also called
the "Crimson Hose" and the "Bosox."

Lou (The Boy Manager) Boudreau

When Roger Peckinpaugh stepped down as manager of the
Cleveland Indians in 1941, twenty-four-year-old infielder Lou

Boudreau applied to team president Alva Bradley for the job and was hired. With only four years of major-league playing experience behind him when he started managing, Boudreau revivified the Indians, finally leading them to the pennant in 1948. The title of "Boy Manager"—first applied in 1924 to Stanley (Bucky) Harris, the twenty-eight-year-old player-manager of the Washington Senators—devolved on Boudreau, who sometimes, depending on individual opinion, shared Marty Marion's nickname of "Mr. Shortstop."

Dennis (Oil Can) Boyd

The tall, skinny pitcher didn't get his nickname because of the shape of his body. In his hometown of Meridian, Mississippi, "oil" was slang for beer, and it was said that as a young man Boyd often could be seen draining an "oil can." Also referred to as "The Can," Boyd tried to discourage people from using his nickname, but to no avail.

Cletis (Spike) Boyer

When Boyer was playing for the A's in the mid-1950s, Kansas City radio broadcaster Merle Harmon noted the similarity between Boyer's nickname of "Clete" and the name "Spike," a natural substitute.

The Boys of Summer

One of baseball's most storied teams, the Brooklyn Dodgers of the 1950s, found an eloquent chronicler in Roger Kahn, whose 1972 book *The Boys of Summer* is a classic of sports literature. Profiling several members of the team from the bittersweet vantage point of their postbaseball years, Kahn took his theme from the haunting words of Welsh poet Dylan Thomas: "I see the boys of summer in their ruin . . ." The phrase "the boys of summer" since has come to be synonymous with the fleeting glory of baseball stardom.

Ralph (Hawk) Branca

Best known for yielding the 1951 pennant-clinching homer to the Giants' Bobby Thomson, Dodgers pitcher Branca was a star basketball player during his college days at New York University, when he became known as "Hawk" because of his deadly accuracy in hitting the basket. John Deal, John Jorgenson, and Roy Sievers were other major leaguers who acquired their nicknames in basketball. Deal's deft moves on the court made him "Snake," the slender Jorgenson was tenacious as a "Spider," and Sievers was called "Squirrel" at St. Louis's Beaumont High because it was said he always "hung around the cage like a squirrel."

Roger (The Duke of Tralee) Bresnahan

Born in Toledo but proud of his Irish ancestry, this Giants catcher always claimed he was born in Tralee, Ireland, and sportswriters obligingly called him "The Duke of Tralee."

Everett (Rocky) Bridges

While Bridges played for Greenville of the Sally League in 1948, going by his middle name of LaMar, one of his teammates heard "LaMar Bridges" over the public address system and said, "That's no name for a ballplayer—you're Rocky from now on." Pitcher John Coppinger's father nicknamed him "Rocky" because he "looked all beat up and ugly" at birth.

The Bronx Zoo

The uninhibited fans at Yankee Stadium are known for venting their feelings in ways that resemble the rumblings of the animal kingdom. Fans in the Bronx ballpark may have given rise to the expression "Bronx cheer" with the most famous of their razzing techniques (blowing contemptuously with the tongue stuck through closed lips). The august Yankee ballpark, long known as "The House That Ruth Built" in honor of Babe Ruth, was irreverently renamed "The Bronx Zoo" in pitcher Sparky Lyle's 1979 book of that title (written with Peter Golenbock). The felicitous phrase was the brainstorm of the book's editor, Larry Freundlich.

Jim (Professor) Brosnan

Brosnan's two books about baseball from the modest, deglamorized viewpoint of a journeyman player—*The Long Season* (1960) and *Pennant Race* (1962)—displayed a candor that was refreshing at a time when virtually all baseball memories were cliché-ridden, romanticized, ghostwritten jobs. (It was said that the first book Mickey Mantle ever finished reading was his own autobiography.) Later, Jim Bouton's *Ball Four* took a harsher, more iconoclastic bent, but it was Brosnan who provided the first truly inside look at modern baseball the way the players see it. Since, in addition to his literary habits, Brosnan wore glasses and a beret and smoked a pipe, the nickname "Professor" was inevitable.

Hector (Skinny) Brown

Because nicknaming is a playful pastime, many nicknames mean exactly the opposite of what they seem. Players named "Happy" are morose types as often as jovial ones, stupid fellows and bright ones are both dubbed "Professor," and well-built players are sometimes known as "Skinny." One of the latter was 6′2″, 185-pound pitcher Hector (Skinny) Brown, who was given the nickname by his parents because he was a chubby baby. Carlton Fisk was more accurately nicknamed "Pudge" in his childhood (because he was pudgy), and even though his baby fat turned to muscle, the nickname stuck.

Mordecai (Three-Finger) Brown

When this Cubs pitcher was young, he lost half of his right index finger in an Indiana coal mine accident. After he made the majors, his unusual grip of a thumb and three fingers became an asset, as it helped him throw one of the widest curves in baseball history. "Three-Finger" Brown was also known as "Miner" because of his prior occupation.

Tommy (Buckshot) Brown

Among the players given identical nicknames for opposite reasons were Tommy Brown and Glenn Wright. Brown, who became a Dodgers shortstop in 1944 at the age of sixteen, had a strong but wild arm that "sprayed buckshot" around the field. Wright, an earlier Dodger, was called "Buckshot" because he had a fast throwing arm that rarely missed its target. Another Dodger, George Shuba, was known as "Shotgun" because line-drive hits jumped from his bat like bullets.

Rick (Rooster) Burleson

Boston Red Sox coach Johnny Pesky tagged Burleson "Rooster" because of his cocky, competitive spirit. Doug Rader became "Rooster" in his early years with the Houston Astros because of his reddish hair.

George (Tioga) Burns

Burns lived on Tioga Street in north Philadelphia when he played for the Athletics.

William (Sleepy Bill) Burns

Burns is notorious as the middleman between the players and the gamblers in the 1919 World Series fix by the Chicago "Black Sox." But earlier, as a pitcher for five lackluster years in the majors, he was renowned for being, in the words of Thomas P. Shea, the "all-time goldbricker of baseball." Shea explained how Burns received his "Sleepy Bill" nickname: he "followed two simple rules on the bench—on days he didn't pitch, he slept through the game; on days he did pitch, he slept only between innings."

Bill (The Singing Umpire) Byron

One of baseball's most colorful umpires, Byron was fond of singing his decisions. After rookies took called third strikes, he would croon: "You'll have to learn before you're older / That you can't hit the ball / With the bat on your shoulder." After ejecting Casey Stengel from a game, Byron once sang, "To the clubhouse you must go / You must go / You must go / To the clubhouse you must go / My fair Casey." Because of his odd habit, Byron was called "The Singing Umpire," "Hummingbird," and "Lord Byron."

Joe (Pongo Joe) Cantillon

While Cantillon, an Irishman, was playing minor-league ball in San Francisco, a fan wrote to sportswriter Charley Dryden, asking the outfielder's nationality. The whimsical Dryden, one of the most prolific coiners of nicknames in the early days of the game, wrote facetiously, "Cantillon's real name is Pelipe Pongo Cantiliono. He is an Italian nobleman who fled to America to escape an idle life of social ease." The Italians in the Bay Area took Dryden seriously and adopted Cantillon as one of their own, cheering "Pongo, Pongo" whenever he came to the plate. From then on, Cantillon sneered at every Italian fan he met, but the name "Pongo Joe" clung to him throughout his career, even when he managed the Washington Nationals from 1907 through 1909.

Lee (Buzz) Capra

A neighbor in Chicago when Capra was growing up, watching the future pitcher play ball with his father, remarked that the youngster swung at the ball "just like a buzz saw." Clyde Wares, a Cardinals shortstop in 1913 and 1914, was dubbed "Buzzy" by Jack O'Leary because he was always talking about baseball.

Robert (Parisian Bob) Caruthers

A star pitcher and outfielder of the nineteenth century, Caruthers was from Memphis, but his dandified dressing habits made him "Parisian Bob," since Paris was regarded as the center of fashion. Other baseball dandies have included Thomas (Dude) Esterbrook, Lewis (Sport) McAllister, Clydell (Slick) Castleman, Samuel (Duke) Derringer, Leo (Broadway Leo) Durocher, and Charlie (Broadway) Wagner. Alexander (Broadway Aleck) Smith, on the other hand, was called that because he doubled as a bookie.

Lou Gehrig made his farewell to baseball on July 4, 1939, while dying of amyotrophic lateral sclerosis, a rare progressive paralysis now known as Lou Gehrig's disease. Babe Ruth and other members of the 1927 Yankees were among the emotional Yankee Stadium crowd of 61,808 that day. Gehrig, visibly shaken, told the crowd, "Today I consider myself the luckiest man on the face of the earth. I might have been given a bad break, but I've got an awful lot to live for. Thank you." Within two years, he was dead. His famous speech, by the way, has often been misquoted as the "luckiest guy" speech.

George (Ug) Caster

The medical connotation of the pitcher's last name—castor oil, infamous for its bad taste—gave him his nickname.

Orlando (The Baby Bull) Cepeda

Cepeda's ballplayer father was sometimes known as "The Babe Ruth of Puerto Rico" because of his great reputation as a slugger. He also was nicknamed "The Bull," and when son Orlando became a star, he was called "The Baby Bull."

Ron (Penguin) Cey

This slugging third baseman had short legs and a waddling walk, like a penguin. Cey was given his nickname in college, and Dodgers manager Tom Lasorda revived it while managing him in the minors. At one point early in Cey's career, the Dodgers tried to sell him to the Milwaukee Brewers, but Milwaukee general manager Frank (Trader) Lane vetoed the deal, saying, "We ain't buyin' no duck!"

Henry (Father) Chadwick

Pioneer baseball writer Henry Chadwick, who codified many of the game's rules, was considered "The Father of Baseball." The title seemed to have been grafted onto him by popular consent, and during his long years as editor of baseball guide-books, Chadwick was known to ballplayers as Father Chadwick.

The short tenure of A. Bartlett (Bart) Giamatti as baseball commissioner is fondly remembered by those who revere the game's traditions. While his most significant action as commissioner, shortly before his sudden death in 1989, was to banish Pete Rose for allegedly betting on baseball ("People will say I'm an idealist. I hope so"), Giamatti, a former president of Yale University, also brought an indelible eloquence to his commentaries on the sport. His most oft-quoted words were written in 1977 for his *Yale Alumni Magazine* article "The Green Fields of the Mind": "It breaks your heart. It is designed to break your heart. The game begins in the spring, when everything else begins again, and it blossoms in the summer, filling the afternoons and evenings, and then as soon as the chill rains come, it stops and leaves you to face the fall alone."

Frank (Husk) Chance

This husky Cubs first baseman once picked a café brawl with heavyweight boxing champ James J. Corbett. After he accused Corbett of rigging a boxing match, they pummeled each other, and Chance had to be dragged away to stop the fight. Afterward, players began to call him "Husk." The star Negro Leagues first baseman Napoleon Cummings became "Chance" in his honor. As manager of the Cubs, Frank Chance was highly esteemed, and Charley Dryden gave him the nickname of "The Peerless Leader." Years later, when Red Smith wanted to poke fun at Leo Durocher, he called him "The Practically Peerless Leader."

Jack (Death to Flying Things) Chapman

The left fielder for the Philadelphia Athletics of the 1860s, Chapman played barehanded, as was then the custom, and thrilled fans with his spectacular one-handed catches. Sportswriters gave him the quaint nickname of "Death to Flying Things."

Hal (Prince Hal) Chase

In his early years as first baseman for the New York Highlanders (later the Yankees), Hal Chase exhibited such grace and authority both in the field and at bat that he was given the Shakespearean nickname of "Prince Hal." He was also known as "Peerless Hal." But the frequent allegations that Chase was involved with gamblers in throwing ball games finally led to his expulsion from major-league baseball in the summer of 1919.

> Screwball Yankees left-hander Vernon (Goofy) Gomez was frank about baseball success: "I'd rather be lucky than good." He also said that to win ball games, a pitcher needed "clean living and a fast-moving outfield."

Jack (Happy Jack) Chesbro

Known as "Happy Jack" because of his perpetual grin, this tough pitcher was also called "Algernon" or "Algy," once-popular slang names for "sissy," because he was exactly the opposite. Other happy-go-lucky players everyone liked included the Giants' captain "Laughing Larry" Doyle (who once said, "Gee, it's great to be young and a Giant!") and the Cardinals' first baseman "Sunny Jim" Bottomley. Pitcher Burt (Happy) Hooton, however, received that nickname from Dodgers manager Tom Lasorda because he was morose.

Chicago Cubs

In 1876, when they formed the National League, A. G. Spalding and William A. Hulbert nicknamed the Chicago team the "White Stockings." In 1890, when Pop Anson was managing the club, he had to hire so many young players to replace veterans who had defected to the Players' League that the team was known as Anson's "Babes," "Cubs," and "Colts." The "Colts" nickname also gave rise to "Broncos" and "Cowboys"; and the Windy City team was also known briefly as the "Rainmakers." When Anson quit after the 1897 season, the team was called the "Orphans" because its "father" had departed. *Chicago Daily News* sports editor Fred Hayner revived popularity for the "Cubs" nickname in 1901.

Chicago White Sox

When the American League was formed in 1901, the Chicago team's owner, Charles A. Comiskey, tried to adopt the Cubs' original nickname of "White Stockings" but ran into opposition from the National League, which he evaded by naming his club the "White Sox." The name often is shortened further to "Chisox," and *The Sporting News* calls them the "Pale Hose." The eight Chicago players who fixed the World Series of 1919—Shoeless Joe Jackson, Chick Gandil, Swede Risberg, Lefty Williams, Happy Felsch, Eddie Cicotte, Fred McMullin, and Buck Weaver—were known as the "Black Sox" after the scandal broke at the end of the 1920 season and they were expelled from baseball.

Clarence (Cupid) Childs

Childs became "Cupid" because of his "lovable" (i.e., fierce) temper. His last name may have helped, too.

Eddie (Knuckles) Cicotte

This ace Chicago pitcher, expelled from baseball for his part in the Black Sox scandal of 1919, was called "Knuckles" because he threw the now-illegal "shine ball," a pitch that had the effect of a knuckleball. The illustrious knuckleballer Phil Niekro later acquired the nickname "Knucksie."

Cincinnati Reds

The first professional baseball club began on an amateur basis when it was organized by Harry Wright in 1866 as the "Red Stockings." Wright introduced knickers into baseball, borrowing from the design of cricket uniforms, and the stockings gave the team its distinctive nickname, soon abbreviated to "Reds" in common usage. The club turned pro in 1869 but folded in the fall of the following year because of financial problems. Wright took the nickname "Red Stockings" along to Boston when he formed a National Association team there in 1871. By the time the National League was organized in 1876, the NA had collapsed, and the new Cincinnati NL franchise reassumed the nickname of "Reds." In 1953, during the McCarthy-era "Red scare," club officials changed the name to "Redlegs" because they thought "Reds" sounded like a bunch of Communists. "Redlegs" never caught on, and in 1959 sanity returned and the team was renamed "Reds."

Baseball scouts often make tremendous expenditures trying to sign young prospects. Mike Gonzalez, however, exercised frugality when he wired the Cardinals after looking over minor leaguer Moe Berg in 1924. His pithy telegram read: "GOOD FIELD. NO HIT." Berg, perhaps the most erudite player in baseball history, was a graduate of Princeton and the Sorbonne, had a Ph.D., and could speak a dozen languages. During World War II he undertook top-secret spying missions for the U.S. government. To fellow players, however, he was just another whiffer. One day a White Sox teammate, tobacco-chewing Buck Crouse, approached Berg after the young catcher had fanned twice with the bases loaded. "Moe," confided Crouse, "I don't care how many of them college degrees you got. They ain't learned you to hit that curveball no better than me."

Roberto (Arriba) Clemente

The late Pittsburgh Hall of Famer came from Puerto Rico, and his fans yelled "*Arriba!*" (Spanish for "Let's go!") as encouragement when he played.

Cleveland Indians

Early Cleveland teams were called the "Spiders" because most of the players were tall and skinny. Later, when the club was in the new American League, its uniform colors led to the nickname of "Blues" or "Bluebirds." In 1902, the players changed the nickname to "Broncos," but the fans didn't like it and a poll conducted by a local newspaper in 1903 led to the nickname of "Naps," in honor of star second baseman (and later manager) Napoleon Lajoie. "Naps" had 365 votes to 281 for its closest competitor, "Buckeyes" (Ohio is the Buckeye State). Other runners-up included "Emperors," "Metropolitans," "Giants," and "Cyclops." Lajoie left the team after the 1914 season, so another fan poll was conducted and the name "Indians" was chosen in honor of 1890s Spiders player Louis (Chief) Sockalexis, a Penobscot Indian, and because several nearby teams were called the "Redskins." Some say that the rowdy behavior of members of the team at a party held by owner James C. Dunn also figured in the choice of the nickname. Also-rans in that poll included "Grays" and "Hustlers."

Ty (The Georgia Peach) Cobb

Generally considered the greatest player in the history of baseball, Cobb came from Georgia, the "Peach State," and since "peach" was a slang term for a sensational person, the nickname won wide acceptance.

Gordon (Mickey) Cochrane

When he was a Boston University football star, the future catcher was called "Kid." Taking note of Cochrane's swarthy features, however, his manager at Dover of the Eastern Shore League dubbed Cochrane "Mickey," saying, "You don't have to come from Ireland to be Irish." Cochrane also became known as "Black Mike." After he established himself as one of the greatest backstops in the history of the game, he lent his nickname of "Mickey" to younger catchers such as Arnold Owen, Thompson Livingston, and Newton Grasso, in the same way promising young pitchers were named after Cy Young or Rube Waddell. Yankees great Mickey Mantle was named by his father in honor of Mickey Cochrane (Mantle's first name is not a nickname).

Jim (Sky Hook) Colborn

Shortly after Colborn joined the Kansas City Royals, he inadvertently "sky-hooked" a spring-training pitch high over a protective screen and hit teammate Andy Hassler in the back of the neck. A fellow Royal, Amos (Famous Amos) Otis, gave Colborn the nickname. Otis, by the way, was nicknamed after a brand of chocolate-chip cookies. Teammates and fans called him "A.O."

James (Rip) Collins

Fastball pitcher Harry (Rip) Collins was in his final year with the St. Louis Browns when Jim Collins joined the Cardinals in 1931. The Sportsman's Park fans made the natural connection, and slugging first baseman Jim Collins became the second local "Rip" or "Ripper." The nickname, which generally refers to speed or power, in those days also connoted a "wonderful person," probably because of the British slang term "ripping." The third "Rip" Collins in baseball was 1940s catcher Robert Collins. Other players nicknamed "Rip" have included pitchers John Egan, Zeriah Hagerman, and Truett Sewell; catcher Alva Williams; and outfielders Wirt Cannell, Dick Wade, Ray Radcliff, and Eldon Repulski.

Brusque Yankee Bob Meusel showed signs of mellowing as he neared the end of his career. Writer Frank Graham observed, "He's learning to say hello when it's time to say good-bye."

John (Shano) Collins

Collins's nickname resulted from a comparison of his first name with its equivalent in Gaelic, Sean. Other players nicknamed through plays on their first names included Ulysses Simpson Grant (Lil) Stoner and Owen (Donie) Bush, who was progressively called "Owen," "Ownie," and "Donie."

Phil (Fidgety Phil) Collins

This Phillies pitcher was known for his nervous habits on the mound, as were Jittery Joe Berry, Shufflin' Phil Douglas, Elmer (Herky Jerky) Horton, Daniel (Jumping Jack) Jones, George (Jerky Jake) Northrop, and Allen (Fidge) Sothoron. Other jittery players have included catcher Darrel (Nerve) Porter and outfielder Richard (Twitchy Dick) Porter, who was also called "Wiggles." John Donahue was known as "Jiggs" because he constantly "jiggled" his feet while playing first base.

Colorado Rockies

The Denver-based expansion team, which entered the National League in 1993, was nicknamed after Colorado's glorious Rocky Mountains. "Rockies" was among several names that drew strong fan support in surveys conducted by Colorado newspapers. "Grizzlies" and "Bears" (the name of an old minor-league team in Denver) were among the other leading suggestions. Some thought the team should be called the Rocky Mountain Grizzlies (or Bears), but the team owners finally decided to combine the names of the state and the mountain range.

Charles (The Old Roman) Comiskey

While Comiskey, later boss of the Chicago White Sox, played for the St. Louis Browns, his imperial appearance and bearing led Charley Dryden to call him "The Noblest Roman of the Baseball Empire." Popular usage shortened it to "The Old Roman."

John (Jocko) Conlan

As a player with Rochester of the International League, the future umpire was an accomplished "bench jockey" (one who "rides" the opposition by shouting insults from the dugout), and local sportswriters began calling him "Jocko."

Joseph (Coaster Joe) Connolly

Connolly was nicknamed "Coaster Joe" in the Texas League because he came from "the coast"—San Francisco, California.

Harry (The Giant Killer) Coveleski

Unlike his younger brother, Stanley, pitcher Harry Coveleski isn't in the Hall of Fame, but he won lasting distinction as "The Giant Killer." In the closing week of the 1908 season—soon after the infamous "Merkle boner"—the twenty-two-year-old Coveleski won three games for the Phillies against the Giants, although his record for the entire season was only 4–1. The losses left the Giants in a dead heat with the Cubs, who whipped them in a playoff game to win the pennant. Ever after that, Harry Coveleski was "The Giant Killer," a phrase derived from the fairy tale "Jack and the Beanstalk."

Roger (Doc) Cramer

When Cramer was a teenager he used to accompany the Beach Haven, New Jersey, physician on his daily rounds, and teammates impressed by Cramer's medical knowledge called him "Doc." Philadelphia sportswriter Jimmy Isaminger dubbed him "Flit" because the outfielder disposed of flies like the once-common insecticide of that name.

Sam (Wahoo Sam) Crawford

Many ballplayers' nicknames have resulted from the names of their birthplaces and hometowns, most memorably that of

"Wahoo Sam" Crawford, who came from Wahoo, Nebraska. Similarly named were Clyde (Pea Ridge) Day, from Arkansas; James (Hub) Hart, from Boston ("The Hub"); Coldwater Jim Hughey, from Michigan; Mickey (The Commerce Comet) Mantle, the speedy slugger from Oklahoma; Rudy (Mr. Coffeeville) May, from Kansas; future congressman Wilmer (Vinegar Bend) Mizell, from Alabama; Joe (The Gause Ghost) Moore, a skinny player from Gause, Texas; Gettysburg Eddie Plank, who jumped from Gettysburg College into the majors; Phil (The Duke of Paducah) Roof, from Paducah, Kentucky; Carvel (Bama) Rowell, from Alabama; Joseph (Arky) Vaughan, from Arkansas; and Bill (Old 96) Voiselle, who lived in Ninety-Six, South Carolina, and insisted on wearing uniform number 96. An even odder nickname was that of Clifford (Gavvy) Cravath. Called "Cactus" when he reached the majors in 1908, a time when his native state of California was still considered the Wild West, Cravath was nicknamed "Gavvy" by eastern sportswriters who jokingly claimed he came from the town of Gaviota, California. Actually he was born in Escondido, but Escondido Cravath just doesn't sound right.

Frank (Creepy) Crespi

It wasn't his personality that gave Frank (Creepy) Crespi his nickname, but rather the way he "crept" around while playing the infield for the Cardinals.

In 1948, the success of the Boston Braves' pitching staff rested on Warren Spahn and Johnny Sain; beyond them, there wasn't much. Boston sportswriter Gerry Hearn, sympathizing with manager Billy Southworth's dilemma, called the Braves' rotation "Spahn and Sain and two days of rain." The quote often was rephrased "Spahn and Sain and pray for rain."

Alvin (General) Crowder

Gen. Enoch H. Crowder originated the conscription lottery for the U.S. military in World War 1, and Alvin Crowder, an American League pitcher who made his debut in 1926 with the Washington Senators, was called "General" because he had the same last name.

William (Candy) Cummings

Called "Candy" because he was fond of sweets, the Hall of Fame pitcher was also known as "The Father of the Curveball," a pitch he invented in 1862.

Hazen (KiKi) Cuyler

As a boy Cuyler was called "Cuy," and while he was with Nashville in 1923, the newspapers began printing his nickname "Ki," eventually doubling it to "KiKi."

Elbridge (Arbie) Dam

"Bill" Dam, as friends called him, had one hit in two at-bats for the Boston Doves in 1909, and that was the extent of his major-league career. He has a more lasting place in baseball lore because of his amusing nickname, "Arbie" Dam, a play on the expression "I'll be damned." Another player whose last name inspired a jocular nickname was Negro Leaguer George (Never) Sweatt.

Harry (The Horse) Danning

The stocky Danning acquired his nickname after one of Damon Runyon's fictional characters, Harry the Horse, featured in the musical *Guys and Dolls*. The name was earlier given to beefy slugger Harry Heilmann.

Charles (Chili) Davis

When he was a sixth-grader, Davis received a bowl haircut and a friend dubbed him "Chili Bowl." Later abbreviated to

"Chili," the flavorful nickname seemed a perfect fit for the peppery-hitting outfielder's zesty playing style.

Jay (Dizzy) Dean

Baseball's most famous screwball was nicknamed "Dizzy" (slang for "crazy") by an Army sergeant, Jimmy Brought, while Dean was serving at Fort Sam Houston in Texas during the late 1920s. After he joined Houston of the Texas League, Dean bombarded Cardinals executive Branch Rickey with letters imploring Rickey to call him up to the majors. Each letter was signed "The Great Dean." Rickey, furious, told the brash young pitcher, "Don't you ever again sign a letter 'The Great Dean'!" But another letter arrived two days later with the same signature. Dean's incorrigible antics at St. Louis attracted so much attention that when he was joined on the Cardinals by his younger brother Paul—a sedate, quiet, well-mannered player—Paul was nicknamed "Daffy" so the Cards would have a matching pair. The two of them became known as "The Daffiness Boys," or, as Dizzy called them, "Me 'n' Paul." There has been much confusion over Dizzy's given name, some sources listing it as "Jay Hanna Dean" and others as "Jerome Herman Dean." According to Curt Smith's book *America's Dizzy Dean,* the pitcher began life as Jay Hanna Dean, but when he was seven, a neighbor's son named Jerome Herman died and Dean changed his name to please the boy's father. But he eventually reverted to Jay

Hanna Dean, the name he used when he filled out a questionnaire for *The Sporting News* in 1939. Pitchers Paul (Dizzy) Trout and Howard (Diz) Reed reminded people of Dean; Trout's son Steve, who also pitched in the majors, was dubbed "Rainbow."

Ed (The Wild Irishman) Delahanty

One of the greatest hitters in the early days of the game, and a member of the Hall of Fame, "Big Ed" Delahanty was known as "The Wild Irishman" because of his flamboyant, hell-raising personality. His drinking habits led to his untimely death on July 2, 1903, when the Washington Senators' train stopped at the suspension bridge across Niagara Falls. Delahanty got off the train and tried to walk across the bridge, but fell to his death after a scuffle with the bridge's night watchman.

The name of utility player Woodie Held won't be found on the walls of the Hall of Fame, but it is fondly remembered because of some advice he once offered to fellow batsmen. A .240 hitter with various American League teams between 1954 and 1969, Held said, "Don't forget to swing hard, in case you hit the ball."

Detroit Tigers

Originally called the "Wolverines," after the animal that symbolizes the state of Michigan, the team adopted blue-and-orange-striped socks in 1901, and *Detroit Free Press* writer Philip J. Reid, noticing the colors' resemblance to those of Princeton University, called the team the "Tigers," which is the nickname of that school's athletic squads. During Ty Cobb's long tenure with the club, reporters occasionally dubbed them the "Tygers." And old-time AL fans still refer to the team sometimes as the "Bengals," after an Indian breed of tiger.

Martin (El Maestro) Dihigo

A member of the Baseball Hall of Fame, the Cuban-born Dihigo was, in the words of Negro Leagues historian James A. Riley, the "most versatile man ever to play the game of baseball . . . [and] was considered by many to be the greatest all-around Negro player of all time." In his twenty-two-year career, the switch-hitting Dihigo played every position and dazzled at every facet of the diamond. He was known simply as "El Maestro"—"The Master."

Dom (The Little Professor) DiMaggio

Joe DiMaggio's younger brother was nicknamed "The Little Professor" because he was boyish-looking and wore thick wire-rimmed glasses. A sportswriter once said of him, "Looking through Dom's glasses is like looking through fifty pounds of ice."

Joe (The Yankee Clipper, Joltin' Joe) DiMaggio

Broadcaster Arch McDonald nicknamed DiMaggio "The Yankee Clipper," after a speedy Boston–to–New York train, because of DiMaggio's swiftness in covering the outfield. Yankee teammates, for the same reason, called him "Cruiser." When he joined the Yanks in 1936, the club had two other Italian stars from San Francisco; since Tony Lazzeri was affectionately known to fellow Yanks as "Big Dago," and Frank Crosetti was "Little Dago," DiMaggio was simply called "Dago." The slugger was also known as "Joltin' Joe DiMaggio," the title of a popular 1941 song in his honor by Alan Courtney and Ben Homer, introduced by Les Brown and his orchestra. The lyrics went: "He'll live in the Hall of Fame / He got there blow by blow / Our kids will tell their kids his name / Joltin' Joe DiMaggio." In 1967, another hit song brought DiMaggio's name back to the forefront when songwriter Paul Simon used him as a symbol of lost American heroism. The song was "Mrs. Robinson," performed by Simon and Art Garfunkel for the film *The Graduate*: "Where have you gone, Joe DiMaggio? / A nation turns its lonely eyes to you." The question was answered in an anticlimactic manner when DiMaggio turned up on TV as the pitchman for a coffee-brewing machine named Mr. Coffee. Sportswriters reported that young people seeing DiMaggio in person would often exclaim "There's Mr. Coffee!" not knowing of his previous fame as a baseball player.

Mike (Turkey Mike) Donlin

Star Giants infielder Mike Donlin left baseball in the 1909 and 1910 seasons to appear in vaudeville with his wife, Mabel Hite. According to Fred Lieb, Donlin received the nickname "Turkey Mike" (which he hated) because his stage walk resembled a turkey strut. When Donlin rejoined the Giants in 1911, Harry Cross of the *New York Times* wrote, "Turkey Mike has been dancing the boards with his wife for two seasons, but he still does the turkey trot when he walks on the diamond." Donlin confronted Cross the next day and warned, "Don't you call me 'Turkey' in your paper again!" Norman Stearnes, a star in the Negro Leagues, was nicknamed "Turkey" and "The Gobbler" because he flapped his arms when he ran.

Brian (The Incredible Hulk) Downing

Downing embarked on a strenuous bodybuilding program in the winter after the 1978 season, adding weight and muscle to his chest and upper arms. When the catcher arrived in spring-training camp, Angels teammates could hardly believe their eyes. "Gee, Brian," said Nolan Ryan, "you don't have to wear your chest protector under your uniform." They took to calling him "The Incredible Hulk," after the green behemoth played by weight lifter Lou Ferrigno on the popular TV series of the same name. The nickname gained wide currency when Downing's newfound strength gave a dramatic boost to his batting average.

Judd (Slow Joe) Doyle

Some sources say Slow Joe Doyle was nicknamed because he pitched a slow ball, but actually the New York Highlanders right-hander was known for his dilatory habits on the mound.

The 1949 Yankees won the pennant despite the incredible total of seventy-three injuries during the season. Leaving a hospital in August, outfielder Tommy Henrich remarked prophetically, "The Yankees will win because we are a team of destiny."

Walt (Moose) Dropo

Dropo's University of Connecticut teammates named him "Moose" because he was born in Moosup, Connecticut, and because he stood 6'5" and weighed 225 pounds. Yankee Bill

Skowron received the same nickname in his childhood after his grandfather jokingly called him "Mussolini," and the family shortened it to "Moose." Other big players nicknamed "Moose" have included pitchers George Earnshaw and Bryan Haas. Another hefty pitcher, Jim Vaughn, was called "Hippo."

Joe (Jumping Joe) Dugan

The thin-skinned young Dugan was so upset by the fans' razzing that he "jumped" the 1917 Athletics several times. Old-time Tiger Davy Jones was called "Kangaroo" because he jumped from team to team; likewise, Roscoe Miller was known as "Rubberlegs."

Bob (Ach) Duliba

Duliba's last name bore a similarity to the title of the German song "Ach, Du Lieber Augustine," and manager Whitey Kurowski began calling him "Ach" Duliba while he was pitching for Peoria in 1954.

Leo (The Lip) Durocher

Will Wedge of the *New York Sun* gave the voluble Durocher his nicknames of "The Lip" and "Lippy Leo" while Leo was a rookie, "the cockiest player on the training field." Durocher's fondness for fine clothes (he once claimed that anyone who didn't change his shirt three times a day was a slob) gave him the nicknames of "Broadway" and "Fifth Avenue." Harry Heilmann reportedly was the man who dubbed Durocher "The All-American Out" in his less-than-dazzling playing days, and after Durocher became a manager, Red Smith, recalling Frank (The Peerless Leader) Chance, called The Lip "The Practically Peerless Leader." Another baseball character with a penchant for popping off is the irrepressible Atlanta Braves owner Ted Turner, mockingly known as "The Mouth from the South" or "The Mouth of the South."

Don (Duffy) Dyer

Pittsburgh catcher Duffy Dyer, an Irishman, was nicknamed by his family after its favorite radio show, *Duffy's Tavern*. Billy (Digger) O'Dell was another ballplayer named after a radio character; Baltimore teammate Chuck Diering gave him the nickname.

Jimmie (The Oakmont Orator) Dykes

The cigar-chomping Dykes was a loudmouth from Oakmont, Pennsylvania; hence his nickname of "The Oakmont Orator." Similarly named were garrulous catchers Orator Jim O'Rourke and Tim (Timosthenes) Donohue, the latter in a pun on the name of the ancient Greek orator Demosthenes.

Lenny (Nails) Dykstra

The fiercely competitive Phillies outfielder, one of the best all-around players in the game, prided himself on being "tough as nails." The nickname of "Nails" stuck even after he missed much of the 1995 season because of knee and back trouble.

General William D. (The Unknown Soldier) Eckert

When the obscure retired Air Force general was named as a figurehead baseball commissioner in 1966, press-box wags quickly dubbed him "The Unknown Soldier." In his brief tenure as commissioner at the height of the Vietnam War era, the ineffectual Eckert did little to live down that nickname, or to live up to his other moniker, "Spike."

Eric (Swat) Erickson

Born in Gothenburg, Sweden, the pitcher came to America as a youngster. Because he was a fair hitter, someone called him "that swattin' Swede," which later evolved into "Swat."

Hank (Popeye) Erickson

Erickson used to entertain his Cincinnati teammates with facial contortions resembling those of the cartoon character Popeye. (Don Zimmer doesn't have to contort his jowly face to be called "Popeye.") Marty (Duck) Pattin and John (Duke)

Wathan were nicknamed because of their penchants for imitating Donald Duck and John (Duke) Wayne.

John (The Crab) Evers

Charley Dryden called Evers "The Crab" because of the crab-like way the Cubs second baseman gripped the ball. Later the name took on more significance when John K. Tener, president of the National League, described the feisty Evers as "my number-one player problem—when they call Evers 'The Crab,' they're only telling half of it." Evers was also dubbed "The Keystone King" by Dryden because of his prowess at second base (the keystone), and "The Trojan," because he was born at Troy, New York.

Fred (Cy) Falkenberg

Good young right-handed pitchers, including Fred Falkenberg, Henry Morgan, and Darrell Blanton, were often nicknamed "Cy" after Denton (Cy) Young, the righty who amassed a record 507 victories between 1890 and 1911. Irving Young was called "Cy ii" or "Young Cy," and Harley Young became "Cy iii." The original Cy Young also lent his name to the awards given each year to the outstanding pitcher of each league. When Jim Palmer won his third Cy Young Award in 1976, he was nicknamed "Cy Old," even though he was still only thirty. Other players, including James Seymour and Fred Williams, have been named "Cy" because of their rustic origins.

The Family

The 1979 Pirates had a happy, raucous clubhouse filled with the sounds of disco music. To celebrate the team's unusually close-knit spirit, captain Willie Stargell in June of that year suggested using "We Are Family," a disco song by the four-woman group Sister Sledge, as the team song. It caught on with the fans, and the club was widely called "The Family"— a phrase that was painted on the roof of the home dugout and seen all over Pittsburgh on T-shirts as the team rolled to a pennant and the world championship.

Bob (Rapid Robert) Feller

In the late 1940s, Feller's fastball was clocked by a U.S. Army measuring device at 98.6 miles per hour, the record until Nolan Ryan threw a 100.9 mph pitch in 1974 (Ryan said later, "I don't feel my fastest pitch was ever timed"). Feller was known as "Rapid Robert" or "Bullet Bob," and Ryan was occasionally tagged "The Ryan Express," after a World War II movie called *Von Ryan's Express*. Similarly named for their speedballs were Walter (The Big Train) Johnson, Leslie (Bullet Joe) Bush, Bullet Bob Gibson, Bullet Bill Singer, Richard (Cannonball Dick) Redding, Gus (Cannonball) Weyhing, Sudden Sam McDowell, and Roger (The Rocket) Clemens. Fireman Aurelio Lopez was known as "Señor Smoke," and among Latin players as "El Lanzallama," or "The Flame-thrower." Virgil (Fire) Trucks was nicknamed by Birmingham sportswriter Jack House because of Trucks's excellent "fireball." Smokey Joe Wood and the Negro Leagues' Smokey Joe Williams also acquired their nicknames because of the "blazing" speed of their pitches. Walter Johnson once said, "Listen, my friend, there's no man alive can throw harder than Smokey Joe Wood."

Oscar (Happy) Felsch

From his early childhood the future member of the Chicago "Black Sox" was known as "Happy"; his father told him that he had been born laughing. Felsch was called "everybody's friend," and some feel it was his easygoing disposition that led him to be talked into joining the conspiracy to fix the 1919 World Series. After that, having the nickname of "Happy" was a cruel irony.

Dave (Boo) Ferriss

Charles (Bubba) Harris, Ralph (Bruz) Hamner, and Dave (Boo) Ferriss all received their nicknames because of childhood mispronunciations of the word "brother." In the case of Darrel (Bud) Harrelson, it was his brother who stumbled over the word, calling him "Bubba" and finally "Bud." Harold (Tookie) Gilbert, at the age of two, slipped on the word "cookie." Willie (Mookie) Wilson bobbled the word "milk" in his childhood.

Babe Herman was the man who kept lighted cigars in his pocket, forgot his son in the ballpark after a game, was hit on the shoulder by a fly ball, and doubled into a double play. When Dodgers owner Charles Ebbets offered him a trip around the world as a bonus, small wonder that he replied, "Frankly, I'd prefer someplace else."

Mark (The Bird) Fidrych

One of the most colorful players to come along in modern baseball, the Tigers' Mark Fidrych took the game by storm in his rookie year of 1976, when he won nineteen games and delighted the fans with his antics on the mound. Among his many eccentricities, Fidrych talked to the ball between pitches, telling it such things as "Flow, gotta flow now, gotta flow." The lanky young pitcher's frizzy hair and goofy behavior had already supplied him with his nicknames of "The Bird" or "Big Bird" in the minor leagues when a coach at Bristol, Jeff Hogan, noted his resemblance to the "Big Bird" character on the children's television show *Sesame Street*. "So that's your nickname," Hogan told him. "Fidrych is too hard to, y'know, *say*." Dave Kingman, the 6'6" Cubs slugger, also became known as "Big Bird."

Charles (The Golden Goose) Finley

The ebullient Finley, known as "Alabama" in his youth because of his southern drawl, was nicknamed "The Golden Goose" when he owned the A's in Kansas City. His equally exuberant pitcher John Wyatt gave him the nickname because Finley contrived the team's green-and-gold uniforms and since, to Wyatt, an important person was a "goose." Leon Goslin and Rich Gossage both became known as "Goose" because it jibed with their last names. During the 1977 season, Gossage kept a pet goose in the Pirates' bullpen.

Florida Marlins

In 1956, when the Syracuse minor-league franchise moved to Miami, it was nicknamed the "Marlins" after the majestic deep-sea sport fish prevalent in the southern Florida coastal waters. After the team moved to Puerto Rico in 1960, other Miami minor-league squads continued to use the nickname intermittently through 1988. Florida's first major-league franchise made its debut in 1993, and owner H. Wayne Huizenga, an avid sport fisherman, turned naturally to the name "Marlins" for the Miami-based National League expansion team. Huizenga said he liked the moniker because the marlin is "a fierce fighter and an adversary that tests your mettle."

Tim (Crazy Horse) Foli

In 1969, when he was nineteen and playing for Visalia of the California League, Tim Foli became so upset after going hitless and making two errors in one game that he went back to the empty diamond and played records to soothe his temper before falling asleep at second base. The story was widely circulated and helped build Foli's reputation as a "flake." He joined the Mets the following year, and teammates began calling him "Crazy Horse" because his fierce competitive spirit reminded them of the Indian warrior of that name. Foli was prone to throwing bats and helmets, and often engaged in fistfights. "That guy's so hyper he brings his bat back to the room," claimed teammate Ed Kranepool after a tussle with Foli. In later years, Foli showed signs of mellowing, but he was still called "Crazy Horse."

Edward (Whitey, Slick) Ford

The Yankees' Hall of Fame pitcher, commonly called "Whitey" because of his hair color, was dubbed "The Chairman of the Board" by teammate Elston Howard. But that term of respect was used less frequently by his teammates than "Slick," a nickname inspired by his strenuous carousing. Angered by the antics of Ford, Mickey Mantle, and Billy Martin, manager Casey Stengel once told a club meeting, "Damn it, some of you guys are drinking so much you're getting whiskey-slick." "After a while," recalled Mantle, "Billy and I picked up on it and we began to call Whitey 'Slick,' and the name just stuck." Ford even titled his autobiography *Slick*.

George (Corky) Foster

Foster uncorked one of his tape-measure home runs on June 2, 1979, at Riverfront Stadium in Philadelphia. Phillies manager Danny Ozark accused Foster of using a bat loaded illegally with cork, and the slugger's Cincinnati teammates gleefully seized upon the remark to give him the nickname of "Corky." Johnny Bench commented, "Danny's all wrong. George has cork in his arms, not his bat." Foster's slugging prowess also gave him the nickname "The Destroyer."

Jimmy (Double X) Foxx

Early in the slugger's career, his unusual last name was erroneously listed in the scorecard as "Fox." He was then called "Double X" to emphasize the variation. A native of Sudlersville, Maryland, he was also nicknamed "The Sudlersville Swatsman," "The Maryland Strong Boy," and "The Maryland Mauler," but more commonly was known as "The Beast."

> Asked what a ballplayer needs most in a slump, feisty manager Miller Huggins snapped, "A string of good alibis."

Gene (Augie) Freese

Freese had the rare distinction of being nicknamed after an umpire. When the Pirates infielder played at Brooklyn's Ebbets Field in his rookie year of 1955, Dodgers public address announcer Tex Rickards asked Brooklyn players what Freese's first name was. August (Augie) Donatelli was umpiring behind home plate that day, so the players jokingly said "Augie," and Rickards announced the rookie as "Augie" Freese.

Frank (The Fordham Flash) Frisch

Frisch captained the baseball, football, and basketball teams at Fordham University. New York sportswriters called him "The Fordham Flash," a name that persisted through his major-league career, partially because college-educated ballplayers were a rarity in those days. When he was player-manager of the St. Louis Cardinals, teammates called him "The Dutchman" or "Onkel Franz."

Carl (The Reading Rifle) Furillo

The outfielder with the magnificent throwing arm became known as "The Reading Rifle" after he played minor-league ball at Reading, Pennsylvania. His teammates on the Dodgers had two less-complimentary nicknames for him: "Skoonj," an Italian word for snail, because of his slowness on the base paths; and "The Rock," a nickname given him by Pete Reiser because Reiser thought Furillo's lack of education (he never attended high school) made him "rock-headed."

Jim (Bad News) Galloway

Before making the major leagues in 1912, Galloway, who came from Texas, worked in a telegraph office and played semipro ball. So that he could get away from work to play ball, Galloway had another telegrapher send him fake messages about illness in the family. Galloway pulled the trick so often that he was known as "Bad News." Arvel Hale, on the other hand, became "Bad News" because of his effect on Cotton States League pitchers. Steve Boros was called "News" because he was an avid reader of newspapers and magazines.

Jim (Pud) Galvin

Lee Allen, the late historian of the Baseball Hall of Fame, speculated that the pitcher was called "Pud" because he "made pudding of the batters." Galvin was a tireless worker, winning him the nickname of "The Little Steam Engine," and his mild-mannered habits made him "Gentle Jeems."

Ralph (Road Runner) Garr

The speedy outfielder was named after the lightning-quick bird of the Chuck Jones cartoon series. Gene Clines had the same nickname for the same reason.

Steve (Mr. Clean) Garvey

Although risqué revelations about his personal life eventually tarnished his image, Dodgers first baseman Steve Garvey presented himself as a paragon of rectitude. He inspired both admiration and sarcasm with his chiseled good looks, peerless play, and ostensibly squeaky-clean living. Caustic comedian Don Rickles, a frequent visitor to the Los Angeles clubhouse, dubbed Garvey "Mr. Clean," after a household scrubbing substance. Rickles described Garvey as "the only first baseman who washes his glove."

The Gas House Gang

There are varying accounts of how the rowdy 1934 St. Louis Cardinals came to be known as "The Gas House Gang," but the most authoritative one appears in a book by St. Louis sportswriter J. Roy Stockton, *The Gas House Gang and a Couple of Other Guys.* According to Stockton, sportswriter

Frank Graham and several players were comparing the National and American Leagues in June of that year. The Cards were then in fifth place, but Dizzy Dean said, "If we was in the other league, we would win the pennant." Pepper Martin retorted, "They wouldn't let us in the other league. They would say we were a lot of gas house ballplayers." Martin was referring to their uniforms, which, because of the team's aggressive playing habits, were as dirty as those worn by filling station ("gas house") mechanics. Graham then referred to them in print as "The Gas House Gang."

After an especially arduous game, umpires Tim Hurst and Silk O'Loughlin were taking a walk together. "It's a dog's life we have, Tim," moaned O'Loughlin. "Worse than that, for some people are kind to dogs. But every afternoon between three and five, standing out there, taking the insults . . ." "I know," agreed Hurst, "but Silk, me boy, you can't beat them hours."

Lou (The Iron Horse) Gehrig

"The Iron Man" played in a record 2,130 consecutive games before being felled by amyotrophic lateral sclerosis in 1939 (his mark was broken in 1995 by the Orioles' Cal Ripken, Jr.).

Gehrig also was nicknamed after the powerful and durable locomotive of the Old West, "The Iron Horse." Because of his slugging he was known as "Larrupin' Lou" and "Buster Lou," and his college education made him "Columbia Lou." When some players jocularly compared his rear end to hard, lumpy biscuits, he became "Biscuit Pants." Teammates, not-ing his uniform number, dubbed him "Little Joe," which is slang for the number four in Parcheesi. Gehrig was also known as "The Pride of the Yankees," which was the title of a movie about his life, starring Gary Cooper. Eleanor Gehrig's nickname for her husband was "Luke."

Charlie (The Mechanical Man) Gehringer

The Detroit second baseman, superbly graceful in both hit-ting and fielding, was so methodically perfect that most fans took him for granted. Teammate Doc Cramer said of "The Mechanical Man": "All you have to do is wind him up on opening day and he runs on and on—doing everything right."

Bob (Hoot) Gibson

The ace Cardinals pitcher was nicknamed after the cowboy movie star Edward (Hoot) Gibson, who died in 1962. Gib-son, former holder of the National League record for most lifetime strikeouts by a pitcher, also was known as "Bullet Bob" because of his speed. Two other players were called

"Hoot" in the actor's honor: Monte Pearson was fond of Western songs and movies, and Walter Evers used to pretend to be Hoot Gibson while playing after school, so an uncle began calling him by that name.

Josh (The Black Babe Ruth) Gibson

In the days when baseball's color bar kept black players out of the major leagues, comparisons were often made between Negro Leagues stars and their white counterparts, whom they sometimes faced in exhibition games. The legendary home-run hitter Josh Gibson, who hit 75 homers in the 1931 season, became known as "The Black Babe Ruth," "The Babe Ruth of the Negro Leagues," and "The Black Bomber." Three players—Oscar Charleston, James (Cool Papa) Bell, and Spotswood Poles—shared the title "The Black Ty Cobb" (an honorific with an unintended irony, since Cobb was a notorious racist). Louis Phillips and Burnham Holmes wrote of Charleston in *Yogi, Babe, and Magic: The Complete Book of Sports Nicknames*, "Some say he was the best player ever to play the game, and a few writers have suggested that Ty Cobb should be known as the White Oscar Charleston." Satchel Paige was sometimes called "The Black Matty" (after Christy Mathewson) or "Black Magic." Another Negro Leagues pitching ace, Cuban José Mendez, was known as "Mathewson in Black" or "El Diemente Negro" ("The Black Diamond"). First baseman Walter (Buck) Leonard was called "The Black Lou Gehrig," shortstop John Henry (Pop) Lloyd was "The Black Honus Wagner," and third baseman William (Judy) Johnson was "The Black Pie Traynor." Johnson became "Judy" in a play on the nickname of Negro Leagues player-manager Robert (Jude) Gans.

Jim (Junior) Gilliam

Gilliam was only seventeen when he joined the Baltimore Elite Giants of the Negro National League in 1946. During a tryout session, the switch-hitting youngster was struggling with right-handed pitchers when manager George Scales shouted, "Hey, Junior, get over on the other side of the plate." His teammates kept calling him "Junior," a nickname he detested but couldn't shake all through his major-league playing career with the Dodgers. As a Dodgers coach, however, Gilliam managed to pick up another moniker. An avid gambler, he walked into a pool hall one day, slapped down a bill, and asked, "Who wants the Devil?" His teammates always called him "Devil" after that, but the nickname never was used by the fans. Negro Leagues star shortstop Willie Wells earlier had been nicknamed "The Devil," after his diabolically good fielding led Mexican League fans to call him "El Diablo."

John (Pebbly Jack) Glasscock

The old-time shortstop had a habit of picking up and throwing away imaginary pebbles in the infield, giving him the name of "Pebbly Jack" or "Pebbles." Because of his hit-the-dirt baserunning habits, he was also called "Clayback Jack."

Since 1976, ballplayers have not been bound by the reserve clause, and are able to conduct negotiations for their services on a free-agent basis after playing out their contracts. As a result, salaries have escalated and attitudes have changed. No one expressed the modern player's pragmatic attitude more bluntly than slugger Reggie Jackson, who became the game's highest-paid player when he left Baltimore to sign a five-year, $2.9 million contract with the Yankees after the 1976 season. "It's become a business with us," Jackson admitted. "I used to dream how good it would be to be Willie Mays or Mickey Mantle. My dreams have died. Even the rotten [World Series] rings aren't what they're supposed to be. I'll buy my own diamonds. I can afford it now. No one gives you anything; you've got to get it for yourself."

William (Kid) Gleason

This White Sox manager was small and wore his cap on the back of his head, like a little boy. Other "Kids" have included Clarence Baldwin, Frank Butler, Wilfred Carsey, Blaine Durbin, Mal Eason, Norman Elberfield, Eddie Foster, Roy Henshaw, Mike Madden, Bill Nance, Charles Nichols, Jim Peoples, and George Spear. Both Ted Williams and Gary Carter were known as "The Kid."

Vernon (Lefty, Goofy) Gomez

Gomez is the only baseball player who owes his nickname to Albert Einstein. Generally called "Lefty," the Yankees' south-paw pitching ace had a reputation as a zany. Manager Joe McCarthy once found Gomez sitting nude in a phone booth outside the Fenway Park dressing room before a game he was scheduled to pitch. Understandably surprised, McCarthy asked what he was doing, and Gomez replied that he was going to stay in the phone booth until game time, "and then when I get out on the field, Fenway will look big to me." Sportswriters began to realize that Gomez was good copy, and they encouraged his antics. Gomez recalled how the "Goofy" nickname originated: "We were on a train to Washington. Albert Einstein got on and one of the writers asked me if I knew who Einstein was. I said sure I did, that he was an inventor. The writer asked if I ever invented anything and I told him I invented a fishbowl that added ten years to the lives of tropical fish. It was a rotating fishbowl. That way, the fish doesn't have to waste all that energy swimming around. He just sits still and the bowl does all the work. I guess the writer thought that sounded a little goofy." Because of his Latin blood, "Goofy" Gomez was also known as "El Goofo," and to Yankees teammates, the half-Spanish, half-Irish Gomez was affectionately called "Spic and Mick."

Dwight (Doc) Gooden

As a teenager, the future Yankees pitcher already was fast on his way to superstardom. While Gooden was playing Little League ball at age fourteen in the Belmar Heights section of East Tampa, Florida, a local reporter wrote, "What Dr. J. is to basketball, Dwight Gooden is to baseball" (Julius Erving's adroit ballhandling made him "Dr. J."). Gooden, in turn, became known as "Doctor K," a reference to his strikeout prowess ("K" is the scorer's symbol for strikeout); the nickname eventually was abbreviated to "Doc." Among the famous pitchers previously called "Doc" was Bobby (Doc) Brown, a Yankee who later became a surgeon and president of the American League. George (Doc) Medich also combined pitching with medicine; the fact that his last name sounded liked "medic" helped make his nickname popular. Other baseball-playing physicians have included Al (Doc) Bushong, Mike (Doc) Powers, and Danny (Doctor) Goodwin. There also have been dentists in baseball, such as Eddie Farrell, James Prothro, and Guy White, all nicknamed "Doc."

Otis Crandall, a star Giants reliever from 1908 to 1913, was given the honorary degree because he was renowned for "doctoring sick ball games." Some fans may have thought pitcher Dock Ellis was so called for similar reasons, but Dock was his actual first name. Ellis went to the Yankees from Pittsburgh as part of a deal involving Doc Medich, and one night in 1976, when Medich was having a hard time with Mets batters, an exasperated Pittsburgh sportswriter cracked, "Ellis is a better *doctor* than this guy!"

Joe (Flash) Gordon

Because of his flashy bat and glove work for the Yankees in the late 1930s and early 1940s, second baseman Joe Gordon was compared to the comic-strip and movie-serial outer-space hero Flash Gordon.

George (Piano Legs) Gore

Nineteenth-century outfielder George Gore had thick, stubby legs, like a piano. Utility player Cheerful Charles Hickman later acquired the same nickname, because, as Thomas P. Shea put it, "His underpinning was heavy Victorian." Players nicknamed because of their big feet included John (Footsie) Marcum, Clarence (Shovel) Hodge, and Joe (Poodles) Hutcheson (also called "Slug" because he ran like a worm).

Hank (Old Goldenrod) Gowdy

Gowdy, the first major leaguer to enlist in World War 1, had reddish-sandy hair, like Clarence (Ginger) Beaumont and some of the innumerable "Reds," who range from Adams (Charles D.) to Worthington (Robert L.). Emil Meusel was "Irish" because of his reddish hair.

Mark (Amazing) Grace

The words of the stately old hymn "Amazing Grace" ("how sweet the sound") came naturally to the lips of those describing the fielding and hitting style of the Cubs' star first baseman.

Jim (Mudcat) Grant

Grant was from Florida, the Sunshine State, but Bartow Irby, a teammate in 1954 at Fargo-Moorhead, thought Grant was from Mississippi, the Mudcat State. Also noting the pitcher's liking for fish, Irby came up with the "Mudcat" nickname.

Samuel (Dolly) Gray

Players on the A's dubbed their teammate "Dolly" when they slurred the title of the song "Oh, My Darling ('Dolly') Nellie Gray."

Elijah (Pumpsie) Green

Best known for being the first black player on the last major-league team to hire a black player (the Boston Red Sox, in 1959), Green for a while kept mum about the explanation for his nickname. Eventually it emerged that his childhood nickname had been "Pumpkin," which his mother affectionately modified to "Pumpsie."

William (Zaza) Grey

The infielder, also called "Reddy" because of the color of his hair, was nicknamed "Zaza" after a play in which redheaded Mrs. Leslie Carter took the title role. Erwin Harvey, who made the majors in 1900, two years after Grey retired, was another "Zaza."

Clark (The Old Fox) Griffith

Most famous for his later position as president of the Washington Nationals, Griffith was an outstanding pitcher around the turn of the century, and he combined occasional pitching stints with managing until he was forty-four. His crafty technique and personality, plus his age, gave him the title of "The Old Fox." Chicago Orphans teammates gave him an earlier nickname, "Dago," because of his swarthy features and dark hair.

Burleigh (Old Stubblebeard) Grimes

Grimes never shaved on days he was scheduled to pitch because, he said, "I had a heavy black beard and, when I shaved, resin would irritate my skin." Writers took notice of this habit and referred to him as "Bluebeard," "Cutthroat," "Wirewhiskers," and "Old Stubblebeard." "Boily," as he was known to Brooklyn fans, went along with the nicknames because batters believed what they read and became afraid of him. Someone searching for a gentler nickname called him "Senator," described by historian Thomas P. Shea as Burleigh's "Sunday-go-to-meeting name."

Fight manager Joe Jacobs attended the 1935 World Series in Detroit while nursing a miserable cold. He had bet on Chicago, but the Tigers won. On his return to New York, he told reporters who had come to interview him, "I should of stood in bed." Jacobs's other famous quotation came on June 21, 1932, when his boxer, Max Schmeling, lost to Jack Sharkey. Grabbing the radio mike, he told a nationwide audience, "We was robbed!"

Ross (Crazy Eyes) Grimsley

One of the leading "flakes" in contemporary baseball, Grimsley became known as "Crazy Eyes" while pitching for the Reds because he resorted to witchcraft in order to break a slump. Turning "crazy eyes" on someone means to cast a spell.

Robert (Lefty, The Wild Oriole) Grove

Lefty Grove pitched for the minor-league Baltimore Orioles from 1920 to 1924, and had control trouble, which he overcame before joining the Athletics. He was named "The Wild Oriole" because of his early habit and "The Maryland Mountaineer" after his birthplace at Lonaconing. As he aged, his middle name of Moses gave rise to the nickname of "Old Mose." Connie Mack always called him "Groves."

Ron (Louisiana Lightning) Guidry

Cajun pitcher Ron Guidry had such a spectacular year in 1978, turning in a 25–3 record for the Yankees, that sportswriters had to come up with nicknames for him, even if none really caught on with the fans. The Louisiana native's speed made him "Louisiana Lightning" and "The Bayou Blazer," and because of his diminutive build, he also was dubbed "The Little Cajun."

Larry (Slider) Gura

In 1975 spring training, Kansas City Royals rookie Jamie Quirk belted a homer off Gura, who was then pitching for the Yankees. After the game, Quirk told reporters the home-run pitch had been a slider, and when Gura, who couldn't get along with Yankees manager Billy Martin, was swapped to the Royals the following year, his new teammates razzed him by calling him "Slider." For the record, Gura did not rely primarily on his slider, and he insisted the pitch Quirk hit was a fastball.

George (Mule) Haas

In 1925, while Haas was playing for Birmingham of the Southern League, a sportswriter commented that the out-fielder had "the kick of a mule in every wallop." Later, team-mate Jimmie Dykes called Mule Haas "Donkey" or "Donk." Haas's last name is German for "rabbit," a fact that escaped the attention of nicknamers. Pitcher John (Mule) Watson was a muledriver in the cotton fields of his native Louisiana.

Harvey (The Kitten) Haddix

Haddix broke into the majors with the Cardinals in 1952, when veteran left-hander Harry (The Cat) Brecheen was pitching his last season for the club. Brecheen was given his nickname by J. Roy Stockton, sports editor of the *St. Louis Post-Dispatch*, because he was small, crafty, and a nimble fielder. Since Haddix had the same qualities, it was fitting that he became "The Kitten." His overall major-league performance didn't equal Brecheen's, but Haddix will always be remembered for pitching the greatest game in baseball history, his twelve-inning perfect game against the Milwaukee Braves on May 26, 1959. Haddix lost the heartbreaker to Lew Burdette in the bottom of the thirteenth through a bizarre succession of events: an error by Pirates third baseman Don Hoak, a sacrifice, an intentional walk of Hank Aaron, and a home run by Joe Adcock. The final score, however, was 1–0, because Aaron failed to cross home and Adcock passed him in the confusion on the base paths.

Frank (Noodles) Hahn

"Noodles" Hahn, a star left-handed pitcher for the Cincinnati Reds in the early 1900s, did not know how he received his nickname. "All I know is they always called me Noodles," he said. But Lee Allen discovered the source of the nickname, quoting a friend of Hahn's: "When Hahn was a boy in Nashville, he always had to carry his father's lunch to him. His father worked in a piano factory, and the lunch was always noodle soup. You never saw the boy without the noodle soup, so the nickname was a natural."

U.S. Marines, it is claimed, screamed insults to Emperor Hirohito at Guadalcanal to incense the Japanese troops. In reply, the story goes, the Japanese directed the "supreme blasphemy" of "To hell with Babe Ruth!" at the Americans. That may have been the sanitized version.

Ed (Ho-Ho) Halicki

Giants teammates thought the towering 6'7" pitcher resembled the Jolly Green Giant of TV commercial fame. Since the TV Giant's trademark was "Ho, ho, ho!," the players called Halicki "Ho-Ho."

Charley (Sea Lion) Hall

This pitcher often coached between turns on the mound, and his bellowing voice was compared to the roar of a sea lion. Similarly, loudmouthed Bill Schuster became "Sabu" because his yell recalled that of Sabu, the movies' elephant boy. One wag called Schuster "baseball's most voluble player."

Luke (Hot Potato) Hamlin

New York sportswriter Jimmy Cannon wrote that Hamlin "juggled the ball like a hot potato" before every pitch. Later, the pitcher's tendency to give up home-run balls gave the nickname of "Hot Potato" an added meaning. His manager at Brooklyn, Leo Durocher, exasperated by his pitching lapses, once saw an old-time political poster for the 1860 Republican ticket of Abraham Lincoln for president and Hannibal Hamlin for vice president. "That shows you what a great man Lincoln was," The Lip quipped. "He was able to win even *with* Hamlin!"

Eugene (Bubbles) Hargrave

The strong-hitting Reds catcher was a stutterer, and his nickname of "Bubbles" stemmed from his difficulties with the letter *b*. His brother Bill, also a catcher, was known as "Pinky" because of his red hair.

Mike (The Human Rain Delay) Hargrove

One reason ball games last so long these days is that players often waste inordinate amounts of time with their fidgeting rituals on the pitcher's mound or in the batter's box. One of the most egregious offenders was first baseman Mike Hargrove, who was so dilatory at the plate that he became known as "The Human Rain Delay."

Charles (Gabby) Hartnett

Hartnett was so taciturn as a rookie in the Cubs' 1922 spring-training camp that he was jokingly called "Gabby." After he established himself as a star catcher, though, the nickname became accurate because he opened up and was genuinely gabby. Another catcher, Charles Street, won the nickname because he called railroad porters "Gabby" to attract their attention. Frank (The Great Gabbo) Gabler was a talkative pitcher.

When Ban Johnson became president of the newly formed American League in 1901, he summed up his objectives in a succinct phrase: "Clean baseball and more twenty-five-cent seats."

Clint (The Hondo Hurricane) Hartung

When he came to the Giants' training camp in 1947, Hartung, a pitcher-outfielder, was heralded as a combination of Walter Johnson and Mel Ott. Sportswriter Tom Meany quipped, "Why bother to even play the season? He should go straight to Cooperstown." But the boy from Hondo, Texas, whom sportswriters called "The Hondo Hurricane" because of his speed and power, never lived up to his promise, becoming one of the classic examples of the "morning glory" ballplayer. As one writer commented, "He came into spring training as a hurricane and left as a gentle breeze." Hartung was also called "Floppy" because of his large, protruding ears. Another player who started like a storm and faded fast was Bob (Hurricane) Hazle, who hit .403 for the Milwaukee Braves in their first pennant-winning year, 1957, after being called up from the minors in June. One explosive Sunday in Philadelphia, someone in the press box said, "That guy's a regular hurricane," and the next day Bob Wolf of the *Milwaukee Journal* became the first to call Hazle "Hurricane" in print (Hazel had been the name of an actual hurricane). The next season, Hazle hit .179 for the Braves and was swapped to the Tigers in midyear.

Emerson (Pink) Hawley

As youngsters in Beaver Dam, Wisconsin, Emerson and Marvin Hawley, later both pitchers, were dressed with large ribbon-bows, pink for Emerson and blue for Marvin. Playmates named each after the color of his ribbon. "Blue" did not make the majors, but "Pink" won 182 games, including 32 in 1895.

The Heavenly Twins

Hugh (.329) Duffy and Tommy (.294) McCarthy played together in the Boston Beaneaters' outfield from 1892 to 1895, and their talents were so angelic that they became known as "The Heavenly Twins." The modern-day Oakland slugging duo of Jose Canseco and Mark McGwire were dubbed "The Bash Brothers."

Don (Jeep) Heffner

Red Kress, a teammate of Heffner's on the 1938–39 St. Louis Browns, called him "Jeep" because Heffner bounced around the infield like the jeeps used in the Army. The word "jeep" stems from G. P. (general purpose) vehicle. Another infielder, Lee Handley, was called "Jeep" for the same reason as Heffner.

Rickey (The Man of Steal) Henderson

When he left the single-season and career stolen-base records of Lou Brock far behind him in the dust, Oakland's Rickey Henderson took on the stature of a true baseball Superman, inspiring a pun on the comic-book character's sobriquet "The Man of Steel." Henderson's flamboyant play on the base paths and in the outfield led fellow players to tag him "Style Dog."

Tommy (Old Reliable) Henrich

Tommy Henrich always seemed to come through with the clutch play during his eleven-year tenure with the Yankees, and broadcaster Mel Allen nicknamed him "Old Reliable."

Henrich was also called "The Clutch." Just how much the team valued him can be gleaned from some advice that manager Casey Stengel once gave him: "Tommy, I don't want you to sit in a draft. Don't slip and fall in the shower. And under no circumstances are you to eat fish, because them bones could be murder. Drive carefully, and stay in the slow lane, and sit quietly in the clubhouse until the game begins. I can't let anything happen to you." Mel Allen came up with a similar nickname for another Yankees outfielder, Gene Woodling, calling him "Old Faithful," after the geyser that erupts daily at Yellowstone Park.

Floyd (Babe) Herman

This brash rookie came to the majors with special bats weighing more than forty-five ounces. When Ty Cobb said that they were heavier than the bats Babe Ruth used, Herman shot back, "I figure if I use heavier wood I'll hit 'em farther than Ruth." The players quickly began calling him "Babe."

The Heroic Legion of Baseball

Pitcher Jim McCormick and catcher Mike (King) Kelly were idols of the public when they played together on the White Stockings, the predecessors of the Cubs. Fans called the two "The Heroic Legion of Baseball."

Umpires have taken abuse since the beginning of baseball, but in the 1880s, conditions became unbearable. An 1882 sign on the outfield wall of a Kansas City ballpark became widely quoted: "Please Do Not Shoot the Umpire; He Is Doing the Best He Can." No umpire has ever been shot during a game, but two have been murdered. At Lowdensborough, Alabama, in 1899, an irate player slew umpire Samuel White at home plate with a bat, and the act was repeated two years later when Ora Jennings died at Farmersburg, Indiana.

Ed (The Wild Elk of the Wasatch) Heusser

Pepper Martin, "The Wild Horse of the Osage," was a Cardinals teammate of pitcher Ed Heusser's when Heusser came up to the majors in 1935. Some fanciful writers, noting that Heusser came from Murray, Utah, near the Wasatch mountain range, tagged him "The Wild Elk of the Wasatch."

The Hitless Wonders

The 1906 Chicago White Sox, relying on a fantastic pitching staff, won the pennant with a season batting average of only .228. The National League champs that year, the Cubs, had another of the all-time great teams, finishing the season with 116 victories, yet they lost the World Series to the weak-hitting Sox. The club's strange abilities led Charley Dryden to label them "The Hitless Wonders," a title first applied the previous year, when the Sox finished in second place, but more widely and accurately used in the championship season of 1906. The Philadelphia Phillies of 1930, on the other hand, were called "The Pitchless Wonders." The team batting average was .315, but the pitching staff's ERA was a dismal 6.71, and they finished in last place.

Don (Tiger) Hoak

A prizefighter before he became a ballplayer, Hoak continued his pugnacious habits in the majors, often getting into brawls, including a memorable one under the Ebbets Field stands with Dodgers teammate Clem Labine. Hoak's feistiness gave him the nickname of "Tiger," and he later hosted a Pittsburgh television show called *Tiger by the Tail.*

Urban (Jupe) Hodapp

This pitcher told a newsman one afternoon that he was praying for rain, so the writer named him "Jupe" after Jupiter Pluvius, the rain god.

James (Shanty) Hogan

New York sportswriter Frank (Buck) O'Neil nicknamed Hogan, a Massachusetts native whom he considered a typical "shanty Irishman."

Tommy (Kelly) Holmes

Some major leaguers, including Lou Gehrig, played semipro ball under assumed names in order to protect their amateur standing while going through school. Tommy Holmes was another to do so, playing under the name of "Kelly" during his high school days in Brooklyn. After he joined the Boston Braves, he was called "Kelly" Holmes.

Burt (Night Owl) Hooton

The Dodgers pitcher's last name made some kind of "owl" nickname inevitable (teammates called him "Hoot"), and since Hooton liked to stay up half the night watching television, manager Tom Lasorda dubbed him "Night Owl." Lasorda also called him "Happy," because he was the opposite.

Rogers (The Rajah) Hornsby

With a lifetime batting average of .358, second only to Ty Cobb's .367, Hornsby was one of baseball's "royalty," and accordingly he was called "The Rajah," a play on his first name.

Engraved on Wee Willie Keeler's Cooperstown plaque are the words "Baseball's Greatest Place-Hitter; Best Bunter." Keeler summed up his theory of batting with "Keep your eye on the ball and hit 'em where they ain't."

Frank (Pig) House

When hefty American League catcher Frank House was a baby, his family used to say he was "big as a house." He twisted the word "big" into "pig," resulting in his nickname.

Houston Astros

When the Texas club was formed in 1962, it took its names, the Colt ".45s" or "Colts," from the Colt .45 revolver, "the gun that won the West." In 1964, however, the gun company objected to the use of its emblem on team souvenirs. Judge

Roy Hofheinz, the club owner, decided to give the team a more modern nickname, and came up with "Astronauts," in honor of Houston's thriving National Aeronautics and Space Administration mission-control center. But after realizing that "Astronauts" would be changed in headlines to "Astros," Hofheinz settled on the latter and named the team's enclosed stadium the "Astrodome." The artificial playing surface in the Astrodome, called "AstroTurf," was later adopted by many other ballparks. One of the players who objected to AstoTurf, first baseman Dick Allen, declared in 1970, "If a horse can't eat it, I don't want to play on it."

Frank (Hondo) Howard

In 1953, John Wayne starred in a Louis L'Amour Western movie called *Hondo*, which means "big" in Spanish. Basketball player John Havlicek, who attended Ohio State before going on to pro ball with the Boston Celtics, became known as "Hondo," and 6'7" baseball player Frank Howard, who also played basketball for Ohio State, acquired the same nickname. During his days with the Washington Senators, the slugging Howard was also called "The Capital Punisher" and "The Washington Monument." Larry Herndon of the San Francisco Giants was called "Hondo" because when he was playing high school basketball in Memphis, fans and teammates thought he bounced the ball like Hondo Havlicek. The Giants' Clint Hartung was "The Hondo Hurricane" because he came from Hondo, Texas.

William (Dummy) Hoy

Some of the early baseball nicknames seem cruel by today's standards. Such was that of William Hoy, a deaf-mute who was a superb outfielder and base stealer for various teams between 1888 and 1902. Despite his nickname, "Dummy" Hoy was respected and well liked by his fellow players, who learned sign language to communicate with him. At the time of his death in 1961, five months short of his 100th birthday, he was the oldest living former major-leaguer. Another early player, Tim O'Rourke, was nicknamed "Voiceless Tim" because his vocal cords were damaged when a ball hit him in the throat.

Waite (Schoolboy) Hoyt

While still a student at Brooklyn's Erasmus High, Hoyt pitched batting practice at Ebbets Field, giving him the nickname of "Schoolboy," which stuck even after he made the major leagues. Another "Schoolboy" was Lynwood Rowe. First known as "Newsboy," Rowe was a star pitcher at fifteen, and during a game between Methodist and Baptist teams at El Dorado, Arkansas, around 1927, some of the fans yelled to the batters, "Don't let that schoolboy strike you out!"

Al (The Mad Hungarian) Hrabosky

Hrabosky's career as a relief pitcher was on the skids in 1974 when he came up with a gimmick that made him famous and successful. During a game against the Dodgers, the Cardinals pitcher walked off the mound, turned his back to the batter, and gave himself a spirited pep talk before slamming the ball into his glove and returning to the rubber with a fierce scowl. He found that his "mad" behavior helped to intimidate hitters, so he cultivated the image by growing longer hair and a bushy, pointed goatee. Hrabosky soon picked up the nickname of "The Mad Hungarian." As he explained, "I want the batters to think I'm crazy. I want them to think I'd hit my own mother if she was up at the plate. And I would. There's supposed to be a dark side in every person. In me, it's The Mad Hungarian. I express my ego through him and, I suppose, my hate and my contempt and all those other evil things. I do things through him that I can't do as Al Hrabosky. He's insane, a menace to society. But he's just on the field when I'm pitching. When I walk off the field, I'm Al Hrabosky again." During his splendid 1974 season, he became a favorite of St. Louis fans, and "I Hlove Hrabosky" bumper stickers began appearing all over town. The following year, after he failed to make the All-Star team despite continued success on the mound, the fans honored him with a "We Hlove Hrabosky Hbanner Hday." But his personality was too abrasive for the Cardinals' management, and he attributed his subpar 1977 season to manager Vern

Rapp's insistence that he shave off the wild foliage. After he was swapped to the Royals at the end of that season, the facial hair returned and "The Mad Hungarian" was in full flower again. His Royals teammates called him "Hungo," a nickname rhyming with that of another Kansas City reliever, Steve (Mingo) Mingori.

Ralph Kiner either led the National League in homers or tied for the lead in each of his first seven seasons, 1946 through 1952. He hit 369 lifetime homers and was elected to the Hall of Fame in 1975. Yet his career batting average was a relatively modest .279. Asked once why he never choked up on the bat and tried to hit for average, Kiner made a famous reply: "Cadillacs are down at the end of the bat." The remark has been paraphrased into the baseball axiom, "Home-run hitters drive Cadillacs." A slugger's stately progress around the bases after hitting a homer is known as the "Cadillac trot."

Miller (The Mite Manager) Huggins

The scrappy little second baseman and Yankees manager was only 5'4" and 148 pounds, but he fought his way through the majors. He was called "Rabbit," "Little Everywhere," "The Mighty Mite," and "The Mite Manager."

Jim (Catfish) Hunter

George (Catfish) Metkovich received his nickname because a catfish bit him while the Braves rookie was fishing in the Manatee River near his Bradenton, Florida, spring-training camp. Players sometimes shortened the name to "Cat" or "Catso." Umpire Bill Klem was dubbed "Catfish" in 1904 by Bill Clymer, manager of the American Association Columbus team, because of Klem's large, fishlike mouth. (Klem hated the nickname, and saying "Catfish" in his presence on the diamond was grounds for immediate ejection from the game.) The origin of Jim (Catfish) Hunter's nickname was more arbitrary. After Hunter was signed to a $75,000 bonus contract by the A's in 1964, club owner Charles O. Finley, always on the lookout for a promotional gimmick, decided to call him "Catfish," telling Hunter, "If anyone asks, just say you always had a string of catfish over your shoulder when you were a kid." Hunter, a country boy from North Carolina, was an avid fisherman, which lent the nickname some appropriateness. (Finley even tried, without success, to persuade Vida Blue to change his first name to "True" in 1971; Blue, who already possessed one of the most interesting names in baseball, retorted, "How about if you change your name to True O'Finley?") "Catfish" Hunter, who became a Yankee in 1975, spawned an imitator in May of that year, when pitcher

Jim Hughes, then with the Minnesota Twins, was having a hot streak. St. Paul sportswriter Pat Reusse remarked that if the Yankees could have their Catfish, the Twins should have a "Bluegill," and he conferred that nickname on Hughes (the bluegill, common in Minnesota waters, is another name for the sunfish).

Joe (Shoeless Joe) Jackson

This South Carolina farm boy, whose great career was ruined by his participation in the 1919 "Black Sox" scandal, played for Greenville before making his major-league debut with the Athletics in 1908. While breaking in a new pair of shoes in his minor-league days, Jackson developed blisters, so he played one game in the outfield barefoot, even though the field his team played on was a former dump littered with sharp rocks and broken glass. Ever after, he was "Shoeless Joe."

Reggie (Mr. October) Jackson

Reggie Jackson usually seemed to rise to the occasion in postseason play, even though Yankees teammate Chris Chambliss caustically observed that Jackson didn't try as hard in the regular season as he did in October. Because of his heroics in the playoffs and World Series, the slugger was widely known as "Mr. October." The nickname was first bestowed with sarcastic intent by another Yank, Thurman Munson,

Every true baseball fan's most cherished fantasy—having the chance to watch the fabled players from the distant past, and perhaps even to play with them—was realized in W. P. Kinsella's 1982 novel *Shoeless Joe.* The book's protagonist, an Iowa farmer named Ray Kinsella, carves a baseball diamond from his cornfield in order to conjure up the ghost of Shoeless Joe Jackson. The apparition comes after Ray hears a mysterious voice: "Three years ago at dusk on a spring evening, when the sky was a robin's-egg blue and the wind as soft as a day-old chick, I was sitting on the verandah of my farm home in eastern Iowa when a voice very clearly said to me, 'If you build it, he will come.'" Those haunting words were given added resonance when heard in the film version of the novel, *Field of Dreams* (1989), starring Kevin Costner as Ray and featuring Ray Liotta as Shoeless Joe.

after Jackson performed poorly in the 1977 league playoffs. But Jackson's heroics in that year's World Series—including three homers in the final game, each on the first pitch—made the nickname an indelible honorific. Known to his teammates as "Buck," Jackson, much to their disgruntlement, cockily dubbed himself "The Straw That Stirs the Drink." Like Josh

Gibson before him, Jackson also was called "The Black Babe Ruth." He acquired the nicknames of "The Candy Man" and "Mr. Candy" after a confections company put out a "Reggie!" chocolate bar in 1978. When Bill Veeck passed out the bars to White Sox fans at Comiskey Park that summer, the fans retaliated by throwing the bars at Jackson.

Vincent (Bo) Jackson

The multitalented Jackson, one of the few players to be simultaneously a star in professional baseball and football, originally was nicknamed "Boar" by a cousin who considered him "tough as a boar." "Bo" was the abbreviated version that made everyone forget that his real name was Vincent.

Bill (Baby Doll) Jacobson

This Browns outfielder was called "Baby Doll," a 1910s slang term for a baby-faced blonde. Handsome Yankees pitcher Marvin Breuer was known as "Baby Face" or "Adonis." Another baby-faced player was Tracy (Kewpie) Barrett.

Harold (Childe Harold) Janvrin

Janvrin was eighteen and fresh out of a Boston high school when he joined the Red Sox in 1911. He was dubbed "Childe Harold," after the poem by Lord Byron. Billy Purtell became

Umpire Bill Klem, who insisted, "It ain't nothin' till I call it," made some famous retorts to players disputing his calls. Once, when the young Al Lopez threw his bat high in the air after taking a called third strike, Klem said, "Son, if that bat comes down you're out of the game." Another time Hack Wilson shouted that Klem had missed a pitch. "Maybe," the umpire said, "but I wouldn't have if I had a bat." In 1949, Polo Grounds fans gave the "Old Arbiter" a "day," and sportswriters presented him a plaque. Accepting the award, Klem exclaimed, "Baseball is more than a game to me—it's a religion!"

"The Child Athlete" because of his fresh-faced appearance at the time of his debut.

Tom (Tut) Jenkins

The tall, thin Jenkins, a Red Sox outfielder in 1926, was said to resemble the mummy of the Egyptian king Tutankhamen, which was discovered in 1922.

When Stan Musial joined the Cardinals in 1941, fans and players laughed at his unorthodox, crouching batting stance. White Sox pitcher Ted Lyons remarked, "Musial's batting stance looks like a small boy looking around the corner to see if the cops are coming." Fred Hutchinson, then pitching for Detroit, claimed Musial would never last; ironically, when Musial made his 3,000th hit in 1958, Hutchinson was his manager.

Hugh (Ee-Yah) Jennings

As a pugnacious Baltimore shortstop, Jennings was nicknamed after his motto of "Hit or Get Hit." As Detroit manager, he coached in the third-base box plucking grass, clenching both fists, and raising a leg in the air as he gave his famous Tiger Yell, "Ee-Yah!" Also nicknamed for his shouts in the coaching box was Joe (Move Up) Gerhardt. White Sox second baseman Nellie Fox was so leather-lunged with his exhortations that he became "The Holler Guy," inspiring a 1955 poem of that title by Ogden Nash.

Forrest (Woody) Jensen

Jensen's nickname was both a play on his first name and a reference to the fact that he once played in the Timber League.

Clifford (Connie) Johnson

Johnson called all his Kansas City Monarchs teammates "Connie," a name, they, in turn, applied to him. It lasted after the pitcher was promoted to the majors by the White Sox. A later player named Clifford Johnson became known as "Heathcliff," after the central character in Charlotte Brontë's novel *Wuthering Heights*, because of his mountainous size. He was also called "Top Cat," and his slugging power made him "Boomer."

Harry (Steamboat) Johnson

The flamboyant "Steamboat" Johnson, also called "The Steamer," was an umpire for forty years, the last thirty in the Southern League. His temper was second in renown only to his booming voice, which was compared to a steamboat whistle. He announced the batteries before each game without the aid of an amplifier.

Walter (The Big Train) Johnson

Sportswriter Arthur (Bugs) Baer memorably declared that Walter Johnson "could throw a lamb chop past a wolf." Johnson's awesome pitching speed cried out for an appropriate sobriquet, and New York sportswriter Grantland Rice provided one. Prior to a Washington–New York series, he wrote, "The Big Train comes to town today." Johnson acquired the nickname of "Barney" in 1911, when he and roommate Clyde Milan bought a Cole Eight, an early speed car. The pitcher took teammate Germany Schaefer for a ride through Washington at the breakneck speed of twenty-five miles per hour. "Whew, Walter!" exclaimed Schaefer, "you drive like Barney Oldfield!" (Oldfield was the most famous auto racer of that era.)

Smead (Guinea) Jolley

When this big slugger was serving his short term with the White Sox, he and pitcher Ted Lyons went to dinner. Jolley ordered a $6 guinea-hen special, and Lyons promptly nicknamed him "Guinea." He was also known as "Big Stud" because of his reputation as a playboy, and the Senators' speedy George (Mercury) Myatt, once a clubhouse aide to Jolley, consequently was called "Stud."

Sam (Sad Sam, Horsewhips Sam) Jones

An American League pitcher from 1914 through 1935, Jones had a curve that snapped and cracked, according to *Boston Herald* sports editor Burt Whitman, who dubbed him "Horsewhips Sam." He was also called "Sad Sam," a common nickname for athletes named Sam Jones, when Bill McGeehan of the *New York Herald-Tribune* dubbed him "Sad Sam, the Sorrowful Sage from Woodsfield [Ohio]." As Jones explained to Lawrence S. Ritter in the book *The Glory of Their Times*, McGeehan "said he used to watch me on the field and I always looked sort of downcast to him: so 'Sad Sam.' Actually, what it was, I would always wear my cap down real low over my eyes. And the sportswriters were more used to fellows like Waite Hoyt, who'd always wear their caps way up so they wouldn't miss seeing any pretty girls."

Sam (Toothpick) Jones

This Sam Jones acquired his "Sad Sam" moniker from sportswriter Bill Phillip while pitching for Wilkes-Barre in 1950. Another nickname was "Toothpick," something he was never without. After he pitched a no-hitter for the Cubs against the Pirates in 1955, he was presented with an appropriate award: a gold toothpick.

One of the most famous foot-in-the-mouth remarks in baseball history was made by Giants pitcher Christy Mathewson, via ghostwriter John N. Wheeler, in a *New York Herald* article during the 1911 World Series. That was the Series in which Frank Baker of the Athletics made his nickname of "Home Run" a household word. Giants manager John McGraw had ordered his pitchers to keep the ball low for Baker, but in the second game Rube Marquard threw him a high fastball and Baker homered to win the game. In the *Herald* the next day (October 17), Matty commented, "Marquard made a poor pitch to Frank Baker on the latter's sixth-inning home run. There was no excuse for it." That very day, protecting a 1–0 lead against the A's in the ninth inning, Mathewson made the same mistake, Baker homered again, and the A's went on to win in the eleventh. Marquard retaliated by having *his* ghostwriter, Frank Menke, attack Mathewson in print. The public feuding between the teammates caused a sensation among baseball fans, and it was a major factor in the Giants' loss of the Series.

Sheldon (Available) Jones

Among cartoonist Al Capp's memorable characters were Li'l Abner, Daisy Mae, Joe Btfsplk, and Available Jones. Baseball players are avid comic-strip readers, and they hung the "Available" tag on Sheldon Jones. Paul Erickson became "Abner" or "Li'l Abner."

Willie (Puddin' Head) Jones

Willie Jones was one of several ballplayers named Jones whose last name evoked comparison with the song "Wooden Head, Puddin' Head Jones."

Kansas City Royals

Sanford Porte of Overland Park, Kansas, submitted the winning entry in 1968 when the Kansas City American League expansion team chose its name. "Kansas City's new baseball team should be called the Royals," he wrote, "because of Missouri's billion-dollar livestock income, Kansas City's position as the nation's leading stocker and feeder market, and the nationally known American Royal parade and pageant. The team colors of royal blue and white would be in harmony with the state bird, the bluebird, the state flag, [and] the old Kansas City Blues [minor-league baseball team]." The words "royal" and "crown" are commonly used in the city primarily because of the American Royal parade, a major event in the livestock world; "Royals" was the name most often suggested by the more than 17,000 entrants in the contest to choose the team's nickname.

Frank (Cactus) Keck

Frank Keck, a native of Missouri, was known as "Cactus" because he once pitched in the Texas League. Another "Cactus," pitcher Jack Kraus, came from San Antonio, Texas.

William (Wee Willie) Keeler

The famous place hitter, known for his slogan of "Hit 'em where they ain't," was a tiny man (5′4½″) known to fans and sportswriters as "Wee Willie." Teammates and friends, however, called him "Billy." Among other players nicknamed for their small size were Tommy (Tommy the Wee) Leach, Elisha (Bitsy) Mott, Norman (Brownie, or Kid) Elberfeld, James (Chappie) Geygan, Anthony (Chick) Cuccinello, Eugene (Half-Pint) Rye, and Milton (Mickey Mouse, or Mickey) Haefner. Many Latin players, in addition, have been nicknamed "Chico," the Spanish word for "little." Sometimes, large players are given diminutive nicknames ironically, including Ernest (Tiny) Bonham, Anthony (Bunny) Brief, and Robert (Junior) Kline. But just as common are straightforward nicknames such as those of Jim (Truck) Hannah, Frank (Blimp) Hayes, Greg (The Bull) Luzinski, John (Ox) Miller, and Bob (Big Foot) Stanley—the latter after the mythical "Big Foot" monster.

William (Wagon Tongue Willie) Keister

One of the slang expressions for a heavy bat in the early days of the game was "wagon tongue," because such a bat was said to be as big as the harnessing pole of a horse-drawn wagon. Infielder Willie Keister used an uncommonly heavy bat, hence "Wagon Tongue Willie."

John (Honest John) Kelly

This umpire, a member of the Hall of Fame, did not receive his nickname on the ball field, but it stood him in good stead there. As Lee Allen tells the story in his book *The Hot Stove League*, Kelly rented a horse for $2 from a farmer outside Akron, Ohio, one winter night after his own horse had bolted. The horse died after getting Kelly to Akron, but Kelly returned and paid the farmer $20. "You're honest, John Kelly," the farmer told him.

Mike (King) Kelly

Baseball writers in the nineteenth century were fond of calling star players "kings." Fred Dunlap was "The King of Second Basemen," Jack Glasscock was "The King of Shortstops," Hoss Radbourn was "The King of Pitchers," and Mike Kelly was simply "The King of Baseball." A colorful, tricky, highly popular slugger, Kelly was commonly referred to as "King" Kelly. After the Chicago White Stockings (later the Cubs) sold Kelly to Boston in 1886, he became known as "$10,000

Milwaukee Journal reporter Ira Kapenstein covered the arrival of the Yankees in Milwaukee prior to the third game of the 1957 World Series. "The Yankees," he recalled, "came into town by train and immediately hustled onto a waiting bus. They brushed past reporters and a small crowd that had gathered. I was the first reporter to get on the bus in search of manager Casey Stengel, but a Yankee bruiser stopped me before I could get very far. He told me that Stengel was not on the bus, which we knew was not true. When we persisted, he blurted out, 'This is strictly bush.' Then he proceeded to forcibly shove us off the bus. At first, we thought the 'bush' quote was made by Charlie (King Kong) Keller, but a little later it was fairly well established that he was Gus Mauch, the Yankee trainer. I phoned in my story, which ended up on page one with the 'bush' quote in the lead. It became the war cry of the Series and was reported all over the world—especially when the 'bush league' team ended up beating the big-city boys." After the seventh game, the *Journal* gloated, "Who's Bush Now?," with an assist from Exodus: "And behold the bush burned with fire, and the bush was not consumed."

Kelly," because of the purchase price, which stood for almost twenty-two years as the highest ever paid for a ballplayer, until the Giants paid $11,000 for Rube Marquard. Kelly's baserunning skills inspired an 1889 hit song by a J. W. Kelly (no relation). The King's fans would chant the lyrics: "Slide, Kelly, on your belly! Slide, Kelly, slide!"

Jim (The Airhead) Kern

The giant relief pitcher, called "Emu" because he resembled an oversized bird, was better known as "The Airhead," a nickname he preferred because it emphasized his supposed craziness. "Since I'm The Airhead," he explained, "the other team is going to read about it and say, 'Here is a guy that is six-five with a grungy-looking beard, looking grungy on the mound and he's throwing hundred-mile-an-hour gas and he doesn't have any idea where it's going and he doesn't care.' It keeps them thinking."

Leo (Black Cat) Kiely

While Kiely was with the Red Sox, he had a habit of carrying a toy black cat to the bullpen every day. When he won his first game in 1956 after a long victory drought, the cat was buried in the Fenway Park bullpen.

Edwin (Twilight Ed) Killian

The Tigers southpaw, who pitched on the pennant-winning teams of 1907, 1908, and 1909, hurled an extraordinary number of extra-inning games, then referred to as "twilight games" because the regular starting time of games was 3 P.M.

Ellis (Old Folks) Kinder

Kinder retired in 1957 at the age of forty-three, which is considered elderly by baseball standards. He was known as "Old Folks," a familiar baseball expression for a veteran. Others nicknamed because of their longevity were William (Dad) Clark, Howard (Old Man) Ehmke, Satchel (Ol' Man River) Paige, Willie (Golden Oldie) McCovey, Herman (Old Folks) Pillette, Robert (Old Mose) Grove, Roy (Pappy) Joiner, Willie (Pops) Stargell, and several players called "Pop": Adrian Anson, Jesse Haines, John Henry Lloyd, Ray Prim, and Ed Tate.

Dave (Kong) Kingman

King Kong, the ape with a penchant for climbing tall New York buildings, lent his name to three Gotham players. The first was Charlie (King Kong) Keller, a hirsute slugger who came in for a great deal of ribbing from teammates and opponents alike. Lefty Gomez, on seeing Keller for the first time, said, "That's the first ballplayer Frank Buck ever brought back alive!" Yogi Berra became known as "Little Kong," after Keller. Dave Kingman, who played for the Yanks briefly in the 1977 season en route to the Cubs, received his "Kong" nickname from sportswriters while he was playing for the New York Mets. Kingman stood a hulking 6'6" and had equal parts of the giant ape's strength and clumsiness. Players called him "Sky King" or "Sky" because of his height and because he worked during the off-season for United Airlines. After he joined the Cubs in 1978, teammates named him "Big Bird" because, like Mark Fidrych, he resembled the *Sesame Street* TV character. Another major leaguer in the King Kong tradition was Earl Averill, a slugger who played most of his career with Cleveland; his simian build led to the nicknames of "Orang-Outang" and "Rock."

The New York Mets threw a "day" in honor of Willie Mays when the legendary player made his farewell appearance at the end of the 1973 season. Gesturing toward the National League–champion Mets, Mays told the Shea Stadium crowd, "I look over there and I see all those kids, and I just think, 'Willie, it's time to say good-bye to America.'"

Lerrin (Lurch) LaGrow

"Lurch," the hulking butler played by Ted Cassidy on television's *The Addams Family*, inspired the nickname of pitcher Lerrin LaGrow, a 6'5", 230-pound behemoth.

Napoleon (Larry) Lajoie

It is quite a turnabout to be named Napoleon and nicknamed Larry. Lajoie, also called "Nap," acquired his nickname of "Larry" from a corruption of his tongue-twisting last name. He was a native of Rhode Island, and New Englanders found it easier to say "Larry" than "Napoleon Lajoie." When Lajoie was player-manager of the Cleveland American League team in the early 1900s, the club was called the "Naps" in his honor.

Don (Perfect Game) Larsen

Larsen pitched the one and only perfect game in World Series history, retiring twenty-seven batters in succession as the Yankees beat the Brooklyn Dodgers, 2–0, on October 8, 1956. "Perfect Game" Larsen had two other nicknames that weren't quite so laudatory. Teammates called him "The Ghoul" because of his fascination with morbid comic books, and he became known as "The Nightrider" after his convertible hit a telephone pole in St. Petersburg, Florida, early one morning during 1956 spring training, five hours after the

Yankees' midnight curfew had expired. The incident provoked two memorable comments from manager Casey Stengel: (1) "He was either out pretty late or up pretty early"; and (2) "Anybody who can find something to do in St. Petersburg at five in the morning deserves a medal, not a fine." Larsen's nocturnal habits persisted, and the night before his perfect game he stayed up until 1 A.M. reading comics and eating pizza.

Frank (Taters) Lary

The Alabama-born pitcher once wrote "taters" for "potatoes" on the order form in a railroad dining car, and Tigers teammates never let him forget it. Casey Stengel, amazed at "The Yankee Killer"'s success against his team, called him "Bulldog" because of his aggressive pitching. Lary was called "Mule" in the army because he turned over beds in the morning when soldiers overslept. Other players who, like "Taters" Lary, were nicknamed because they liked potatoes were pitcher Spurgeon (Spud) Chandler and catcher Virgil (Spud) Davis. Pitcher Howard Krist was called "Spud" because he was a farmer in the off-season. George (Boomer) Scott was known as "The Tater Man" because he hit a lot of "taters," a slang expression for home runs. Scott popularized the term, which was derived from the use of the word "potato" as a synonym for "ball."

Harry (Cookie) Lavagetto

Cookie DeVincenzi, the owner of the old Oakland team in the Pacific Coast League, signed Lavagetto to his first professional contract. Teammates called him "Cookie's boy," later shortened to "Cookie."

> Joe McCarthy, the fantastically successful manager of the Yankees, had a favorite reply to sportswriters' questions about his team: "Let me do the worrying."

Tony (Poosh-'Em-Up Tony) Lazzeri

The Italian American slugger drew large numbers of Italian fans to cheer him when he played for the Yankees. Urging him to drive in runs, they would scream, "Poosh 'em up, Tony!" "Pooshing" means "pushing," or advancing, the runners.

DeWitt (Bevo) Le Bourveau

This outfielder's last name recalled the malt beverage Bevo, which was marketed during the Prohibition era, when Le Bourveau played for the Phillies.

Bill (The Spaceman) Lee

Oddballs of the space age often are referred to as "Spaceman" or "Moon Man." The nicknames stem from the drug culture of the late 1960s, which popularized the term "spaced-out" for mentally unbalanced behavior. Variations included "spacey," "space cadet," "aired out," and "airhead." Pitcher Bill Lee became known as "The Spaceman" because of his widely publicized iconoclastic attitudes, which led to clashes with Boston manager Don Zimmer and baseball commissioner Bowie Kuhn over his beard and his pot-smoking. Lee defended himself by saying, "In baseball, you're supposed to sit on your ass, spit tobacco, and nod at stupid things." Among the players called "Moon Man" have been Jay Johnstone, Steve Hovley, Mike Marshall, and Mike Shannon. Bob Lacey was "Spacey Lacey."

Harry (Nemo) Leibold

The 5'6" American League outfielder was figuratively as small as Little Nemo, the title character of a comic strip originated by Winsor McCay in 1905. Little Nemo always had dreams of quixotic adventures, and pitcher Leslie Munns, who seemed just as naive, became the second baseball "Nemo."

Dennis (Yosemite Sam) Leonard

The mustachioed Royals pitcher resembled the cartoon character Yosemite Sam, a grizzled old sourdough with flamboyant red whiskers.

Walter (Buck) Leonard

The slugging first baseman of the Negro National League's Homestead Grays formed half of "The Thunder Twins" with teammate Josh Gibson. As a child, Leonard was called "Buddy" by his parents, a name his brother Charlie mispronounced as "Buck." A member of the Baseball Hall of Fame, Buck Leonard also was called "The Black Lou Gehrig."

George (Duffy) Lewis

The Red Sox outfielder, who gave his name to "Duffy's Cliff," Fenway Park's unusual left-field incline, acquired his nickname because his mother's maiden name was Duffy.

John Henry (Pop, El Cuchara) Lloyd

The legendary Negro Leagues shortstop, a member of the Hall of Fame, had an uncanny ability to scoop balls out of the infield dirt. When he played with the Cuban X-Giants in 1906, the fans dubbed him "El Cuchara," Spanish for "The Tablespoon." Because of his combination of prowess at his position and power at the plate, Lloyd also was known as

"The Black Honus Wagner"; Wagner himself said, "I felt honored that they would name such a great player after me." Following his long playing career, Lloyd became a manager and was "a master at instilling confidence in younger players," wrote Negro Leagues historian James A. Riley. "In these latter years he became known affectionately as 'Pop' and was considered the elder statesman of black baseball."

Ernie (Schnozzle) Lombardi

"Schnoz" or "schnozzle" is Yiddish for "nose," and Lombardi's was a dilly. The Reds catcher was "Beezer" for the same reason, and "Botcho" because of his fielding lapses, including the famous "Lombardi Snooze" when he was knocked out in a collision at home plate by the Yankees' King Kong Keller during the fourth game of the 1939 World Series. Morrie (Snooker) Arnovich, Zeke (Banana Nose) Bonura, Clay (Hawk) Carroll, Ken (Hawk) Harrelson, and Hank (Horn) Sauer were also nicknamed because of their large noses. William (Wheezer) Dell wheezed because he had a broken nose.

Los Angeles Dodgers

The Brooklyn National League club, founded in 1890, was first called the "Bridegrooms" because most of its players were married, and was later known as the "Superbas," after a hit Broadway musical. In the latter years of the nineteenth

century, residents of Brooklyn became known to Manhat-
tanites as "trolley-dodgers," or simply "dodgers," because of
the many streetcars clogging the public lanes. The problem
was particularly bad in the area around old Washington Park,
where the baseball team played. As a New York newspaper
of the 1890s reported, "The streets around the ballpark have
been made hazardous by these newfangled streetcars, and if
a person isn't an alert dodger his chances of reaching the park
intact are doubtful." The club thus became known as the
"Dodgers," a name that endured but was eclipsed by other
nicknames at different times. During the tenure of beloved
manager Wilbert (Uncle Robby) Robinson, from 1914 to 1931,
the team was called the "Robins" (or the "Flock") in his
honor. After he was replaced by Max Carey in 1932, a fans'
contest to pick a new name came up with "Kings," since
Brooklyn comprises Kings County, but the nickname did not
catch on, and "Dodgers" soon regained popularity. In the
1930s, as the team's fortunes sagged, its irreverent fans began
calling the club the "Bums" or "dem Bums." That nickname
was popularized by *New York World-Telegram* sports cartoonist
Willard Mullin. While returning to his office by cab after the
inept Dodgers had lost another game, Mullin was asked by
the cabbie, "What did our bums do today?" He began drawing a bum for the team's symbol, but after the club moved
to Los Angeles, Mullin gave the bum a sportshirt, a beret,
and dark glasses. The "Dodgers" nickname was kept after the
team moved west, and although the streetcar is a thing of the
past in southern California, the nickname still seems appro-

priate. The traffic problem is so acute in the area, Bob Hope quipped, that "you're either a Dodger or an Angel." After Tom Lasorda became the manager of the Dodgers in 1977, he claimed that he "bleeds Dodger blue," the team color. Sportswriters obliged by calling the team the "Bluebloods."

Harry (Peanuts) Lowrey

When Lowrey's uncle saw him for the first time, he exclaimed, "Why, he's so small, he's no bigger than a peanut!"

Connie (Mr. Baseball) Mack

Manager of the Philadelphia Athletics for fifty years, Mack was a beloved figure who often was honored with the title of "Mr. Baseball." Sportswriter Red Smith, who knew Mack well, explained why he inspired such respect: "He could be as tough as rawhide and gentle as a mother, reasonable and obstinate beyond reason, and courtly, benevolent, and fierce. He was kind-hearted and hard-fisted, drove a close bargain, and was suckered in a hundred deals. He was generous and thoughtful and autocratic and shy and independent and completely lovable." Mack's real name was Cornelius McGillicuddy, and in his playing days, as a catcher, he was called "Slats" because of his tall, gaunt frame (slats are thin, narrow fence-posts, and the word was early baseball slang for "legs"). Later, in the Connecticut State League, Mack and skinny pitcher Frank Gilmore teamed as the "Shadow Battery"; when they played in the National League together, the nickname was modified to the "Bones Battery." Mack's quick tongue and distinctive, high-pitched voice made him known as "The Talking Catcher." And some writers, reaching a bit, later called him "The Tall Tactician."

Garry (Secretariat) Maddox

Speedy center fielder Maddox was compared to Secretariat, the horse that won the 1973 Triple Crown, by his Phillies manager, Danny Ozark. Announcer Bob Prince called Maddox "The Windshield Wiper" for his speed and regularity in covering the outfield. As Prince's fellow announcer Ralph Kiner put it, "Two-thirds of the earth is covered by water; the other one-third is covered by Garry Maddox."

Sal (The Barber) Maglie

Because of his uncanny ability to brush back batters with "gillettes"—close-shave pitches that just scrape their whiskers—and because of his skill at "shaving" the corners of the plate, Maglie became known as "The Barber." The fact that he had heavy whiskers, like Burleigh (Old Stubblebeard) Grimes, perhaps contributed to the formation of the nickname.

The 1973 Mets were last in their division in mid-August but managed to squeak through with the pennant on a winning percentage of only .509. If ever there was a case of faith moving mountains in baseball, this was it. The loyal fans cheered the team to victory under the rallying cry of "You gotta believe!" coined by ace relief pitcher Tug McGraw. The slogan originated as a joke, according to McGraw, but it quickly became serious. One morning as he came through the gate on the way into the park, a fan waiting for autographs shouted, "Hey, what's wrong with the Mets?" McGraw called back, "There's nothing wrong with the Mets—you gotta believe!" The autograph hounds, to McGraw's surprise, began chanting the slogan, and it was picked up by the players on the field during batting practice. Soon it spread through the crowd and became a common sight on ballpark banners during the Mets' surge to victory. Another famous saying by McGraw came when he was asked if he preferred grass or artificial playing surfaces: "I don't know," he said. "I never smoked AstroTurf."

Walter (Duster) Mails

After he beaned a batter named Coltrin in Seattle in 1915, Mails became known as "Duster," a slang term for a knock-down pitch.

August (Gus, Blackie) Mancuso

Caucasian players with dark complexions often acquired racially tinged nicknames in the preintegration days of major-league baseball. Catcher Gordon (Black Mike) Cochrane was one of them, and so was Gus Mancuso, who was nicknamed "Blackie" in his rookie year of 1928 by Cardinals teammate Jim Bottomley. Others included William (Jap) Barbeau, Jay (Nig) Clarke, Tullos (Topsy) Hartzel, and Edward (Inky) Lake. Conversely, Mike Higgins was called "Pinky" because of his extremely fair complexion, and for the same reason Wilfred Ryan was known as "Rosy." "Sunset" Jimmy Burke had a deep-red complexion. Blackie Mancuso, by the way, lent his more-familiar nickname of "Gus" to Cincinnati outfielder David (Gus) Bell. Bell was a catcher in his youth, and since his parents were fans of Gus Mancuso, they gave him that nickname.

Leslie (Major) Mann

Baseball historian Thomas P. Shea, who described Mann as "a stiff, serious sort of guy," thought George Stallings, the outfielder's first big-league manager, tagged him "Major" because of Mann's "rigid bearing." Stallings, Shea said, "used to wax a bit sarcastic on the Major."

> Brooklyn had such weak teams in the 1930s that sportswriter Edward T. Murphy claimed, "Overconfidence may cost the Dodgers sixth place."

James (Rabbit) Maranville

Fans in New Bedford, Massachusetts, called this 5'5", 155-pound pixie "Rabbit" because of the way he hopped around the infield gathering grounders. In the twilight of his career, however, Maranville slowed down considerably, and Red Smith gave him the nickname of "The Ancient Mariner," after Samuel Taylor Coleridge's poem "The Rime of the Ancient Mariner." Recalling the poem's opening lines ("It is an ancient Mariner / And he stoppeth one of three"), Smith called Maranville "an aging shortstop who now stoppeth one in three." The ageless pitching ace of the Seattle Mariners, Gaylord Perry, also became known as "The Ancient Mariner."

Fred (Firpo) Marberry

This 6'1", 190-pound pitcher resembled one of the most feared boxers of his day, Luis Firpo, who was nicknamed "The Wild Bull of the Pampas."

Marty (Slats) Marion

Often considered "Mr. Shortstop" (a name sometimes given to his contemporary Lou Boudreau), the Cardinals star was also called "The Octopus" because of his amazing fielding range. More familiarly, Marion was known as "Slats," like Connie Mack in his early days, because of his thin frame; manager Burt Shotton gave Marion that nickname. A later infielder, Gene Michael, was called "The Stick" because of his taut, upright build.

Richard (Rube, The $11,000 Lemon) Marquard

Rube Waddell, the great Athletics pitcher, gave his nickname to several promising young lefties, including Richard Marquard. After Marquard won his first minor-league game for Indianapolis on opening day in 1908, the *Indianapolis Star* compared him to Waddell, and from then on he was called "Rube." His father, who was chief engineer of the city of Cleveland, said later, "I told him baseball was no good. Now they've even gone and changed his name!" Marquard became

the talk of baseball that September after Giants manager
John McGraw paid a record $11,000 to Indianapolis for his
contract. In his first appearance in the majors, however, Marquard was drubbed by the Reds, 7–1, a defeat that eventually meant the difference between first and second place for
the Giants. Until he won 24 games in 1911, Marquard was
known as "The $11,000 Lemon."

John (Pepper) Martin

Blake Harper, president of the Cards' Fort Smith, Arkansas,
farm team, called Martin "Pepper" in 1925 because of his
aggressive, gung-ho play. St. Louis sportswriter J. Roy Stockton nicknamed him "The Wild Horse of the Osage" because
the firebrand was born in Oklahoma, home of the Osage
Indians.

William (Smokey Joe) Martin

While with the Giants this short-term third baseman was
named "Smokey Joe" after a famous Manhattan fireman. Joe
Wood, the Red Sox pitcher, and Negro Leagues hurler Joe
Williams won the same name because they were fireballers,
or "smokethrowers." Compact slugger Joe (Little Joe) Morgan became "Smokey Joe" because of his speed on the base
paths, like William Benjamin (Blazin' Ben) Chapman, Maurice (Flash) Archdeacon, and Sam (The Jet) Jethro.

Christy (The Big Six) Mathewson

"The Big Six" was a famous fire brigade in New York during the early 1900s, popular and celebrated among New Yorkers, as was the great Giants pitcher Christy Mathewson. Sportswriter Sam Crane drew the connection when he wrote, "Mathewson is certainly the 'Big Six' of pitchers." The name was seldom used except in the press; most people called Mathewson "Matty." Players sometimes called him "Husk," like Frank Chance, because of his husky build.

Carl (Sub) Mays

The Yankees pitcher threw an unorthodox underhand, or "submarine," pitch. He and his "Sub" nickname became highly publicized after one of his pitches killed Cleveland infielder Ray Chapman in 1920. Later hurlers to use the pitch include Eldon (Sub) Auker, Ted Abernathy, Kent Tekulve, and Dan (The Australian) Quisenberry (whose delivery came "from down under").

Willie (The Say Hey Kid) Mays

Tremendous press ballyhoo heralded the arrival of Willie Mays in the Polo Grounds on May 25, 1951. He had been hitting .477 for Minneapolis when the Giants called him up. The twenty-year-old Mays was overwhelmed by the pressure and went hitless in his first twelve at bats—before homering off Warren Spahn. So many faces were greeting Mays those first few days that he often seemed bewildered. Barney Kremenko, who covered the Giants for the *New York Journal-American*, recalled, "Willie was cautious in communicating with reporters. He didn't want to say the wrong things and on occasion preferred that [manager Leo] Durocher talk for him. However, when you could get through to him that first week, he would blurt, 'Say who,' 'Say what,' 'Say where,' 'Say hey.' In the next day's *Journal-American*, I tabbed him the 'Say Hey Kid.' It stuck." The nickname acquired wider popularity when broadcaster Russ Hodges began using it every time Mays came to the plate. And it seemed to express Mays's breezy, engaging personality so well that it was engraved on his plaque when he entered the Hall of Fame in 1979.

Jack Norworth wrote the lyrics to baseball's anthem, "Take Me Out to the Ballgame," in 1906 (the music was supplied by Albert Von Tilzer). As sung in vaudeville by Norworth and his wife, Nora Bayes, the song was an immediate success. Norworth, however, had never seen a ball game in his life, ignoring the message of the song until 1940.

Bill (No Hands) Mazeroski

Among the fans, Mazeroski was most famous for hitting the homer that won the 1960 World Series for the Pittsburgh Pirates, but among his fellow players the second baseman was most renowned for his ability to get rid of the ball quickly. His lightning-quick movements gave him the nickname of "No Hands" or "No Touch." Ironically, a less-skillful second baseman, Chuck Hiller, was also called "No Hands," because of his clumsiness (he was also nicknamed "Dr. No," after a James Bond book and movie, and "Iron Hands").

John (Windy) McCall

This pitcher appeared in only six games with the Red Sox, but he acquired the nickname of "Windy" from Ted Williams because of his constant questions about the slugger's bats.

Joe (Marse Joe) McCarthy

Chicago American sportswriter Harry Neily compared McCarthy's efficient managing to that of a southern plantation master, or "marse" in southern dialect. It was a rather incongruous nickname for the manager of a team called the "Yankees."

Willie (Stretch) McCovey

Giants teammates Leon Wagner and Willie Kirkland called the 6′4″ first baseman "Stretch" because of his elongated reach for infield balls. As Jim Murray explained in the *Los Angeles Times*, "On ground balls hit down to the second baseman, there's no need to throw, the second baseman just hands it to Willie." McCovey was also known as "Big Mac" (after the McDonald's extra-large hamburger) and "Golden Oldie" (because he played past his fortieth year). In 1979, when the Giants platooned McCovey with Mike (The Blond Bomber) Ivie at first base, sportswriters began referring to McCovey and Ivie by the joint nickname of "McIvie."

Joe (Iron Man) McGinnity

It's generally believed that McGinnity's nickname resulted from his spectacular feats of endurance on the mound, such as the six-day period in which he won five games, or the three times in one month that he pitched and won both games of a doubleheader for the Giants. McGinnity was called "Iron Man," however, even before he reached the majors in 1899, because he spent winters working in his father-in-law's iron foundry in Rock Island, Illinois. His later heroics gave the nickname a new currency.

Frank (Tug) McGraw

As a baby, McGraw tugged at his mother's breast so strenuously while being nursed that his parents nicknamed him "Tugger," later shortened to "Tug."

John (Muggsy) McGraw

The squat, fierce-tempered Orioles and Giants manager was known as "Little Napoleon" and "The Little Corporal" because of his militaristic discipline. As a player, he acquired the nickname "Muggsy," which he always hated, because he looked like a corrupt Baltimore politician of that name. Whenever McGraw and umpire Bill Klem had an argument, McGraw would provoke Klem's wrath by calling him "Catfish," and Klem would retort with "Muggsy," until both men were in a lather. McGraw also popularized the nickname "Mastermind."

Marty (The Baseball Caruso) McHale

More celebrated for his singing voice than for his pitching ability, McHale teamed with Turkey Mike Donlin in a vaudeville act called "Donlin of the Giants and McHale of the Yankees." The show-business trade paper *Variety* dubbed McHale "The Baseball Caruso," after Italian opera singer Enrico Caruso.

Timeless pitcher Satchel Paige gave six famous tips on "how to stay young." The first, and most widely quoted, was "Don't look back. Something might be gaining on you." The others, quoted in a 1953 *Collier's* magazine article titled "The Fabulous Satchel Paige," were

2. Avoid fried meats which angry up the blood.
3. If your stomach disputes you, lie down and pacify it with cool thoughts.
4. Keep the juices flowing by jangling around gently as you move.
5. Go very light on the vices, such as carrying on in society. The social ramble ain't restful.
6. Avoid running at all times.

John (Stuffy) McInnis

As a youngster, McInnis already showed the skill that made him a .308 big-league hitter, and fans used to yell, "That's the stuff, kid."

Bill (Deacon) McKechnie

During his playing days, the future Cincinnati manager and Hall of Fame member sang in the choir of his Wilkinsburg, Pennsylvania, church. Charlie Grimm nicknamed Claude Passeau "Deacon" because of the pitcher's stern, ascetic face. Charles (Deacon) Phillippe, Vernon (Deacon) Law, James (Deacon) White, and Emmett (Parson) Perryman were known for their sedate dispositions, and Elwin (Preacher) Roe once considered becoming a minister.

Don (Boob) McNair

McNair's last name was similar to that of Boob McNutt, a Rube Goldberg cartoon character.

Hal (Fly Crow) McRae

McRae's nickname resulted from a boast that backfired. When he joined Kansas City in 1973, he told his new teammates that he was going to cover the outfield "like a sky hawk." But when he trotted to his position in left field to shag fly balls that day, McRae had to eat crow: he dropped the first fly and quickly became known as "Fly Crow."

Joe (Ducky) Medwick

Slugging outfielder Joe Medwick, one of the bulwarks of the 1934 St. Louis Cardinals "Gas House Gang," much preferred to be called "Muscles" rather than "Ducky." But he was stuck with the latter nickname forever after a girl watching him play minor-league ball in Houston exclaimed when he made a hit, "Isn't he a ducky-wucky of a ballplayer?" The sportswriters got wind of the story and began calling him "Ducky" or "Ducky-Wucky." His Hungarian descent also made him "The Menacing Magyar," but that fanciful title never caught on.

Sabath (Sam) Mele

The first letters in Mele's three names—Sabath Anthony Mele—were combined into "Sam." Charles Andrew Peterson was nicknamed "Cap" in the same manner.

Oscar (Spinach) Melillo

Melillo became ill in 1927 with Bright's disease, a kidney inflammation, and was in danger of death. The next season he was permitted to return to baseball if he followed a strict diet—nothing but spinach for several months if he wanted to live. For variety, he boiled it for breakfast, made a salad of it for lunch, and baked it for dinner. Besides his nickname of "Spinach," Melillo was called "Ski" because he admired a Polish football player in Chicago.

Fred (Bonehead) Merkle

Fred Merkle is one of the most tragic figures in baseball history. His life was blighted by a nickname, "Bonehead," which was given to him by Charley Dryden in the aftermath of the most controversial game ever played. On September 23, 1908, the Giants played the Cubs, who trailed them by a scant six percentage points. Merkle, replacing ailing Fred Tenney at first base for New York, was a rookie of nineteen playing his first full major-league game. With Moose McCormick on third and Merkle on first in the last of the ninth, Al Bridwell singled to center, apparently scoring McCormick with the winning run. But Merkle, seeing McCormick cross the plate, neglected to touch second base and headed for the dugout to avoid the crowd streaming onto the field. Quick-thinking Cubs second baseman Johnny Evers began shouting to center fielder Artie Hofman for the ball Bridwell had hit. According to some accounts, Giants third-base coach Joe McGinnity intercepted Hofman's throw and tossed the ball into the bleachers. But Evers came up with a ball—some say it was thrown to him by Cubs relief pitcher Floyd Kroh—and touched second base with it. After being challenged by Evers and Cubs manager Frank Chance, plate umpire Hank O'Day, who had been in the umpires' dressing room during the previous chaotic minutes, called Merkle out for not completing the play that would have scored McCormick. O'Day had been confronted with a similar decision nineteen days earlier and had announced that he would enforce the base-touching technicality in the future. The game officially ended in a 1–1 tie (it could not be completed because of the mob on the field), and after the regular season ended with the Cubs and Giants deadlocked, it was replayed, and the Giants lost both it and the pennant. Though Merkle went on to play fourteen more years in the majors, winding up with a creditable lifetime batting average of .273 in 1,638 games, his name was permanently clouded by what came to be known as "Merkle's Boner," and he lived in seclusion in Florida until he died in 1956 at the age of sixty-seven. In the aftermath of his blunder, Merkle ruefully predicted, "When I die, I guess my epitaph will be—'Here Lies Bonehead Merkle.'" Umpire Bill Klem, the most respected arbiter in the game, went on record describing the incident as "the worst decision ever made in baseball." Teammates and manager John McGraw defended Merkle, because it was a common practice for players to sprint off the field as soon as the winning run scored, in order to avoid the raucous fans. But you can't live down a nickname like "Bonehead," or the fact that your very name, Merkle, became synonymous with "boner." As Christy Mathewson put it in his book *Pitching in a Pinch*, "It was simply Fred Merkle's misfortune to have been on first base at the critical moment."

Samuel (Sandow) Mertes

The outfielder of the early 1900s was named after Sandow, a strongman managed by Flo Ziegfeld.

Dodgers secretary Harold Parrott marveled at team executive Branch Rickey's uncanny ability for evaluating baseball prospects. "Nobody," Parrott said, "could match his knack for putting a dollar sign on a muscle."

Bob (The Rifle) Meusel

Possessor of perhaps the strongest "rifle" arm of any outfielder in the history of baseball, the Yankees' Bob Meusel was called "The Rifle" for that reason. Hard-throwing Yankees pitcher Vic Raschi, who was born in West Springfield, Massachusetts, was known as "The Springfield Rifle," and Dodgers outfielder Carl Furillo became "The Reading Rifle" after he played minor-league ball at Reading, Pennsylvania. An old-time National League second baseman, Fred Dunlap, was called "Sure Shot" (so strong was his arm that it was said he could knock a man down with a throw while lying prone), and Brooklyn infielder Bill Hart became "True Gun" because of his rifle arm as well as the similarity of his name to that of movie cowboy William S. Hart. Bob (Gunner) Reeves was another hard-throwing infielder.

Clyde (Deerfoot) Milan

Washington teammate Bob Ganley called outfielder Clyde Milan "Zeb" because Milan was from the rustic town of Linden, Tennessee, and Chief Bender sarcastically nicknamed Milan "Deerfoot" because of his lack of speed on the base paths. A contemporary of Milan's, National League catcher Tom Needham, was also called "Deerfoot" for the same reason. Infielder Rick Auerbach, on the other hand, was called "Reindeer" because he actually was a fast runner. Lumbering first baseman Johnny Mize received the ironic nickname of "Skippy," and pitcher Alva Javery was known as "Beartracks" because of his heavy-footed movement.

Felix (The Cat) Millan

Because of the cartoon character Felix the Cat, ballplayers named Felix frequently acquire that nickname, particularly if they are quick and agile, like Felix Millan and Felix Mantilla before him. Hulking first baseman Andres Galarraga became known as "The Big Cat."

Edmund (Bing) Miller

When he was eleven, this future outfielder regularly read a comic strip, "Uncle George Washington Bing, the Village Story Teller," in the *Vinton* (Iowa) *Eagle*. Miller's brother Eugene nicknamed him "Bing."

John (Dots) Miller

When John Barney Miller joined the Pirates in 1909, a sportswriter asked the team's star shortstop, Honus Wagner, to identify their rookie second baseman. Wagner, who spoke with a German accent, replied, "Dot's Miller." Miller was called "Dots" throughout his twelve-year career in the majors.

Milwaukee Brewers

The first major-league team in Milwaukee, a National League club that played one year there in 1878, was called the "Brewers" because Milwaukee was then the self-proclaimed beer capital of the world. The nickname was used again when the city fielded a team in the first year of the American League, 1901. In the interim before the Boston Braves moved to Milwaukee in 1953, the city's minor-league franchise was also called the Brewers. And after the Braves left for Atlanta, a group of Milwaukeeans headed by Bud Selig activated a new organization called the Brewers and tried to get another baseball franchise for the city. Their efforts paid off in 1970, when the Seattle Pilots American League expansion team moved to Milwaukee, assuming the name "Brewers."

Minnesota Twins

The first team in the major leagues to represent two cities (Minneapolis and St. Paul), the Minnesota Twins were originally called the Twin Cities Twins when they moved there from Washington, D.C., in 1960. Uniforms were ordered with "TC" as the team emblem, but then, as a team spokesman put it, owner Calvin Griffith "got the idea that as long as our club was breaking from tradition by naming the team after more than one city we might just as well go all the way and name it after the entire state." While in Washington, the team was first known as the "Statesmen" but became the "Senators" in 1886. A fans' contest in 1905 changed the name to "Nationals" (more familiarly, the "Nats"), but many still referred to the club as the "Senators." Longtime team manager and owner Clark Griffith—in whose honor the club sometimes was called the "Griffs," as the A's were known as the "Macks," after Connie Mack—insisted on the nickname "Nationals." Griffith said in 1939, "They are not the Senators. There's no distinction in a name like Senators. Why, every state capital team has that nickname . . . well, most of them. The Washington baseball club is the Nationals." However, in 1957, two years after Griffith's death, "Senators" became the official nickname again. *The Sporting News* liked to call the team the "Solons," an archaic word meaning "legislators." In a paraphrase of the old saw about George Washington, the Senators were often said to be "first in war, first in peace, and last in the American League."

Branch Rickey was often assailed for selling veteran ballplayers and using promising youngsters in their places. He defended his logic by saying, "Hungry ballplayers win pennants." Another time, Rickey deflated the magical aura that players assign to chance, stating simply, "Luck is the residue of design." Nevertheless, Rickey believed in the intangibles, realizing that some skills cannot be measured in charts or statistics. One of the players whose abilities were most intangible was Eddie Stanky, who helped spark the Dodgers to the 1947 pennant. Rickey commented, "He can't run; he can't throw; he can't hit; but I wouldn't trade him for Hornsby in his prime." Near the end of his executive years, the philosophical Rickey pondered the ultimate meaning of the game of baseball, holding up a baseball as he asked himself and *Sports Illustrated* interviewer Gerald Holland, "This ball—this symbol; is it worth a man's whole life?"

John (The Count) Montefusco

This brash young pitcher received his nickname while playing for Amarillo of the Texas League. His braggadocio—plus the fact that his unusual last name sounds a bit like that of the title character in Alexandre Dumas's *The Count of Monte*

Cristo—led a headline writer in El Paso to label him "Count Monte" when he beat the local team. The nickname eventually fell into disuse but was revived when Montefusco joined the Giants in 1975 and began to be called "The Count of Monte Frisco." Albert (Sparky) Lyle (a name given him in boyhood because of his energetic behavior and his sparkpluglike red hair) was also known to his teammates as "The Count" because his greased-back hairstyle reminded them of Bela Lugosi's Count Dracula. And going way back to the late nineteenth century, ambidextrous pitcher Tony (Count) Mullane, a native of Ireland, was so named because his powerful build and neatly waxed mustache made him the darling of Cincinnati women and the star performer at the Red Stockings' ladies' day games. Indeed, the dashing Mullane is credited by baseball historians with single-handedly popularizing the ladies' day game. He was also called "The Apollo of the Box."

Montreal Expos

This National League expansion team received its franchise in 1968, the year after Montreal played host to a world's fair called Expo '67. With the memory of the event still fresh, it seemed appropriate to call the new team the "Expos."

John (Jug, Jughandle Johnny) Morrison

This Pittsburgh right-hander won 103 games in the majors, including 25 in 1903, relying mainly on his excellent curve. During a 1922 game, Morrison was in a tough spot and infielder Cotton Tierney began yelling, "Throw him that jughandle!" Another "Jughandle" was National Leaguer Freddie Frankhouse.

Ford (Moon) Mullen

The last name of this Phillies infielder provoked a comparison to the comic-strip character Moon Mullins. Lowell (Moon) Miller, on the other hand, was nicknamed because of his round, or "moon," face. He was also called "Moonie."

Murderers' Row

The Yankees' greatest season was 1927, when their powerhouse lineup included Babe Ruth, with his record 60 home runs, and Lou Gehrig, with 47. Covering the team that year, New York sportswriter Arthur Robinson wrote, "This isn't just a ball club! This is Murderers' Row!" Though Robinson was the first to apply the name to the 1927 Yankees, the expression has been traced as far back as 1858 in baseball usage. The game adopted it from the name of the row of cells housing dangerous inmates in New York's Tombs prison.

John (Grandma) Murphy

A number of sources have claimed that the Yankees pitcher was nicknamed "Grandma" because of "his rocking-chair motion when winding up," as *The Official Encyclopedia of Baseball* put it. Murphy himself debunked that theory, explaining, "My good friend (and Yankees teammate) the late Pat Malone tagged me 'Grandma' due to the fact that I was sedate and reserved, and usually complained about poor meals and service. Pat always said that I acted like a grandma. The name in no way had any reference to my pitching motion."

Yankees TV broadcaster Phil Rizzuto made a classic gaffe on the air after a Baltimore–New York game on August 6, 1978, was interrupted by a bulletin announcing the death of Pope Paul VI. "Well," said Rizzuto sadly, "that kind of puts a damper on even a Yankee win."

Stan (The Man) Musial

Musial hit so well in Brooklyn's Ebbets Field that Dodgers fans revered him even when he demolished their pitchers.

Commonly heard around the park when he stepped to the plate was "Here comes that man again!" Eventually just about everyone in baseball called him "Stan the Man," a tribute to his ability and his gentlemanly bearing. In his early days, Musial, who came from Donora, Pennsylvania, had enough running speed to be called "The Donora Greyhound." And because he was Polish, he was sometimes called "Stashu." In the 1940s, Musial and four fellow Poles on the Cardinals (Rip Repulski, Steve Bilko, Erv Dusak, and Ray Jablonski) were collectively known as "The Polish Falcons."

Alfred (Greasy) Neale

When this Cincinnati Reds player and, later, Philadelphia Eagles football coach was a boy in Parkersburg, West Virginia, he called one of his companions "Dirty Face" or "Dirty Neck," and the boy began calling him "Greasy" because Neale worked for a time as a grease boy in a rolling mill.

Lynn (Line Drive) Nelson

Like Walter (Boom-Boom) Beck, Nelson was a pitcher whom batters enjoyed facing. So many balls flew through the air when he pitched that he was called "Line Drive."

Louis (Bobo) Newsom

According to Newsom, when he was a youngster his uncle Jake Newsom nicknamed him "Buck," but he couldn't pronounce "Buck" so he called himself "Bobo" instead, taking that name from a character in a book. Another Newsom nickname, "Ol' Showboat," stemmed from his garrulous, hammy behavior.

Ashby (Skeeter) Newsome

Normally a light-hitting infielder, the diminutive Newsome could hurt a pitcher in a tight spot. He was compared to a mosquito, or "skeeter," because of his pesty batting ability. Similarly nicknamed were infielders Jim (Skeeter) Webb and Ed (Skeeter) Lake.

New York Mets

Because New York is the biggest metropolitan area in the United States, the American Association team established there in 1883 took the name "Metropolitans" (the team lasted only four years). Previous New York clubs in the National Association and the National League were called the "Mutuals"; later, of course, the Mutuals became the Giants. When the National League expanded into New York in 1962, five years after the Giants departed for San Francisco, the old "Metropolitans" nickname was echoed in the shortened form of "Mets" for the new team.

New York Yankees

After the old Baltimore Orioles moved to New York in 1903, the team was first called the "Highlanders" because its park was situated on Washington Heights, the highlands of the Hudson River, and because the name of its first president, Joseph W. Gordon, recalled that of the famous Scottish regiment, the Gordon Highlanders. Highlanders' Park also was called Hilltop Park in those days, and the team was also called the "Hilltoppers." Both names were unwieldy in headlines, however, so in 1909 *New York Press* sports editor Jim Price took it upon himself to dub the team the "Yankees." Other newspapermen gratefully seized upon the new nickname and its even pithier variant, "Yanks." According to sportswriter Fred G. Lieb, beer magnate Colonel Jacob Ruppert was conned into buying a half-interest in the team with Colonel Tillinghast Huston in the winter of 1914–15 in the belief that he could change the nickname to "Knickerbockers," after his most popular brand of beer. Ruppert actually issued an announcement of the name change. But the managing editors of the thirteen New York newspapers met in 1915 and refused to go along with the new nickname. Ruppert grudgingly accepted their decision. After the team, revitalized by Babe Ruth's slugging, occupied Yankee Stadium on April 18, 1923, Lieb soon dubbed the park "The House That Ruth Built." Because its short right-field fence (296 feet from home) was such an inviting target for the Babe, cynics amended Lieb's name for the stadium to "The House Built for Ruth." In the 1920s, the Yankees' legendary batting power gave them the nicknames of the "Ruppert Rifles," "Murderers' Row," and "The Bronx Bombers" or simply the "Bombers." Their domination of the American League gave them the nickname of "The Millionaires," and led to a famous crack by comic Joe E. Lewis in the late 1940s: "Rooting for the Yankees is like rooting for U.S. Steel."

Charles (Kid) Nichols

A Hall of Fame member who won 360 games, Nichols broke in with the Boston Nationals in 1890 and won 27 games at the age of twenty-one. He then reeled off nine straight years of 20 or more victories, making him a "Kid" successful among older men.

> Once Wilbert Robinson, the long-suffering manager of the Daffy Dodgers of the 1920s, was ejected from the game and sat in the clubhouse waiting for news. A coach called "Uncle Robby" and said that the Dodgers had three men on base. Sighing deeply, Robinson asked, "Which base?" Another time, when three Dodgers actually wound up on third together, he tried to laugh it off, saying, "That's the first time all season they've been together on anything."

Hideo (The Tornado) Nomo

The Japanese rookie sensation who bewitched, bothered, and bewildered National League hitters when he joined the Los Angeles Dodgers in 1995 has an unusual body-twisting delivery. Combined with his thunderous fastball, Nomo's deadly corkscrew style already had made Japanese sportswriters dub him "The Tornado" when he pitched for the Kintetsu Buffaloes. The excitement aroused by Nomo in his American debut quickly became known as "Nomomania," since it was reminiscent of the fan frenzy caused in 1981 by the Dodgers' Mexican pitching phenom Fernando Valenzuela ("Fernandomania").

Lou (The Mad Russian) Novikoff

Since Novikoff was eccentric and a sometimes lusty hitter, his Russian descent led to such sobriquets as "The Mad Russian," "The Clouting Cossack," "The Socking Soviet," and "The Mauling Muscovite."

Oakland A's

An amateur local baseball club in Philadelphia first used the title "Athletics" in the 1860s, and the name was adopted successively by the city's National Association, National League, and American Association franchises during the later part of that century. When an American League team was activated there in 1901, manager Connie Mack decided the name was good enough to be used again. The team, casually known as the "A's" all through its existence and the "Macks" or "Mackmen" during Mack's long reign, was later shifted to Kansas City and then to Oakland. Mack's Athletics also were known as "The White Elephants" or "Elephants" and adopted the elephant as their team symbol, because of an ill-timed wisecrack by Baltimore manager John McGraw in 1902. Sportswriters asked McGraw, "What do you think of the Philadelphia A's?" "White elephants!" he replied. "Mr. B. F. Shibe (the owner) has a white elephant on his hands!" McGraw was a poor prophet, for the fast-rising A's won the pennant that year while McGraw's Orioles slumped to last place, costing him his job. Thereafter the A's were proud to be known as "White Elephants."

Jack (Peach Pie Jack) O'Connor

As an amateur, O'Connor played for a St. Louis street team called the "Peach Pies." To distinguish him from another Jack O'Connor then playing baseball, he was referred to as "Peach Pie Jack." His roughhouse personality made him "Rowdy Jack."

John (Blue Moon) Odom

The pitcher had a round, or "moon," face, and as a boy he was called "Moon." Later, his frequent moodiness prompted

friends to lengthen the nickname to "Blue Moon," a nick-
name inspired by the title of a popular song. "I'm intense,"
Odom explained. "I don't feel like laughing and smiling a lot.
I don't find much that's funny in life."

Pedro (Tony) Oliva

The hard-hitting Cuban used his older brother Tony's birth
certificate to get a passport to the United States and then kept
the name for baseball.

Al (Scoop) Oliver

The nickname of "Scoop" or "Scoops" is often given to fielders (usually first basemen or outfielders) with an ability to
make "scooping" snags of difficult grounders or low fly balls.
Outfielder and sometime first baseman Al Oliver was called
"Scoop," as was the Giants' first-sacker Willie McCovey. The
Pirates had two early-day players known as "Scoops": George
Carey, who played first base for the team from 1895 to 1903,
and outfielder Max Carey, who joined the Bucs seven years
later. The "Scoops" nickname and the name of Carey continued their identification in the person of Tom Carey, an
American League infielder from 1935 to 1946.

Frank (Silk) O'Loughlin

The umpire, famous for his bellowing voice, was nicknamed "Silk" after he wore a silk hat to a wedding.

The $100,000 Infield

Though at today's prices it sounds like a piddling sum, the nickname of "The $100,000 Infield" was a high compliment in the 1910s to the Athletics' great quartet of Stuffy McInnis, Eddie Collins, Jack Barry, and Home Run Baker. Similarly named were the Phillies pitcher Grover Cleveland Alexander and catcher Bill Killefer, "The $100,000 Battery."

John (Buck) O'Neil

Best known today for his sagacious reminiscences on Ken Burns's 1994 television documentary *Baseball,* O'Neil was a star player and manager for the Kansas City Monarchs of the Negro Leagues and the first African American to become a major-league coach. He was nicknamed "Buck" in 1934, when he was playing with a barnstorming team called the Zulu Cannibal Giants. Team promoter Syd Pollock confused him with Buck O'Neal, the owner of the Miami Giants, the team for which O'Neil previously had played.

James (Tip) O'Neill

For one season, 1887, walks were counted as hits in the major leagues, which enabled eleven players to hit over .400. The batting champ that year was James O'Neill of St. Louis, who wound up with an astounding .492 record (if walks had not been counted as hits, he would have hit .442, still the best single-season mark in major-league history, though the legendary Josh Gibson hit a mind-boggling .503 for the Negro League Homestead Grays in 1943). Because James O'Neill foul-tipped many balls in order to wait out the pitchers, hoping they eventually would walk him and build up his average, he became known as "Tip." He was a hero to Irish American fans, who frequently named their sons after him. One so named was Thomas P. (Tip) O'Neill, Jr., of Massachusetts, former Speaker of the U.S. House of Representatives and a lifelong baseball fan.

Clarence (Brick) Owens

Owens was on the receiving end of a brick while umpiring a game in Pittsburg, Kansas. It didn't shake his credo: "Call 'em fast and walk away tough."

Jim (Bear) Owens

Chet DiEmidio, a catcher for Miami of the K-O-M League in 1952, once said that teammate Owens always "bears down" on the mound. The pitcher's burly appearance enhanced the nickname's popularity.

A month after Pearl Harbor, baseball commissioner Kenesaw Mountain Landis wrote to President Franklin D. Roosevelt, offering to cancel the baseball season if it would help the war effort to do so. FDR, in his famous "Green Light Letter" of January 15, 1942, replied, "I honestly feel that it would be best for the country to keep baseball going. . . . If 300 teams use 5,000 or 6,000 players, these players are a definite recreational asset to at least 20,000,000 of their fellow citizens—and that in my judgment is thoroughly worthwhile."

Tom (Wimpy) Paciorek

When he was signed by the Dodgers organization in 1968, Paciorek used to go out eating with several older players. Since the veterans had more money, they would order steaks, but Paciorek could afford only hamburgers. So Tom Lasorda, then a coach, nicknamed him in honor of the hamburger-loving *Popeye* cartoon character J. Wellington Wimpy, whose name also inspired that of a popular restaurant chain. Mel

Harder of the Cleveland Indians was also called "Wimpy," because his short haircut reminded a teammate of the cartoon character. Although unlike Allie Reynolds and Charles Bender, he had no Indian blood, Harder also became known as "Chief," simply because he was the Indians' leading pitcher.

Andy (The Brow) Pafko

Charlie Grimm, comparing his Cubs outfielder Andy Pafko to a character in the *Dick Tracy* cartoon, dubbed him "The Brow" because of Pafko's high forehead. A more familiar nickname for the skillful outfielder, known for his fancy sliding catches, was "Handy Andy."

Leroy (Satchel) Paige

The Official Encyclopedia of Baseball claimed that Paige was called "Satchel" because "his feet seemed big as suitcases," but he actually acquired the nickname in childhood while carrying suitcases for tips in the Mobile, Alabama, railroad station. In *The Biographical Encyclopedia of the Negro Baseball Leagues*, James A. Riley explained, "Once he attempted to steal a man's satchel but the owner ran him down and cuffed him about the head while recovering his property. A friend who witnessed the incident gave him the nickname 'Satchel,' which young Leroy hated. In later years he concocted various versions of the origin of his nickname that were more socially acceptable." This is the version Paige printed in his

1962 autobiography, *Maybe I'll Pitch Forever*: "We weren't going to be eating much better if I made only a dime at a time so I got me a pole and some ropes. That let me sling two, three, or four satchels together and carry them at one time. You always got to be thinking to make money. My invention wasn't a smart-looking thing, but it upped my income. The other kids laughed. 'You look like a walking satchel tree,' one of them yelled. They all started yelling it. Soon everybody was calling me that, you know how it is with kids and nicknames. That's when Leroy Paige became no more and Satchel Paige took over. Nobody ever called me Leroy, nobody except my mom and the government." Often called the "ageless" Satchel Paige, he was forty-two when he entered major-league ball in 1948 after pitching for two decades in the Negro Leagues, and he made his last appearance in the majors at the age of fifty-nine. As a result, he was known as "Ol' Man River," after the Jerome Kern–Oscar Hammerstein II song from *Show Boat* that Paul Robeson made famous. Like the Mississippi River in the song, Paige seemed to be forever "rolling along." Among his widely quoted remarks on the subject of aging was, "How old would you be if you didn't know how old you were?"

Dave (The Cobra) Parker

So dangerous at the plate that he was dubbed "Lightning" and "The Cobra," Parker heard the strains of snake-charming music from the Pittsburgh organist every time he came to the plate, and the electronic scoreboard flashed an animated picture of a cobra. Dan Driessen became "Cobra" because of his coiled batting stance.

Francis (Salty) Parker

As a boy in Granite City, Illinois, Parker liked to eat salted peanuts. He was nicknamed "Salty" by local grocers named the Holtzman Brothers.

Mel (Dusty) Parnell

Although the Bosox lefty compiled an outstanding record, including 25 wins in 1949, he had a nagging control problem. He yielded over 100 walks a year three times in his first five years in the majors, and his habit of throwing pitches in the dirt made him "Dusty."

Fred (Midget, Flea) Patek

Until Harry Chappas (5'3") made his debut in 1979, Patek (5'4") was the smallest player in the major leagues. He said philosophically, "I'd rather be the shortest player in the majors than the tallest player in the minors." Called "Flea" and "Midget," he also was known as "The Flying Flea" because of his baserunning skill, and "Spotty," after a spotted, stuffed dog he used to keep next to his locker. "I was in a big slump at the time," he recalled, "so one night I came in and we held services for old Spotty. After that everyone started calling me Spotty. But I've been called Midget for as long as I've been in baseball."

> After terrorizing pitchers and umpires in the majors for sixteen years, Jesse (Crab) Burkett settled down as the owner, manager, and pinch hitter for Worcester of the New England League. One summer, the story goes, his team was trailing 12–0, in the ninth. Infuriated with the inept play of his squad, he sprang from the bench and growled to his players, "I'll show you blind bums how to hit the ball! And I'll show you something else, too, after I hit it." As Burkett strode to the plate, umpire Roaring Red Rorty asked whom he was replacing. "None of your business!" roared Burkett. The witty Rorty then turned toward the stands and bellowed, "Burkett now batting for exercise!" To the delight of the fans and the satisfaction of his players, Burkett struck out.

Ralph (Cy) Perkins

The Old Homestead, a play that was popular when the catcher was on the A's, featured a character named Cy Perkins, and columnist Westbrook Pegler made the connection.

John (Pretzels) Pezzullo

This short-term Phillies pitcher contorted his body "like a pretzel" while winding up. Another hurler with a weird motion was Oscar (Flip Flap) Jones.

Philadelphia Phillies

The alliterative nickname "Phillies" has been used ever since the National League franchise was moved to Philadelphia from Worcester in 1883. "Quakers," a nickname used by an old National Association team in the City of Brotherly Love, occasionally was applied to the NL club, but it was more popular with out-of-town sportswriters than with local fans. In 1943, owner Bob Carpenter became dissatisfied with the name "Phillies," and after polling the fans, renamed the team the "Blue Jays." The public, however, never warmed up to the name, and it was dropped officially in 1950 (the American League's Toronto expansion team was named the "Blue Jays" in 1976). During the 1950 reign of the Phillies' youthful pennant-winners, who were called the "Whiz Kids" by sportswriters, the team was jokingly known as the "Fillies."

Lou (Sweet Lou) Piniella

The player and manager, a Florida native, originally was dubbed "Sweet Lou from Peru" because of his Hispanic ancestry; the nickname eventually was abbreviated to "Sweet Lou." During his days as a Yankees outfielder, the sharp-tongued Piniella was known as "The Needler" because he was always "needling" someone. Len Schulte of the old St. Louis Browns was called "Needle" for the same reason, but Bill (Needle) Clark's nickname had a more esoteric derivation. The Dodgers pitcher's middle name was Watson, and teammates recalled that Dr. Watson supplied Sherlock Holmes with his needle for cocaine injections. Hence, "Needle" Clark.

Charlie (Horse Face) Pittinger

His fellow players called the homely Pittinger "Horse Face," which, according to Fred Lieb, was a favorite nickname of Horace Fogel, a Philadelphia sportswriter who later was the Phillies' president when Pittinger was pitching for the team. A female fan was offended by the nickname and wrote Fogel, "I believe Charlie Pittinger is one of the most handsome of men." "Lady," Fogel replied, "can I help it if he looks like a horse?"

Country-bred Detroit pitcher Schoolboy Rowe, on the radio just before the 1934 World Series, made an aside to his wife, who was listening at home: "How'm I doin', Edna?" Bench jockeys never let Rowe forget his remark.

Pittsburgh Pirates

Previously called the "Alleghenies," after the mountain range, and the "Innocents," because of their newness and ineptitude, Pittsburgh's National League team became the "Pirates" in 1891, the club's fifth year of operation. A large number of players had jumped the previous year to the new Players' League, and the depleted Pittsburgh club hit the cellar, winning only 23 games and losing 114. After the Players' League folded at the end of one season, players were permitted to return to their original clubs if they were on the teams' reserve lists. Since the Philadelphia Athletics of the American Association had failed to place second baseman Louis Bierbauer on its reserve list, Pittsburgh signed him in a move that an AA official called "piratical" and that a Philadelphia newspaper described as "an act of piracy on the high seas." Other papers took up the war cry, and although a board of arbitration upheld Pittsburgh's action, the team was permanently branded the "Pirates" (alternatively, "Buccaneers" or "Bucs").

The Pretzel Battery

Ted Breitenstein and Heinie Peitz were an outstanding pitcher-catcher combination on the Cardinals from 1893 to 1895 and on the Reds from 1897 to 1900. Their German ancestry prompted the nickname of "The Pretzel Battery."

Dick (Monster) Radatz

This Boston strikeout sensation terrified batters with his 6'5" height and 235-pound weight. Radatz became known as "Monster," but he and his family disliked the nickname, so in 1963 a Boston newspaper held a contest to pick a new one for him. The winner was "Smokey Dick" (referring to his speed), but it never caught on. Radatz requested that he be called "Monster" again.

Charles (Hoss) Radbourn

This indestructible nineteenth-century pitcher played the outfield between turns on the mound, and the beyond-the-call-of-duty activity earned him the nickname of "Old Workhorse," later whittled down to "Old Hoss" or just "Hoss." In tribute to his eminence on the mound, the future Hall of Famer was also known in his day as "The King of Pitchers." He compiled a record of 306–192 in twelve years and still holds the single-season victory mark with an incredible 60–12 record for the Providence team of the National League in 1884.

Ted (Double Duty) Radcliffe

Theodore Roosevelt (Ted) Radcliffe was a longtime star in the Negro Leagues who excelled at both catching and pitching, often doing both on the same day in doubleheaders.

Writer Damon Runyon nicknamed Radcliffe "Double Duty" after seeing him catch a game for Satchel Paige and then take the mound himself for the second game.

Arthur (Bugs) Raymond

A pitcher with a severe alcohol problem, Raymond was dropped by the Southern Association Atlanta Crackers in 1906 because of his drinking. Approaching Wilson Matthews, manager of the weak Savannah team of the South Atlantic League, Raymond demanded, "Sign me up." "You have a reputation," Matthews replied. "I know you can pitch, but . . ." "Not only can I pitch," Raymond broke in, "I shall pitch Savannah to the pennant." His "crazy" boast helped earn the pitcher his nickname of "Bugs" (synonymous in those days with "bughouse" or "buggy"), but Raymond did in fact pace the team to the pennant by winning 18 games. He later pitched for the Cardinals and Giants, but his drinking became steadily worse, and in 1911, Giants manager John McGraw had to drop him from the team. It wasn't long before Raymond's uniform appeared in the window of the saloon nearest the Polo Grounds, with a sign attached: "Bugs Raymond Tending Bar Here." He died the following year, at the age of thirty.

Harold (Pee Wee) Reese

At the age of twelve, Reese won a marble-shooting ("pee wee") contest. Although he grew to a full height, 5'10", he kept the nickname throughout his career as a Dodgers short-stop. A later Dodgers infielder, Nate Oliver, was the same height as Reese but was called "Pee Wee" because he seemed small next to the towering players who dominated the team in the mid-1960s. Because of his leadership qualities and his Kentucky background, Pee Wee Reese was sometimes known as "The Little Colonel." Similar nicknames have been given to other players from Kentucky, notably the Yankees' Earle (The Kentucky Colonel) Combs and the Pirates' Howie (The Kentucky Rosebud) Camnitz.

Phil (The Vulture) Regan

In the 1960s, pitchers began calling a save a "vultch," since a reliever who comes in late in the game to pick up a save (or a victory) is acting like a "vulture," figuratively picking over the carcass of the starting pitcher. Regan was given his nickname in the mid-1960s when he came in to relieve Dodgers starter Don Drysdale in the late innings of a game at Pittsburgh. Though Drysdale had pitched well, it was Regan who picked up the win, and teammate Claude Osteen told him, "You're a vulture." The nickname stuck, and it was later passed on to Angels pitcher Dave LaRoche, who didn't like it, asking plaintively, "Can't I be just plain Roachie?"

President Calvin Coolidge once attended a ball game at which the Yankees were lined up for formal introductions. As silent Cal moved down the line, Waite Hoyt said, "How do you do, Mr. President?" Herb Pennock remarked, "Good day, sir." Babe Ruth took off his cap and mopped his forehead with his handkerchief. "Mr. Ruth," said Coolidge. "Hot as hell, ain't it, Prez?" replied the Babe. In 1930, when Herbert Hoover was president and the nation was in a Depression, Ruth demanded an $80,000 salary from Yankees owner Jacob Ruppert. Sportswriters told Ruth the demand would result in bad publicity, and one noted, "That's more money than Hoover gets as president of the United States." Ruth snapped, "What's Hoover got to do with it?" Then a smile crept over his face. "Besides, I had a better year than he did anyway." He got the $80,000.

Rick (Jingles) Reichardt

Bonus baby Rick Reichardt signed with the Angels from the University of Wisconsin campus in 1964 for a record $200,000 in bonus money, and his new teammates said they could hear the money jingling in his pants.

Harold (Pistol Pete) Reiser

As a boy, Reiser was fond of a Western movie serial called *Two-Gun Pete*. He often imitated the cowboy, and was called "Pistol Pete," or simply "Pete," as a result.

Ken (The Zamboni Machine) Reitz

A Zamboni machine is a device that cleans the ice between periods of a hockey game and sucks water from artificial turf at baseball games. Third baseman Reitz earned the nickname with his slick, infield-cleaning defensive play.

Flint (Zorie) Rhem

Watching the scoreboard from the Fort Smith bench, Rhem observed that the opponents were racking up plenty of "zories." Bewildered teammates soon learned that "zorie" was Rhem's word for "zero."

James (Dusty) Rhodes

More often than not, players named Rhodes or Rhoads are called "Dusty," a nickname originally derived from a tramp character in an old comic strip. Bill Rhodes began the tradition in 1893, and since then, Bob Rhoads, Charlie Rhodes, Gordon Rhodes, and James Rhodes have acquired the nickname. Because of his pinch-hitting heroics for the Giants in the 1954 World Series, Jim Rhodes was the most famous "Dusty" Rhodes; his feats inspired another nickname, "The Colossus of Rhodes."

Not long before his death in 1948, Babe Ruth went to Hollywood to help Republic Pictures promote its upcoming biographical film *The Babe Ruth Story*. Studio publicist Dave Kaufman arranged a photo opportunity at which the Babe met the actor who played him on-screen, William Bendix, and joined the press in watching Bendix take batting practice, resplendent in a Yankees uniform. Proving a better actor than hitter, Bendix took mighty swings but, much to the Bambino's disgust, could barely hit the ball out of the infield. After one puny Bendix effort rolled weakly toward the pitcher's mound, Ruth turned to the members of the press and growled, "Hell, I can *piss* farther than he can hit!"

Edgar (Sam) Rice

The Washington outfielder, collector of 2,987 hits in eighteen years, was called "Sam" by a sportswriter who couldn't remember his real name.

J. R. (High Rise) Richard

James Rodney Richard's towering height of 6'8" made him a menace to hitters, and he acquired the tag of "High Rise" for that reason. Richard, sometimes called "J. R. Superstar," also was known as "Bee," because of his "stinging" fastball.

Branch (The Mahatma) Rickey

In a singular tribute by sportswriter Tom Meany, Rickey was nicknamed "The Mahatma" after the great Indian pacifist Mohandas K. (Mahatma) Gandhi. The executive who broke baseball's color bar by bringing Jackie Robinson to the Brooklyn Dodgers in 1947, Rickey had a blend of sagacity and canny political skills that put Meany in mind of the words used to describe Gandhi by John Gunther: "a combination of God, your own father, and Tammany Hall." An example of Rickey's wisdom was his observation to Robinson that "a baseball box score is a democratic thing. It doesn't tell how big you are, what church you attend, what color you are, or how your father voted in the last election. It just tells what kind of baseball player you were on that particular day."

Eppa (Jephtha) Rixey

Rixey was the tallest player of his day—an imposing 6'6"—and his height plus his Virginia birthplace gave him the nickname of "The Eiffel Tower of Culpepper." Charley Dryden, the same man who stuck Joe Cantillon with his hated "Pongo Joe" nickname, engaged in more of his whimsy when he compared Rixey's unusual first name to that of the biblical character Jephtha and tried to convince the fans that Jephtha was Rixey's middle name. Although the pitcher continually and vehemently denied it, "Jephtha" clung to Rixey the way "Pongo Joe" did to Cantillon.

Phil (Scooter) Rizzuto

While an amateur in the Queens Alliance League, the future Yankees shortstop became known for the way he "scooted" after grounders. His speed and his shortness (5′6″) also led him to be called "Flea," as was shortstop Fred Patek. Similarly, shortstop Larry Bowa was dubbed "Gnat."

Brooks (The Vacuum Cleaner) Robinson

Regarded by many as the best-fielding third baseman in baseball history, the Orioles star became known as "The Vacuum Cleaner" (or "Hoover") because of his uncanny ability to dispose of balls hit in his area of the field. Before him, Negro Leagues infielders William (Bonnie) Serrell and Bobbie Robinson were called "The Vacuum Cleaner" and "The Human Vacuum Cleaner," respectively. Shortstop Mario Mendoza was nicknamed "El Espirador," Spanish for "The Vacuum Cleaner." First baseman Charlie (Bushel Basket) Gould was nicknamed for a similar reason, as were boyish-looking glove wizards Jim (The Boy Bandit) Piersall and Roy (The Boy Bandit) McMillan. The latter "soaked up" so many balls at shortstop that he was also called "The Sponge."

On September 29, 1920, a Chicago grand jury continued its investigation of the newly breaking "Black Sox" scandal, involving the eight disgraced Chicago White Sox players who helped gambler Arnold Rothstein fix the previous year's World Series. As outfielder Shoeless Joe Jackson left the hearing chamber, the *Chicago Herald and Examiner* reported, "A small boy clutched at his sleeve and tagged along with him. 'Say it ain't so, Joe,' he pleaded. 'Say it ain't so.' 'Yes, kid, I'm afraid it is,' Jackson replied. 'Well, I never would've thought it,' the boy said."

Frank (The Judge) Robinson

While playing for the Baltimore Orioles—before the Indians hired him as the major leagues' first black manager—the authoritative Robinson presided over a playful "kangaroo court" held in the locker room after every Orioles victory (after a loss, no one was in the mood for clubhouse games). Robinson, who was known for his biting sarcasm, would pass out fines of one "hog" (dollar) to teammates for offenses ranging from fielding errors to walking around nude in the clubhouse food area. The kangaroo court also gave out facetious prizes, such as the "Tater Award," a beat-up ball covered with bandages and aspirins, given to the pitcher who surrendered the most home runs ("taters") in a single week. The money collected by "The Judge" was used for team parties or given to charity. Reliable second-string catcher Jeff Torborg, a future manager, spent so much time on the bench during his playing career that he also became known as "The Judge."

William (Yank) Robinson

Yankee Robinson was the name of a nineteenth-century midwestern circus showman. Old-time St. Louis infielder Bill Robinson acquired the nickname of "Yank" in his honor.

Ed (Sears) Roebuck

Clever bench jockeys used to taunt the Dodgers relief pitcher with the name of "Sears" Roebuck, after the chain of department stores, but it never went into general use. After Roebuck's trade to Washington, however, and his subsequent criticism of his former Dodgers manager, *The Sporting News* headlined the story, "Roebuck Sears Alston."

Stanley (Packy) Rogers

The old Dodgers infielder was as pugnacious as boxer Packy McFarland.

Charlie (Chinski) Root

The ebullient Charlie (Jolly Cholly) Grimm, Root's teammate and manager on the Cubs, tagged the pitcher "Chinski" because of Root's prominent lower jaw.

Pete (Charlie Hustle) Rose

In his rookie year with the Reds, 1963, Rose was playing in an exhibition game against the Yankees. He received a walk and raced to first base. Mickey Mantle and Whitey Ford watched with amazement, and Mantle asked, "Who's that Charlie Hustle?" The nickname stuck (at least in the press) as Rose continued his feisty, all-out playing habits through a stellar career with the Reds, the Phillies, and the Montreal Expos. In the late 1970s, singer Pamela Neal recorded a disco song about Rose called "The Charlie Hustle," which was also the name of a disco dance simulating baseball movements. Rose also achieved the rare distinction of having a flower named after himself when the Atlanta Braves, who ended his hitting streak at forty-four games in 1978, commissioned a California horticulturist to develop a "Pete" rose hybrid in his honor. Rose wound up breaking Ty Cobb's all-time career hit record (with 4,256) but was barred from baseball in 1989 by commissioner A. Bartlett Giamatti for allegedly betting on major-league games.

Perhaps the most elegant prose stylist who ever wrote about baseball was Walter (Red) Smith, who covered the game from 1927 until his death in 1982. In 1979 he won the first Pulitzer Prize ever awarded to a sports columnist. Smith's most frequently quoted observation was, "Ninety feet between home plate and first base may be the closest man has ever come to perfection." And to those who disparaged baseball as dull, he made the classic retort: "Baseball is dull only to those with dull minds."

Al (Flip) Rosen

While in high school, the future Cleveland Indians infielder was a softball pitcher, or "flipper," which teammates shortened to "Flip."

Clarence (Pants) Rowland

During a sandlot game in his hometown of Platteville, Wisconsin, with a large crowd present, Rowland tore his trousers sliding home. Ever after he was "Pants."

George (Nap) Rucker

"Nap" was merely a contraction of Rucker's middle name of Napoleon, but just how it came into general use is interesting. When he was a boy in Alpharetta, Georgia, he was fond of confections called "napoleons," and whenever his playmates saw the ice-cream peddler, they would yell, "There's your napoleon, Rucker!" His first name was soon forgotten, and Brooklyn fans made the contraction of "Nap" from "Napoleon" after Rucker made the major leagues. Pitcher Al (Bozo) Cicotte was nicknamed by an uncle because, as a boy in Detroit, he was partial to ice-cream cones called "bozos."

Herold (Muddy) Ruel

Ruel was anything but a sloppy dresser, but the nickname of "Muddy" clung to him from childhood. He once entered the house dripping with mud, and his father said, "Look at muddy over there!"

Jacob (Four Straight Jake) Ruppert

The millionaire beer baron and Yankees owner was "Colonel" Ruppert because of his position as aide-de-camp to New York governor David Bennett Hill from 1889 to 1892. While his team was sweeping the 1927, 1928, 1932, 1938, and 1939 World Series in four straight games each, writers came to call him "Four Straight Jake."

Bill (Ropes) Russell

Russell's first year in the major leagues, 1969, was also the last year that veteran Ken Boyer played. The Dodgers assigned Russell to room with Boyer "to learn the ropes," and as a result the rookie (and future Dodgers manager) came to be called "Ropes."

George (Babe) Ruth

Manager Jack Dunn signed George Herman Ruth, a pudgy, moon-faced boy of nineteen, to a contract with the minor-league Baltimore Orioles in 1914. As Ruth recalled in his autobiography, *The Babe Ruth Story*, "Dunn already had a reputation for picking up very young players and developing them. Some of his older players used to kid him a lot about the baby-faced kids he concentrated on, and the first time they saw me with him—on the field—was no exception. 'Look at Dunnie and his new babe,' one of the older players yelled. That started it, I guess. But the clincher came a few days later." Ruth became fascinated with the elevator in the Fayetteville, North Carolina, hotel that served as the Orioles' training base. After bribing the operator to let him run the controls, Ruth began cruising up and down. He was almost decapitated on the third floor as he stuck his head out the door, yanking it back just in time after another player screamed. "Dunnie bawled me out until the stuffings ran out of me, and what he didn't say to me the older players said for him. But finally one of them took pity on me, shook his head and said: 'You're just a babe in the woods.' After that they called me Babe." Sportswriters later came up with a variant on the nickname, calling Ruth "The Bambino" (Italian for "little baby"). After Ruth's home run–hitting exploits eclipsed those of Frank (Home Run) Baker, homers were no longer referred to as "bakers"; they were now "babe ruths." Even today, in the Mexican League, homers are called *banbinazos*, derived from "The Bambino." Yankee players usually referred to Ruth as "Jidge." Ruth himself had trouble remembering names, calling young players "Kid" and older ones "Doc." According to Fred Lieb, his favorite name for clubhouse cronies was "Jidge," a corruption of his own first name (George) that they began applying to him. Some players mocked Ruth's outsized visage by calling him "Two Head." A couple of more fanciful Babe Ruth nicknames sometimes used in the press were "The Sultan of Swat" (inspired by an early slang term for hitter, "Son of Swat") and "The Caliph of Clout." The "Sultan of Swat" nickname inspired confusion in a foreign reader of *Time* in 1961 after the magazine referred to Claire Ruth as the "widow of baseball's Sultan of Swat." Mahmood Khan, a citizen of Swat in West Pakistan, wrote: "Being a citizen of Swat, the term Sultan of Swat has greatly aroused my interest. There is no such title as Sultan of Swat in the state. Our ruler is called the Wali of Swat. I hope you would let me know the idea behind the term which you have used." *Time* replied, "His fans believed that there was no one who could swat a baseball like Babe Ruth, the Home Run King." Ruth's popularity was so vast that he even had a candy bar named after him, the Baby Ruth bar. The makers of the bar, Standard Brands Confectionery, insisted that it "was named for Grover Cleveland's daughter who was born in the White House." But Lieb, a close friend of the Babe, said Ruth and his publicist, Christy Walsh, were convinced that the bar was named to cash in on him.

Dominic (Mike) Ryba

According to Lee Allen, when Ryba joined the Cardinals, manager Bill McKechnie constantly called him "Mike." Ryba went to McKechnie and complained, "My name's not Mike. I'm a Pole, not an Irishman." "From now on," McKechnie replied, "your name is Mike. I don't go for that Dominic."

> The .400-hitting Cardinals rookie Don Padgett, the story goes, asked manager Billy Southworth in 1937 why he was riding the bench. "Because you're a .399 fielder," was Southworth's answer.

St. Louis Cardinals

St. Louis clubs in the old American Association and the early National League were called the "Browns" because of their stocking colors. The National Leaguers, also known as the "Maroons," changed their colors to red in 1899. This prompted a new nickname, "Cardinals," which was applied at the suggestion of *St. Louis Post-Dispatch* writer Billy McHale after he allegedly heard a lady in back of the press box during a 1900 St. Louis–Chicago game remark, "Isn't that the loveliest shade of cardinal?" The team adopted not only the name but also the cardinal bird as its symbol; "Redbirds" and "Birds" are used as unofficial alternate nicknames. Upon the formation of the American League in 1901, the new St. Louis AL entry took over the discarded name of "Browns" and kept it until the franchise was shifted in 1954 to Baltimore, where the team took over the traditional local nickname of "Orioles."

San Diego Padres

Like the Milwaukee Brewers, the Padres took their nickname from a minor-league predecessor. The name originally was chosen for the old San Diego Pacific Coast League club because of the predominant Spanish heritage of the city, which is close to Mexico. Padres (priests) were in charge of the many Catholic missions that dot the landscape in the area and helped shape its history.

San Francisco Giants

When the Troy Trojans National League franchise was moved to New York City in 1883, the club became known as the "Gothams," after the traditional name for the city. "Giants" supplanted that nickname after Jim Mutrie became manager of the team in 1885. After a victorious road trip, the team returned to New York and a fan in the box seats told the manager, "Mutrie, your boys played like giants." To which he replied, "My boys are giants in stature and in baseball ability." Sportswriters heard the story and began using the nickname, which quickly won favor. The Giants kept it after moving to San Francisco in 1958.

Al (The Clown Prince of Baseball) Schacht

Schacht played only three lackluster seasons in the major leagues, pitching for the Senators from 1919 through 1921, but he became renowned as a zany, along with such other famous cutups as Babe Herman, Germany Schaefer, and Casey Stengel. Schacht had the business sense to make money out of his antics, and for many years he toured ballparks with partner Nick Altrock, doing a comic baseball routine. Schacht labeled himself "The Clown Prince of Baseball."

After a disappointing season, Boston Braves manager George Stallings suffered a mild heart attack on the way back to his Georgia home. A doctor asked, "What do you suppose was the origin of your condition, Mr. Stallings?" The manager murmured sadly, "Bases on balls. Bases on balls." The remark became famous and other managers, notably Frank Frisch, repeated it incessantly, sometimes modifying it to "Oh, those bases on balls!"

Ray (Cracker) Schalk

Many fans thought the scrappy catcher's nickname of "Cracker" was short for "Whipcracker," "Firecracker," or something similar. Actually, the nickname had a less complimentary origin. When Schalk reported to the White Sox in 1912, he weighed only 140 pounds. After his first game, he stripped for a shower, and outfielder Shano Collins called out to his teammates, "Look at the cracker ass on that kid!"

Bob (Grump) Scheffing

During a 1941 round of golf while the Cubs trained on Catalina Island, Charlie Root missed a putt on the eighteenth green, and Scheffing chewed him out. Root began calling him "Grump."

Fred (Crazy) Schmidt

This Chicago-born pitcher of foreign descent spoke English poorly. When fans laughed at his mispronunciations, he never understood why, and asked, "Am I crazy?" Besides "Crazy," he was called "Tacks," because "tacky" and "tacks" were turn-of-the-century slang terms for eccentricity.

Johnny (Bear Tracks) Schmitz

Schmitz had a peculiar way of walking that led players to call him "Bear Tracks." Alva Javery had the same nickname, because of his heavy stride.

Frank (Wildfire) Schulte

Cubs outfielder Frank Schulte was friendly with actress Lillian Russell, and when she came to Vicksburg, Mississippi, with the play *Wildfire*, she held a party for the Cubs, who were also in town. Schulte named his best trotting horse "Wildfire" in her honor, and Charley Dryden then applied the nickname to Schulte himself.

Hal (Prince Hal) Schumacher

Like Lou Gehrig, who was eclipsed by Babe Ruth, the Giants' Schumacher had to surrender most of the headlines to his more illustrious teammate, Carl Hubbell. Since Hubbell was "King Carl," Schumacher picked up the Shakespearean nickname of "Prince Hal," earlier given to the Yankees' lordly player-manager Hal Chase.

Jim (Death Valley) Scott

The White Sox right-hander was named after the legendary California desert character Death Valley Scotty.

Owners of baseball parks have always found it a lucrative practice to rent out space for advertisements. In the early days, the outfield walls were covered with signs; today, it more often is the scoreboard that plugs commercial products. Probably the most famous ballpark ad was dreamed up by the Tanglefoot Flypaper Company in the 1920s: "Last year Zack Wheat caught 288 flies; Tanglefoot caught 15 billion."

Seattle Mariners

Because Seattle is a major seaport of the Pacific Northwest, the first American League expansion team established there, in 1969, was called the "Pilots." That club went bankrupt, however, and four days before the start of the 1970 season it was shifted to Milwaukee, where it took over the old nickname of the city's former minor-league franchise, the "Brewers." In 1976, the American League decided to expand into Toronto and to give Seattle another chance. Seattle fans were asked to submit ideas for nicknames in an August 1976 essay contest, and from a list of more than 600 entries, the club's six partners chose "Mariners," because of its appropriate nautical connotation. Roger Szmodis of Bellevue, Washington, was selected as the fan who argued most persuasively for the nickname. "Mariners" is often shortened to "M's" in headlines.

Tom (Tom Terrific) Seaver

The masterly pitcher who won 311 games in twenty-one seasons was nicknamed "Tom Terrific" after a 1950s cartoon character, a boy who could change himself into anything he wanted. The animated Tom Terrific made regular appearances on one of the most popular children's shows of that period, *Captain Kangaroo*. Another TV cartoon character who lent his name to a baseball player was McGruff, a crime-fighting dog featured on public-service announcements. After the slugging first baseman Fred McGriff came to the majors in 1986, his last name prompted fellow players to call him "Crime Dog."

Bob (Suitcase) Seeds

Seeds played nine seasons in the majors, shuttling around five different teams. Bibb Falk called him "Suitcase" because of his frequent travels. Later, the peripatetic outfielder Harry Simpson acquired the same nickname.

George (Twinkletoes) Selkirk

Babe Ruth's outfield successor was dubbed "Twinkletoes" or "Twink" by his Newark teammates because of the way he walked and ran, with the weight on the fore parts of his feet.

Truett (Rip) Sewell

The eephus-ball pitcher was called "Little Rip" after an older brother, and in 1936 Buffalo sportswriter Francis Dunn shortened the nickname to "Rip."

Arthur (Tillie) Shafer

When the boyish, reserved infielder joined the Giants in 1909, manager John McGraw told the team, "Men, I want you to meet Arthur Shafer, our new third baseman." Veteran Cy Seymour ran over to him, kissed him on both cheeks, and said, "Hello, Tillie! How are you?" Though he hit a respectable .273 in his four seasons with the Giants, Shafer became so upset by his unshakable nickname, according to Lee Allen, that he finally quit the game to run a haberdashery in his native Los Angeles.

Walter (Skinny) Shaner

Shaner stood 6′2″ and weighed 195 pounds, but he was called "Skinny" because his last name reminded people of Skinny Shaner, a character in a comic strip called *Us Boys*.

Francis (Spec) Shea

In some cases, the nickname "Spec" or "Specs" means that its holder wears glasses. One such player was pitcher Henry

(Specs) Meadows. Francis (Spec) Shea, however, was freckled, or "speckled." Other freckled players included Fred (Speck or Specs) Harkness, Marv (Freck) Owen, and Walter (Huck) Betts, named after Huckleberry Finn. Some fanciful writer also called Spec Shea "The Naugatuck Nugget," after his hometown of Naugatuck, Connecticut, but that nickname never caught on.

Arthur (Art the Great) Shires

A forerunner of Muhammad Ali in the ego department, Shires would boast to sportswriters that he was "The Great Shires," and would fight to prove it.

Burt (Barney) Shotton

Walter Johnson became "Barney" because he drove like race-car driver Barney Oldfield, but Shotton, later a Brooklyn manager, was said to be as fast as Oldfield on the bases when he played for the St. Louis Browns. John Wyrostek's middle name of "Barney" was preferred usage for the same reason.

Clyde (Hardrock) Shoun

Rugged play as a football and baseball player at Mountain City, Tennessee, High School tagged the pitcher "Hardrock."

Ted (Simba) Simmons

The catcher's long mane suggested the nickname "Simba," an African word for lion. While he was burning leaves, however, his hair caught fire, so he cut off the mane but kept the name.

Bill (The Singer Throwing Machine) Singer

The big, hard-throwing right-handed pitcher received his nickname from Bob Hunter of the *Los Angeles Herald-Examiner* early in his major-league career in a pun on the Singer Sewing Machine. He also was dubbed "Bullet Bill."

Gordon (Oskie) Slade

Slade attended the University of Oregon and was nicknamed after a college cheer, "Oskie, Wah Wah!"

Enos (Country) Slaughter

At Columbus in 1936, manager Burt Shotton met the youth from Roxboro, South Carolina, and called him "Country." The name has been given to other players from rural backgrounds, such as relief pitcher Mark Littell, who came from Gideon, Missouri.

Giants manager Bill Terry made a remark prior to the 1934 season that cost his club the pennant. During a press conference in the lobby of New York's Hotel Roosevelt at the annual baseball meetings in February, Roscoe McGowen of the *New York Times* asked Terry, who was discussing his rivals' chances for the pennant, "How about Brooklyn, Bill?" Terry, remembering the Dodgers' sixth-place finish the previous year, cracked, "Brooklyn? Is Brooklyn still in the league?" The remark was widely printed and the source of much amusement. But Casey Stengel, Brooklyn's manager, used it to goad his team all season. The final two games of the year the Dodgers beat New York, knocking Terry's team out of the race and proving that Brooklyn was, indeed, "still in the league." In 1953, Dodgers manager Charlie Dressen courted fate with a similar remark but emerged unscathed. That August, while the Dodgers were basking in a healthy lead over New York, Dressen sneered to *New York Daily News* sportswriter Dick Young, "The Giants is dead." Young put the Dressen quote in a box on the sports page, and though it was frequently repeated, it failed to do anything for the Giants, who wound up with a dismal fifth-place finish as the Dodgers went on to win the pennant.

The Slaughterhouse Nine

The Pittsburgh Alleghenies, an American Association fore-runner of the modern Pirates, joined the AA in 1882. The players of that season's team called themselves "The Slaugh-terhouse Nine"; they used to tell each other before game time, "Let's slide out to the slaughterhouse. It's just twenty min-utes before killing time."

Earl (Oil) Smith

When he was a sportswriter, Westbrook Pegler dubbed the Giants catcher "Oil" because of the way Bronx fans pro-nounced his first name.

Ozzie (The Wizard of Oz) Smith

Unquestionably the best-fielding shortstop who ever played the game, Ozzie Smith performed feats with his glove that left baseball afi-cionados agape with wonder. His first name made people think of the classic 1939 movie with Judy Garland (based on the books by L. Frank Baum), even though Smith, unlike the wizard on screen played by Frank Morgan, was no sham. "The Wizard" of baseball, who played his first four seasons with the Padres before spending fifteen years with the Cardinals, added to his magical image with his acrobatic stunts, such as starting and ending each season with a somersault.

Edwin (Duke) Snider

When Snider was four, his father, seeing him approaching, said, "Here comes the Duke!" He was later known to Brooklyn fans as "The Duke of Flatbush." Leon (Duke) Carmel idolized Snider and was named after him by boyhood friends in Harlem.

Warren (Hooks) Spahn

During a 1941 exhibition game in Texas, a thrown ball hit Spahn in the face, breaking his nose. After he returned to the club, teammates taunted him as "The Great Profile." He became "Hooks" after one player said, "Get a load of the hook on that guy." In later years, players simply called him "Spahnie."

Tris (The Gray Eagle) Speaker

The great outfielder had gray hair by the time he was thirty, and that, combined with his speed, led to the nickname of "The Gray Eagle." Players called him "Spoke," a play on his last name.

Don (Full Pack) Stanhouse

Stanhouse was the fireman on whom Orioles manager Earl Weaver relied in the late 1970s to quell the most threatening opposition rallies. The manager nicknamed him "Full Pack" because, he said, "that's how many cigarettes I smoke when he's on the mound." The flaky Stanhouse also was dubbed "Stan the Man Unusual" (a play on Stan Musial's nickname of "Stan the Man") by fellow Birds pitcher Mike Flanagan in 1979.

Eddie (The Brat) Stanky

New York Sun sportswriter Edward T. Murphy called the pugnacious infielder "that brat from Kensington" after the section of Philadelphia where Stanky was raised.

Fred (The Chicken) Stanley

The plucky Yankees infielder was not lacking in courage, as his aggressive play in the 1977 World Series proved. The reason he was called "The Chicken" was that teammates thought the skinny, pale-skinned Stanley looked and walked like a chicken.

Wilver (Willie, Pops) Stargell

The elder statesman of the Pittsburgh Pirates jokingly dubbed himself "Pops" while, at age thirty-eight, he led the club to the 1979 world championship. Stargell's teammates also called him "Lumber," because he swung such a heavy and powerful bat. Stargell, Dave Parker, and their fellow Pirates sluggers of the 1980s were known collectively as "The Lumber

Company." Cubs coach Gene Clines nicknamed Stargell "Magic," because, he said, "magic things happen around him." But that name didn't gain much currency, since it was more familiar as the nickname of basketball wizard Earvin (Magic) Johnson.

Arnold (Jigger) Statz

The National League outfielder, once considered the best golfer among major-league players, made good use of the iron called a "jigger."

Daniel (Rusty, Le Grand Orange) Staub

Nurses in the New Orleans hospital where he was born gave Staub the "Rusty" nickname because of his red hair, and when he played at Montreal he also acquired the French equivalent, "Le Grand Orange" (roughly translated, "Big Red"). Because he was an excellent cook and owned a restaurant in New York, Staub also was known as "The Galloping Gourmet," after TV chef Graham Kerr. Teammates teasing him about his fussy habits dubbed him "Felix," after the compulsively neat character Felix Unger in Neil Simon's *The Odd Couple*.

Harry (Battleaxe) Steinfeldt

The superb but largely unheralded third baseman in the early-Cubs' Tinker-to-Evers-to-Chance infield, Steinfeldt was called "Battleaxe" after his favorite brand of chewing tobacco. Yankee batting champ George Stirnweiss became known as "Snuffy" because he used snuff for a sinus condition.

Charles (Casey) Stengel

First known as "Dutch" in the minors, Stengel had two theories about how he came to be called "Casey." The first is that he struck out a great deal early in his career, and in an allusion to Ernest L. Thayer's famous poem "Casey at the Bat," he was long known as "Strikeout Casey"—a nickname later amended to "Home Run Casey" after he hit two game-winning homers for the Giants against the Yankees in the 1923 World Series. The more likely theory of how he received the nickname is that since he was from Kansas City, he had "Charles Stengel, K.C." stenciled on his baggage and used to introduce himself to teammates by saying, "I'm from K.C." So they called him "K.C.," and then "Casey." As a manager, Stengel was known as "Ol' Case" and as the "Old Perfesser" because of his manipulations of batting orders and the English language.

Riggs (Old Hoss) Stephenson

As a football star at the University of Alabama, the durable Cubs slugger was "Warhorse," later shortened to "Old Hoss."

Bob (Scrap Iron) Stinson

A rugged catcher and infielder, Stinson was first called "Scrap Iron" in his early years with the Dodgers, because he wouldn't let injuries keep him from playing. Feisty infielder Phil Garner also was known as "Scrap Iron," and the same nickname was given in 1952 to St. Louis Browns catcher Clint Courtney by teammate Duane Pillette and announcer Buddy Blattner. Courtney hurt himself running a race at a train station with Pillette and Blattner but suited up the following day. Dizzy Dean gave Courtney the nickname of "The Toy Bulldog" as a tribute to his fighting spirit. Dodgers manager Tom Lasorda jokingly nicknamed his lanky, mild-mannered rookie pitcher Orel Hershiser "Bulldog," but Hershiser's tenacity on the mound eventually made the name seem fitting.

The Stone Wall

Besides their "Heroic Legion of Baseball" battery of Jim McCormick and Mike (King) Kelly, the old Chicago White Stockings had a fabulous infield, dominated by first baseman Cap Anson and filled out by Dandelion Pfeffer, Ned Williamson, and Tommy Burns. Fans called the infield "The Stone Wall" because it was so hard to penetrate with hits.

Ernest L. Thayer's poem "Casey at the Bat" first appeared in the June 3, 1888, *San Francisco Examiner* under the title "A Ballad of the Republic, Sung in the Year 1888." It caught the national imagination after Shakespearean actor De Wolf Hopper recited it later that year at a New York show honoring the Giants. Hopper made it a part of his repertoire, others began to perform it on stage, and it became one of vaudeville's most popular routines. Many claims have been made about supposed real-life models for "Casey," but none has been authenticated. The most famous of the poem's thirteen stanzas is the last:

> Oh! somewhere in this favored land the sun
> 　　　is shining bright;
> The band is playing somewhere, and somewhere
> 　　　hearts are light,
> And somewhere men are laughing, and somewhere
> 　　　children shout;
> But there is no joy in Mudville—mighty Casey
> 　　　has struck out.

Dick (Dr. Strangeglove) Stuart

A first baseman with a good bat but a bad glove, Stuart was playing for the Red Sox in 1964 when Stanley Kubrick's movie *Dr. Strangelove* appeared. A Boston sportswriter dubbed the clumsy fielder "Dr. Strangeglove." Sox fans sometimes called Stuart "King Richard." Outfielder Willie Norwood later inherited the "Dr. Strangeglove" title.

Billy (Parson) Sunday

During his eight years in the majors, from 1883 to 1890, outfielder Billy Sunday had the reputation of being one of the heaviest drinkers in the game. That all changed one night, so the story goes, while he and his Phillies teammates were carousing in a tavern. A band of gospel singers marched past, and Sunday suddenly declared, "I'm finished with this life. Boys, we've come to the parting of the ways. I'm going into the service of God." His pals laughed, but Sunday was serious. He gave up his large (for that time) salary of $3,500 a season to preach for the YMCA at $83 a month. Eventually becoming the world's leading evangelist, he was known as "Parson" Sunday throughout his thirty-five-year preaching career. Ironically, though his early carousing years in baseball were played at Chicago, Sunday was immortalized in the song "Chicago," with the description of the Windy City as "the town that Billy Sunday couldn't close down."

Tampa Bay Devil Rays

The Florida American League expansion team, scheduled to play its first games in the spring of 1998, was dubbed the "Devil Rays" after a fish prominent in the Gulf of Mexico. Giving the state its second big-league team named after a fish (the other is the Florida Marlins), the nickname was chosen by the Tampa Bay team's managing general partner, Vincent J. Naimoli, after the franchise was awarded in 1995.

George (Birdie) Tebbetts

The catcher and, later, manager had a high-pitched, often-used voice that sounded like the chirping of a bird. An earlier player, William Cree of the Yankees, was also called "Birdie," because his last name is also the name of a bird. Cree once played under the name of William Burdee.

Kent (Mr. Bones) Tekulve

Also called "The Blade," "The Book End," and "The Creature," Tekulve was an oddly elongated (6′4″ and 165 pounds) but highly effective relief pitcher with a sidearm motion often compared to that of another skinny pitcher, the Reds' Ewell (The Whip) Blackwell. At age fifteen, growing up in Cincinnati, Tekulve was called "The Whip" after Blackwell. Later, sportswriters began calling Tekulve "Mr. Bones," a comic moniker dating back to the vaudeville era. To his teammates, Tekulve was known as "Teke." Another tall, lean modern player, John LeMaster, was nicknamed "Bones." Besides Tekulve, other skinny pitchers in baseball have included Tom (The Blade) Hall; William (Lank) Wilson, named after the tall member of the silent-movie comedy team "Hank and Lank"; J. R. (High Rise) Richard; Monty (Gander) Stratton, said to resemble a goose; Russell (Feather) Christopher, also called "Daddy," as in "Daddy Long Legs"; Dave (Scissors) Foutz; and George (Scissors) Shears, whose last name also contributed.

Bill (Memphis Bill) Terry

Although a native of Atlanta, Terry owned an estate near Memphis.

Charles (Jeff) Tesreau

This Giants pitcher, 6′2½″ and 230 pounds, reminded people of heavyweight boxing champion Jim Jeffries. Three other pitchers of the early 1900s were nicknamed after the boxer: Orval (Jeff) Overall and the brothers Ed (Jeff) Pfeffer and Francis (Big Jeff) Pfeffer. Tesreau's nickname became so ingrained in fans' minds that nobody knew who "Charles Monroe Tesreau" was when he later ran for public office. Because of a regulation forbidding nicknames on ballots, Tesreau's campaign fizzled. His size and his mountain origin also gave him the less-used nickname of "The Ozark Bear."

Texas Rangers

The Washington Senators expansion team of 1961–71, which replaced the old Nats after their move to Minnesota, relocated to Arlington, Texas, a suburb of Dallas, in 1972. The team then took the name Texas Rangers, after the legendary lawmen of the Western frontier.

Frank (The Big Hurt) Thomas

During his sophomore season in the majors, 1991, the White Sox slugger walloped a tremendous home run that made broadcaster Ken (Hawk) Harrelson exclaim, "O-o-o-oh, Frank put the big hurt on that ball." Delighted that people started calling him "The Big Hurt," Thomas remarked, "It's what I do with the baseball, hit line drive after line drive."

Gorman (The Perch Man) Thomas

The flaky slugger, whose power at the plate made him "Stormin' Gorman," also became known as "The Perch Man" because he liked to meditate on top of his locker before going out onto the field.

Bobby (The Flying Scot) Thomson

Garry Schumacher, later the Giants' publicity director but then a sportswriter for the *New York Journal-American*, nicknamed Thomson "The Royal Scot," later modified to "The Flying Scot." Schumacher explained, "Bobby was a native Scotsman, born in Edinburgh, though he grew up in Staten Island, New York. In those days and for a quarter of a century before, the fastest and best-equipped train in the British Isles was the 'Royal Scot,' which made the overnight run between London and Edinburgh. Like the 'Twentieth Century' in this country. Along with his hitting power and other baseball attributes, Bobby Thomson was a streamlined speedster—extremely fast. In the circumstances, I thought the name was apropos. I guess not enough of the readers were familiar with the Scotch train connotation. It never really did catch on." However, Thomson's more popular nickname, "The Flying Scot," was most likely a compromise of Schumacher's nickname. What Thomson said in the locker room after his 1951 pennant-winning homer certainly helped to fix the nickname in the public's mind: "I was flying coming around third base. I didn't touch the ground once."

Marvin (Marvelous Marv) Throneberry

No player better typified the hapless 1962 New York Mets (of whom manager Casey Stengel sighed, "Can't anyone here play this game?") than first baseman Marvin E. Throneberry, whose very initials, a sportswriter pointed out, spelled "MET." Perhaps Throneberry's most famous moment came in a game against the Cubs in June 17 of that year, when after one of his fielding blunders cost the Mets four runs, he atoned by slamming what appeared to be a triple with two men on base. Arriving at third, however, Throneberry was called out because he had failed to touch first base. Stengel ran out of the dugout to protest, but the first-base coach stopped him by saying, "Forget it, Casey, he didn't touch second either." Sportswriter Jack Lang rose to Marvelous Marv's defense: "How could he be expected to remember where the bases were? He gets on so infrequently." On Throneberry's birthday that year, teammate Richie Ashburn said, "We were going to give him a cake, but we were afraid he'd drop it." Throneberry's bumbling play endeared him to the fans, won him the New York sportswriters' "Good Guy" award for his cheerfulness, and gave him the nickname of "Marvelous Marv." (His older brother, Maynard Faye Throneberry, an American League outfielder, subsequently was dubbed "Fabulous Faye," even though Faye was hardly in Marv's class.)

Hollis (Sloppy) Thurston

Thurston's nickname was misleading because his dressing habits were anything but "Sloppy." He inherited the name from his father, a kindhearted restaurant owner in Tombstone, Arizona, who became known as "Sloppy" because he gave free soup to bums at the back door. William (Bucky) Walters, Forrest (Smoky) Burgess, James (Pete) Runnels, and John (Champ) Summers were other players nicknamed after their fathers.

Toronto Blue Jays

The expansion team chose its nickname in a 1976 contest from more than 4,000 names submitted by 30,000 fans. A total of 154 suggested "Blue Jays," which had a multiple appropriateness to the area: several other local teams used the color blue in their uniforms, the blue jay is a common bird in southern Ontario, and, not least important, one of the team's principal owners was Labatt's Breweries, which made a beer called "Blue." The team's board of directors, who made the final name choice, noted that the club's feathered namesake "dares to take on all comers, yet is down-to-earth, gutsy, and good-looking."

Harold (Pie) Traynor

When the Hall of Fame third baseman was a boy in Somerville, Massachusetts, he idolized a baseball-playing son of the local grocer and carried the boy's bats to games. Every morning Traynor would go to the store for his family and, when running down his mother's list, always ended with, "And one pie!" The grocer's son began calling his young companion "Pie."

> The greatest baseball showman of the modern era, Bill Veeck, was also one of the game's most eloquent defenders. After he returned to baseball in 1976 as president of the Chicago White Sox, Veeck declared, "Baseball is the only game left for people. To play basketball now, you have to be 7'6". To play football, you have to be the same width."

Thurman (Joe E.) Tucker

Tucker bore a startling resemblance to bigmouthed comedian Joe E. Brown, who played the title role in the 1935 movie version of Ring Lardner's classic baseball story "Alibi Ike."

George (Jerry) Upp

"Jerryup," like "giddyup," was an old expression used to get horses moving. The last name of George Upp, who pitched briefly for Cleveland in 1907, invited the nickname of "Jerry."

Fernando (El Toro) Valenzuela

While playing in his native Mexico before coming to the major leagues, the stocky, seemingly indefatigable pitcher was known as "El Toro" ("The Bull"). In his sensational rookie season of 1981 with the Dodgers, Valenzuela became such an instant legend that sportswriters tried to popularize the nickname anew. But it never really caught on, since his American aficionados were content to call him simply Fernando (the Americanization "Freddie" was trotted out and generally ignored). The fervor stirred in Los Angeles by the stylish left-handed phenom was dubbed "Fernandomania." After ten full seasons with the Dodgers (not counting his 1980 cup of coffee), "El Toro" moved on to other arenas, and in time the dazzling Japanese import Hideo Nomo prompted an outbreak of "Nomomania," but the memory of Fernandomania is still cherished.

Arthur (Dazzy) Vance

The firethrowing pitcher's nickname was often thought to refer to his "dazzling" speed, but according to Lee Allen, it actually can be traced back to his boyhood. As a Nebraska youngster, he imitated the speech of a cowboy who would say of his pistol, "Ain't that a daisy?" As the cowboy pronounced it, "daisy" sounded like "dazzy." Vance became "Dazzy" after repeating the expression so often, usually in reference to his curveball.

Bill (Sportshirt) Veeck

Baseball's Barnum had a skin condition on his neck that made it irritating for him to wear tight collars. His trademark was his habit of wearing only open-necked sportshirts, never ties. *The Sporting News* called him "The Burrhead" because of his curly, close-cropped hair. American League pitcher Joe Dobson was "Burrhead" for the same reason.

Zoilo (Zorro) Versalles

A Washington clubhouse attendant in the late 1950s compared this Cuban shortstop in speed, grace, and name to Zorro, the fictional Mexican vigilante then popular because of a Walt Disney television series.

George (Rube) Waddell

The zany left-hander was a gangling young hick when he started playing pro ball, and as he strode to the mound, fans would heckle him, yelling, "Hey, Rube!" He always bowed politely to them, but he would punch a stranger who called him "Rube" off the field. To his friends, Waddell was "Eddie," from his middle name of Edward. Eventually, however, Waddell grew to like being called "Rube," and he painted signs on St. Louis sidewalks proclaiming brashly, "Come and see Rube fan 'em out." Later, other young left-handers became known as "Rube" in Waddell's honor, including John Benton, Ray Bressler, Floyd Kroh, Richard Marquard, and George Walberg. Andrew Foster, father of the Negro Leagues, was nicknamed "Rube" after he outpitched Rube Waddell in a 1902 exhibition game.

John (Honus) Wagner

The German nickname for Johannes (John) is "Honus" or "Hans," and a "big Honus" is an affectionate term roughly equivalent to calling someone a "big oaf." The Pirates' great shortstop John Wagner was called both "Honus" and "Hans," as well as "The Flying Dutchman," after the opera by Richard Wagner. John Lobert, a third baseman who looked like Honus Wagner, was nicknamed "Honus," "Hans," or "Little Hans" in his honor. Another "Hans" was Harry Ables, a big American League pitcher who was so nicknamed because he was said to have the biggest hands in baseball history.

Leon (Daddy Wags) Wagner

Wagner owned a clothing store in Los Angeles whose slogan was "Get Your Rags from Daddy Wags." Giants trainer Frank Bowman named him "Cheeky" because of his high cheekbones.

Fred (Dixie) Walker

Walker, born on a plantation in Georgia, waited two years, the story goes, before he could admit to his old grandmother that he played for the Yankees. He was dubbed "Dixie" after his father, Ewart, a nondescript Washington pitcher who, as an eighteen-year-old playing at Zanesville, Ohio, in 1909, won his nickname when a morning newspaper headlined,

"Dixie Walker Pitches Today." After son Fred hit .436 against the Giants in 1940, his second year with the Dodgers, he was called "The Peepul's Cherce," Brooklynese for "The People's Choice."

Harry (The Hat) Walker

According to cap manufacturer Tim McAuliffe, the roughest player on hats was Harry Walker, whose habit of removing his hat or tugging at it between every pitch while batting made him wear out twenty caps per year, in contrast to the three that the average player wears out. In addition to his nickname of "Harry the Hat," Walker was called "Little Dixie" after his older and equally talented brother.

Joe (Tarzan) Wallis

His Oakland teammates named Wallis "Tarzan" because he liked to dive into swimming pools from motel windows. "Just make sure you clear the cement," he said of his diving technique. The bearded outfielder and ten other hirsute A's became known collectively as "The Bearded Bunch." An earlier baseball "Tarzan," LeRoy Parmelee, was a pitcher whose performance on the mound, New York sportswriters said, usually left him "out on a limb." Charlie (King Kong) Keller was sometimes known as "Tarzan" because of his "apelike" appearance. Jungle Jim Rivera was called that because the muscular outfielder had a loud voice and frequently used it in disputes with bleacher fans.

Paul and Lloyd (Big and Little Poison) Waner

A sportswriter once overheard an Ebbets Field fan saying when the Waners were playing, "Every time you look up, those Waner boys are on base. It's always that little poison on thoid and the big poison on foist." That was Brooklynese for "little person" and "big person." Although each was 5′8½″ tall and their weights were almost identical, Paul was considered "The Big Poison" because he was three years older than Lloyd and the better hitter.

Lon (The Arkansas Hummingbird) Warneke

Warneke's nicknames of "Dixie," "Country," and "Ol' Arkansas" were derived from the fact that he was born in Mt. Ida, Arkansas. Teammates on the 1934 Cardinals called him "The Arkansas Hummingbird" because he played the guitar and sang in Pepper Martin's "Mudcat Band" of Cardinals players.

Arthur (Six O'Clock) Weaver

Weaver was a tall catcher whose build was likened to the hands of a clock at dinnertime. Other picturesque labels for elongated players included those of first basemen George (High Pockets) Kelly and Howard (Steeple) Schultz. Like Willie McCovey, Schultz was also called "Stretch."

Earl (Son of Sam) Weaver

Often called "The Genius" because of his managerial brilliance with the Baltimore Orioles, Weaver acquired a less complimentary nickname during the 1979 season. Because Weaver's fierce temper brought him into frequent conflicts with the men in blue (he was ejected from nine games that year), umpire Jim Evans retaliated by describing him as "the Son of Sam of baseball." The reference was to New York mass murderer David Berkowitz, who claimed that he took his commands from a demon inhabiting the body of a dog named Sam.

Bob (Mr. Ice) Welch

The twenty-two-year-old pitcher had a brilliant rookie year in 1978, helping the Dodgers to the pennant. The youngster's cool composure on the mound astonished baseball observers, and by season's end Welch was known as "The Iceman" and "Mr. Ice." The latter nickname gained wide currency after his dramatic performance in coming in from the bullpen with two outs in the ninth inning of the second game of the World Series. The Dodgers were clinging to a 4–3 lead, but the Yankees had two men on base and the batter was Reggie Jackson. As 55,982 fans rose to their feet and shouted—a pressure-packed situation for a youngster if ever there was one—"Mr. Ice" entered the history books by striking out "Mr. October."

Joyner (Jo-Jo) White

Teammates thought the outfielder pronounced the name of his native Georgia as "Jo-Jo."

Ted (Cork) Wilks

His great ability to stop enemy rallies gave the relief pitcher the nickname of "Cork."

Mitch (Wild Thing) Williams

The boisterous relief pitcher, a 1980s throwback to the colorful ruffians of the Gas House Gang, was nicknamed after the popular song "Wild Thing," which his fans often crooned when he marched in from the bullpen. He once explained, "I pitch like my hair's on fire."

Baseball has always inspired American poets to eloquence. "I see great things in baseball," Walt Whitman wrote in the nineteenth century. "It's our game—the American game. It will take our people out-of-doors, fill them with oxygen, give them a larger physical stoicism. Tend to relieve us from being a nervous, dyspeptic set. Repair these losses, and be a blessing to us."

Ted (The Kid) Williams

Williams was tall, lean, and boyish when he joined the Red Sox in 1939. Johnny Orlando, Boston's equipment manager, was the first to call him "The Kid." Later, because of his slugging heroics and his slender frame, *The Sporting News* nicknamed Williams "The Splendid Splinter" (Lee Lacy became known as "The Splendid Splint," since he was a good reserve player, adept at "propping up" an ailing team). A friend's young son was the first to call Williams "Teddy Ballgame."

Walt (No-Neck) Williams

This stocky, 5'6" infielder was described as "No-Neck" while playing for the White Sox. He didn't like the nickname.

Lewis (Hack) Wilson

This Cubs muscleman, a Hall of Famer who still holds the record for most RBIs in a season (190 in 1930, the year he also hit 56 homers), was short for a slugger at 5'6", but he was powerfully built and weighed 195 pounds. When he broke into baseball at Martinsburg, West Virginia, he was known as "Stouts" because of his build and also because of his fondness for beer drinking. He subsequently became "Hack" after his physique was compared to that of the great wrestler George Hackenschmidt. Larry Miller, a player who left the Cubs the year before Wilson joined the team, also was called "Hack" because of his prodigious strength. It was claimed that Miller could twist an iron spike in his hands. Hack Wilson acquired a less complimentary nickname during the fourth game of the 1929 World Series. The Cubs were leading the Philadelphia A's, 8–0, in the seventh inning at Shibe Park when the A's ignited an incredible ten-run rally, the biggest single-inning spree in Series history until the Tigers equaled it in 1968. The Philadelphia hitters were helped in large measure by Wilson, never an impressive fielder, who outdid himself on this occasion by losing two fly balls in the sun during that one inning. The A's won the game, 10–8, and Wilson became known as "Sunny Boy."

George (Hooks) Wiltse

One of the game's most renowned curveball pitchers, Wiltse was proficient with the "hooks." Similarly named were Allyn (Fish Hook) Stout and Charles (Hooks) Beverly of the Negro Leagues. Negro Leaguer Ray Dandridge, on the other hand, was dubbed "Hooks" because he was so adept at "hooking" the ball at third base.

Dave (The Rave) Winfield

Like Art (The Great) Shires in an earlier era, Winfield immodestly nicknamed himself, in this case because the fans were "raving" about him and he thought "Dave the Rave" had a pleasant ring to it.

Charles (Spades) Wood

While a student at Wofford College in Spartanburg, South Carolina, Wood skipped the mandatory religious services for a game of bridge. To his misfortune, he was dealt thirteen spades (a one-in-635,013,559,600 chance) and was expelled after a paper printed the news. Ever after, he was "Spades" Wood.

Early (Gus) Wynn

Ellis Clary, a teammate of Wynn's at Sanford of the Florida State League in 1937, wasn't sure why he nicknamed the pitcher "Gus." The stocky Wynn may have reminded him of wrestler Gus Sonnenberg, said Clary, but in any case, Wynn simply looked like a "Gus."

Jim (The Toy Cannon) Wynn

Although only 5'9", Wynn was a powerfully built slugger. Hence, "The Toy Cannon."

Carl (Yaz, Irish) Yastrzemski

When Yastrzemski joined the Red Sox in 1961, a Boston sportswriter made a suggestion about his last name: "You don't pronounce it, you sneeze it." Soon called "Yaz," Yastrzemski was nicknamed "Irish" by Gene Mauch because Yaz, though Polish, was an alumnus of Notre Dame University. Like Carl Hubbell before him, Yastrzemski was also honored with the nickname "King Carl."

Eddie (The Walking Man) Yost

Though Yost was anything but a superstar during his tenure in the American League, winding up with an average of .254, he had an uncanny ability to draw bases on balls. In one decade, 1950–60, he led the league in walks six times, and his total of 1,614 career walks places Yost behind only seven other players in the history of baseball. Most of the others were primarily known for their hitting power, but Yost was "The Walking Man."

Denton (Cy) Young

While trying out for the Canton team of the Tri-State League in 1890, twenty-three-year-old Denton Young threw the ball so hard that it splintered the backstop. The club's owner later asked manager George Moreland, "How's that kid pitcher?" Pointing to the backstop, Moreland replied, "Just look at the grandstand." After surveying the damage, the owner muttered, "'Pears as though a cyclone struck it." It was not long before the "Cyclone" nickname was abbreviated to "Cy." After Young went on to become, by general consensus, the greatest pitcher in the history of the game, winning a record 511 major-league games, promising new pitchers were often called "Cy" in his honor. Since 1956 the Cy Young Memorial Award has been given to the game's top pitchers; originally given to only one pitcher each year, in 1967 it was expanded to include a pitcher from each league. Once, at an old-timers' game, a reporter asked Cy Young how many games he won. Young's lordly reply was, "I won more games than you ever saw."

Joe (Mad Dog) Zdeb

Royals manager Whitey Herzog, watching the rookie out-fielder in 1977 spring-training camp, commented, "He plays like he's mad all the time—always hustling and going all out." Recalling that Norm Larker had been called "Mad Dog" for similar reasons, Herzog passed the name on to Zdeb. Bill Madlock and John Stearns were two other players named "Mad Dog." Stearns received the nickname while playing football at the University of Colorado.

Rollie (Bunions) Zeider

The Chicago infielder was often called "Hook" because of the shape of his nose, and friends in Garrett, Indiana, comparing his beak to that of a parrot, labeled him "Polly." While a member of the White Sox in 1913, Zeider spent six weeks in a hospital with blood poisoning after Ty Cobb's spikes nearly cut off his bunion. Known as "Bunions" or "The Bunion King" because of the foot ailment, Zeider was swapped that year to the Yankees with a nondescript first baseman, Babe Borton. Yanks manager Frank Chance gave up his contentious star first baseman Hal Chase for the two members of the Sox, and *New York Globe* sportswriter Mark Roth wrote in disgust, "Chance traded Chase for a bunion and an onion."

Gus (Ozark Ike) Zernial

Zernial was from Texas, not the Ozarks, but it was close enough for Fred Haney to dub him "Ozark Ike," after the rustic cartoon character, when Haney was broadcasting games for the Hollywood Stars. Another "Ozark Ike" was Jackie Brandt, a Nebraska native who was nicknamed by Rochester teammate Allie Clark in 1955.

Don (Popeye) Zimmer

Zimmer's bulging jowls, augmented with a hefty chaw of tobacco, made him the spitting image of Popeye, the cartoon character. He had some disciplinary problems with various players while managing the Boston Red Sox, and Ferguson Jenkins began calling him "Buffalo Head." Sox teammates Jenkins, Bill Lee, Bernie Carbo, Rick Wise, and Jim Willoughby formed a group called "The Loyal Order of the Buffalo" in sarcastic reference to Zimmer. Zimmer's friends more kindly called him "Zim."

Only one time in his life was Casey Stengel struck completely dumb by a question. On October 8, 1956, after Don Larsen's perfect-game World Series victory, swarms of reporters interviewed everyone connected with the game, asking every conceivable question. An unidentified young reporter asked Stengel, "Casey, do you think this was the best game Larsen ever pitched?"

BIBLIOGRAPHY AND
ACKNOWLEDGMENTS

The groundwork for the study of baseball slang was laid by Edward J. Nichols in his 1939 Pennsylvania State College doctoral thesis "An Historical Dictionary of Baseball Terminology" (University Microfilms, Ann Arbor, Michigan), which traces about 2,500 slang expressions back to the earliest printed references the researcher could find. Nichols did not, however, attempt to trace the etymology of baseball language, noting that "another investigation [will have] to battle over the origins of much of the terminology." Nichols's primary sources included the records of the first formal baseball team, Alexander J. Cartwright's Knickerbocker Club, dating from 1845; the A. G. Spalding collection of baseball material, including the 1858–68 scrapbooks of pioneer baseball writer Henry Chadwick; the Frank Merriwell series of boys' fiction books by Burt L. Standish; various eastern newspapers; and periodicals including *Sporting Life*, its successor *The Sporting News*, and *Baseball Magazine*.

Among the first significant attempts to catalog baseball slang were Thomas W. Lawson, *The Krank: His Language and What It Means* (Rand Avary Co., 1888); Henry Chadwick, *Technical Terms of Baseball* (American Sports Publishing Co.,

1897); John B. Foster, "Glossary of Base Ball Terms" in *Collier's New Dictionary of the English Language* (P. F. Collier & Son, 1908); Rollin Lynde Hartt, "The National Game," *The Atlantic Monthly*, August 1908; and Hugh S. Fullerton, "The Baseball Primer," *The American Magazine*, June 1912. The baseball writings of Ring W. Lardner contain the most accurate and colorful reflection of the speech of early ballplayers, especially his short stories "Alibi Ike" and "My Roomy" and his epistolary novel *You Know Me, Al* (Charles Scribner's Sons, 1916). George W. Hilton was editor of *The Annotated Baseball Stories of Ring W. Lardner, 1914–1919*, Stanford University Press, 1995. The 1921 and 1923 editions of H. L. Mencken's *The American Language* (Alfred A. Knopf) include Lardner's "Baseball-American," a whimsical two-page imaginary dialogue between a manager and his players.

The most comprehensive dictionary of baseball is Paul Dickson's *The Dickson Baseball Dictionary* (Facts on File, 1989), which includes about 5,000 baseball terms. Dickson's book, which builds impressively on the foundation established by Nichols fifty years earlier, provides definitions, etymologies, citations of first usages, and other historical background for baseball terms. Additional dictionaries of baseball terms include Jerome H. (Dizzy) Dean, *The Dizzy Dean Dictionary and What's What in Baseball* (Falstaff Brewing Co., 1943 and 1949), and *Dizzy Baseball: A Gay and Amusing Glossary of Baseball Terms Used by Radio Broadcasters, with Explanations to Aid the Uninitiated* (Greenberg,

1952); Parke Cummings, *Dictionary of Baseball* (A. S. Barnes, 1950); Bert Dunne, *Folger's Dictionary of Baseball* (Folger's Coffee and Stark-Rath Printing Co., 1958); Zander Hollander, *Baseball Lingo* (W. W. Norton, 1967); Joe Archibald, *Baseball Talk for Beginners* (Pocket Books, 1969, republished in 1974 as *Baseball Talk*); Richard Scholl, *The Running Press Glossary of Baseball Language* (Running Press, 1977); Mike Whiteford, *How to Talk Baseball* (Dembner Books, 1983); Jerry Howarth, *Baseball Lite* (Protocol Books, 1986); and Patrick Ercolano, *Fungoes, Floaters and Fork Balls: A Colorful Baseball Dictionary* (Prentice-Hall, 1987). Lawrence Frank analyzed field usage of baseball slang in *Playing Hardball: The Dynamics of Baseball Folk Speech* (Peter Lang, 1984).

General dictionaries of sports with baseball definitions include John S. Salak, *Dictionary of American Sports* (Philosophical Library, 1961); Robert Copeland, ed., *Webster's Sports Dictionary* (G. & C. Merriam Co., 1976); Zander Hollander, ed., *The Encyclopedia of Sports Talk* (Corwin Books, 1976), including a section on baseball slang by Phil Pepe; Graeme Wright, *Illustrated Handbook of Sporting Terms* (Hampton House, 1978, republished as *Rand-McNally Illustrated Dictionary of Sports*, Rand-McNally, 1979); Harvey Frommer, *Sports Lingo: A Dictionary of the Language of Sports* (Atheneum, 1979); and Tim Considine, *The Language of Sport* (Facts on File, 1982). *The American Thesaurus of Slang* by Lester V. Berrey and Melvin Van Bark (Thomas Y. Crowell, 1953) contains a fifteen-page listing of baseball terms, and

Mencken's *The American Language* includes brief listings of baseball slang terms as well as a few notes on derivations.

In addition to the Nichols thesis, another seminal source for this study was *Baseball Nicknames*, a pamphlet by Thomas P. Shea published in 1946 by Gates-Vincent Publications of Hingham, Massachusetts. The pamphlet was so obscure when I started my research that the Baseball Hall of Fame library in Cooperstown, New York, did not even possess a copy; through the help of the late Hall of Fame historian Lee Allen, I was able to locate Mr. Shea, who graciously supplied me with an annotated copy of the pamphlet, correcting apocryphal stories that had found their way into it and supplying additional information. (That pamphlet is now in my collection of *High and Inside* research material at the State Historical Society of Wisconsin, and I have donated another copy of the pamphlet to the Baseball Hall of Fame.) Mr. Shea was also kind enough to respond to numerous questions about the nicknames of other players who were not included in his pioneering survey. Other books with useful information on baseball nicknames include Louis Phillips and Burnham Holmes, *Yogi, Babe, and Magic: The Complete Book of Sports Nicknames* (Prentice-Hall, 1994), and David H. Martinez, *The Book of Baseball Literacy* (Plume, 1996); Martinez's entertaining compendium also includes information on baseball terminology.

The most complete collection of baseball quotations is Paul Dickson's *Baseball's Greatest Quotations* (Edward

Burlingame Books, 1991). Other useful collections include Bert Randolph Sugar, *The Book of Sports Quotes* (Quick Fox, 1979); Kevin Nelson, *Baseball's Greatest Quotes* (Fireside Books, 1982); Bob Chieger, *Voices of Baseball: Quotations on the Summer Game* (Atheneum, 1983); David H. Nathan, ed., *Baseball Quotations* (Ballantine Books, 1991); and David Plaut, ed., *Speaking of Baseball: Quotes and Notes on the National Pastime* (Running Press, 1993).

The scholarly periodical *American Speech* has published several articles on baseball language, including Joseph Curtin Gephart, "Nicknames of Baseball Clubs," April 1941 (first published as "Baseball Nicknames" in the *New York Times Magazine*, February 23, 1941); Franklin P. Huddle, "Baseball Jargon," April 1943; and David Shulman, "Baseball's Bright Lexicon," February 1951. Other noteworthy articles include Anon., "English and Baseball," *The Nation*, August 21, 1913; Anon., "Peril of the Baseball Lingo," *The Literary Digest*, September 6, 1913; William G. Brandt, "That Unrecognized Language—Baseballese," *Baseball*, October 1932; J. Willard Ridings, "Use of Slang in Newspaper Sports Writing," *Journalism Quarterly*, December 1934; and Russell Baker, "Come Back, Dizzy," *New York Times*, October 9, 1979.

The Sporting News, the weekly trade paper published in St. Louis since 1886, is a consistently useful source of information on baseball and its language. Particularly valuable for this study was an article by Frederick G. Lieb, "Noah's Ark Spawned Big-Time's Nicknames," in the December 21, 1963, issue. *Baseball Digest, Sport, Sports Illustrated, Time, Newsweek,* the *New York Times,* the *Los Angeles Times,* the *Chicago Tribune,* the *Milwaukee Journal, USA Today,* and other periodicals also were consulted. Annual publications that were helpful include *The Complete Handbook of Baseball* series, edited by Zander Hollander and published by New American Library and (later) by Signet; the *Petersen's Pro Baseball Annual* series, edited by Chuck Benedict and published by Petersen Publishing Co.; and Bill James's *The Bill James Baseball Abstract* series, published by Ballantine Books.

The reference books published by *The Sporting News*—including *Official Baseball Register, Official Baseball Guide, Official Baseball Rules, Official Baseball Dope Book,* and *Daguerreotypes*—served as authoritative sources of records and other factual information. Various editions of the *Official Baseball Register* were helpful on some nickname derivations, and the "Inside Corner" column of *The Sporting News* answered a few of my questions about slang origins. Other sources of baseball records included Hy Turkin and S. C. Thompson, *The Official Encyclopedia of Baseball* (A. S. Barnes, first published in 1951 and subsequently updated); Frank Menke, *The Encyclopedia of Sports* (A. S. Barnes, first published in 1953); Joseph L. Reichler, *The Baseball Encyclopedia* (Macmillan, first published in 1969); David S. Neft, Roland T. Johnson, Richard M. Cohen, and Jordan A. Deutsch, *The Sports Encyclopedia: Baseball* (Grosset & Dunlap, first published in 1974); Rick Wolff, editorial director,

The Baseball Encyclopedia (Macmillan, first published in 1969); John Thorn and Peter Palmer, eds. (with Michael Gershman), *Total Baseball: The Official Encyclopedia of Major League Baseball* (Viking, first published in 1989); and James A. Riley, *The Biographical Encyclopedia of the Negro Baseball Leagues* (Carroll & Graf, 1994).

Too many books on baseball history and other aspects of the game have been consulted for a complete listing here, but the most helpful have been *The Hot Stove League* by Lee Allen (A. S. Barnes, 1953), which contains a chapter on nicknames that is reprinted in *The Fireside Book of Baseball*, edited by Charles Einstein (Simon & Schuster, 1956); Einstein's other anthologies, *The Second Fireside Book of Baseball* and *The Third Fireside Book of Baseball* (Simon & Schuster, 1958 and 1969); James P. Brosnan, *The Long Season* (Harper & Brothers, 1960) and *Pennant Race* (Harper & Brothers, 1962); Joe Garagiola, *Baseball Is a Funny Game* (J. B. Lippincott, 1960); Frank Graham and Dick Hyman, *Baseball Wit and Wisdom: Folklore of a National Pastime* (David McKay, 1962); Lawrence S. Ritter, *The Glory of Their Times* (Macmillan, 1966); Roger Angell's collections *The Summer Game* (Simon & Schuster, 1972), *Five Seasons* (Simon & Schuster, 1977), *Late Innings* (Simon & Schuster, 1982), and *Season Ticket* (Houghton Mifflin, 1988); Jordan A. Deutsch, Richard M. Cohen, Roland T. Johnson, and David S. Neft, *The Scrapbook History of Baseball* (Bobbs-Merrill, 1975); Fred Lieb, *Baseball As I Have Known It* (Coward,

McCann, and Geoghegan, 1977); David Lamb, *Stolen Season: A Journey Through America and Baseball's Minor Leagues* (Random House, 1991); Henry Aaron and Lonnie Wheeler, *I Had a Hammer: The Hank Aaron Story* (HarperCollins, 1991); Bill James, *The Politics of Glory: How Baseball's Hall of Fame Really Works* (Macmillan, 1994, reissued in 1995 by Simon & Schuster as *Whatever Happened to the Hall of Fame: Baseball, Cooperstown, and the Politics of Glory);* and Geoffrey C. Ward, *Baseball: An Illustrated History*, based on the documentary film script by Ward and Ken Burns (Alfred A. Knopf, 1994).

My most patient, knowledgeable, and encouraging source throughout the writing of this book's first edition was my father, Raymond E. McBride, a veteran reporter, sportswriter, and fan who answered countless questions about the game and its language. Without his guidance in the early stages of the writing, and his prodding in the 1970s, this book would not have been written or published. Dr. Patrick McBride, my brother and a former batboy and clubhouse manager for the Milwaukee Brewers, was an invaluable source of inside information. He also read the manuscript and suggested important changes, as did my father; my brother Dennis McBride; my high school English teacher and journalism adviser, Thomas L. Book; Todd McCarthy; and Meredith Brody. My father's *Milwaukee Journal* colleagues Ira Kapenstein, Cleon J. Walfoort, Robert W. Wells, and Bob Wolf also were generous with their assistance.

In preparing the revised edition, I was greatly helped by my two children, John and Jessica. After I introduced them to baseball, they reciprocated by sustaining my interest in the game with their own innocent enthusiasm. At John's urging, we eventually resumed making the five-minute drive to Dodger Stadium after I swore off baseball because of the disillusionment brought on by the 1994 strike. I also am grateful to Kendall Hailey, who inspired me anew every day with her beautiful soul and her literary brilliance; and her scholarly uncle Thomas Hailey, who regaled me with his delightful stories and kindly lent me his library of reference books on baseball. Betsy, Brooke, and Hallie May welcomed me into their family with warm Hailey hospitality and literary fellowship.

Others who were generous with their information and assistance include Randy Adamack of the Cleveland Indians; Sylvia Adamson of the Atlanta Braves; Professor Ralph Andreano of the University of Wisconsin; Jim Bagby, Jr.; Edward Bernds; Joe Bodolai of the Toronto Blue Jays; Carey Brandt of the Colorado Rockies; Steve Brener of the Los Angeles Dodgers; Larry Chiasson of the Montreal Expos; Hal Childs of the Seattle Mariners; Bob Crawford of the Arizona Diamondbacks; Bill Crowley of the Boston Red Sox; Don Davidson of the Houston Astros; Jim Enright of the Chicago Cubs; Walter A. Evers of the Cleveland Indians; Jim Ferguson of the Cincinnati Reds; William J. Guilfoile of the New York Yankees and the Pittsburgh Pirates; Eileen Hackart of the Kansas City Royals; Mary Hunt of the Wauwatosa, Wisconsin, Public Library; Barbara Kaiser of the State Historical Society of Wisconsin; Dave Kaufman; Sally N. MacNichol; Jack Malaney of the Boston Red Sox; Steve Matesich of the Tampa Bay Devil Rays; Patrick McGilligan; Tom Mee of the Minnesota Twins; Hal Middlesworth of the Detroit Tigers; Gerry Murphy of the New York Yankees; John J. Murphy; Diana Price; Arthur Richman of the New York Mets; Steve Ritter; Bill Robertson of Anaheim Sports, Inc.; Mike Ryan of the San Diego Padres; Julio C. Sarmiento of the Florida Marlins; Garry Schumacher; Tom Seeberg of the California Angels; Truett B. (Rip) Sewell; Larry Shenk of the Philadelphia Phillies; Tom Skibosh of the Milwaukee Brewers; Stu Smith of the San Francisco Giants; Don Unferth of the Chicago White Sox; Dean Vogelaar of the Kansas City Royals; and Ellen Whitman.

For finding this book its publishers, I am indebted to my agent for the original 1980 edition, Candace Lake, and my agent for the revised edition, Richard Parks. At Contemporary Books, this edition was in the good hands of Craig Bolt, Kara Leverte, Kathy Willhoite, Nancy Crossman, Alina Cowden, and Peter Grennen.

INDEX